BECOMING VISIBLE

"Kevin Jennings has written an informative, highly readable, and much needed book. It is useful both for general faculty members who are committed to making schools better places for gay and lesbian students, and for teachers of history and social science who want to ensure that all students — gay, lesbian, straight — receive a complete and accurate education. *Becoming Visible* helps to fill a large, important gap in the curriculum."

—Ernest Van B. Seasholes, principal,
Newton South High School
Newton, Massachusetts

BECOMING VISIBLE

A Reader in Gay & Lesbian History for High School & College Students

Kevin Jennings, editor

Boston ♦ Alyson Publications, Inc.

Cover design by Catherine Hopkins.

Typeset and printed in the United States of America.

This is a trade paperback original from Alyson Publications, Inc.,
40 Plympton Street, Boston, Massachusetts 02118.
Distributed in England by GMP Publishers,
P.O. Box 247, London N17 9QR, England.

First edition: April 1994

5 4 3 2 1

ISBN 1-55583-254-7

Library of Congress Cataloging-in-Publication Data

Becoming visible : a reader in gay & lesbian history for high school & college students / Kevin Jennings, editor. — 1st ed.
p. cm.
Includes bibliographical references.
ISBN 1-55583-254-7 (pbk.) : $9.95
1. Gays—History. I. Jennings, Kevin, 1963–
HQ76.25.B425 1994
305.9'0664'09—dc20 94-8579
CIP

For my mother,
who taught me to love history,
&
for Bob,
who taught me to love

CONTENTS

ACKNOWLEDGMENTS

Writing this part of the book has caused me more anxiety than any other. It simply is not possible to express my gratitude to the many people who have helped make this book possible, and listing them all is equally unfeasible. With apologies to anyone omitted, here we go!

The obvious place to begin is with Alyson Publications. First, Sasha Alyson had the vision to conceive of this project, and I had the good luck to be the person he sought out to complete it. I am deeply appreciative of being afforded this opportunity. Karen Barber was a godsend, thanks to her talent, persistence, and diligence. Her ability to keep on top of a thousand details has amazed me, and I always was thankful for her encouraging words when I thought we would never surmount the technical obstacles that lay between conception and publication.

The next group which needs thanks are the writers and publishers who have generously shared their work with me. A complete list of them follows this foreword. In particular, Martin Duberman and Neil Miller went above and beyond the call of duty to help me to pull this book together.

Always in the back of my mind were a group of very special students whom I have been privileged to teach during my career. To Brewster, Devin, Lee, and Morgan: I wanted to write this book so that you would have a sense of our history, and take pride in our past. You have each made history in your own way, and I am enormously proud of you.

Among my friends, special thanks go to: Cynthia Katz, for the photos and the friendship; Miriam "Air" Messinger, who must be thanked for her courier service, without which the manuscript literally would not have made it to publication; Mark Melchior, who is commended for his ability to withstand endless kvetching; John DiCarlo, who has become the brother I never really had before; and The Fabulous Pam Shime, without whose support I could never have done any of this.

Bob, I simply have no words to say how I feel. "Thanks" will have to suffice.

PERMISSIONS

"A Discussion about Differences: The Left-Hand Analogy," from *Looking at Gay and Lesbian Life* (pp.23–33), copyright © 1988, 1993 by Warren J. Blumenfeld and Diane Raymond. Published by Beacon Press, Boston. All rights reserved. Reprinted with permission of the authors.

Excerpts from *Christianity, Social Tolerance, and Homosexuality: Gay People in Western Europe from the Beginning of the Christian Era to the Fourteenth Century,* by John Boswell, copyright © 1980 by The University of Chicago. Reprinted and abridged by permission of the author and The University of Chicago Press.

Excerpts from *Passions of the Cut Sleeve: The Male Homosexual Tradition in China,* by Bret Hinsch, copyright © 1990 by the Regents of the University of California. Reprinted by permission of the Regents of the University of California and the University of California Press.

Excerpts from *The Spirit and the Flesh,* by Walter Williams. Copyright © 1986 by Walter Williams. Reprinted by permission of Beacon Press.

"She Even Chewed Tobacco," by the San Francisco Lesbian and Gay History Project, from *Hidden from History: Reclaiming the Gay and Lesbian Past,* edited by Martin Duberman, Martha Vicinus, and George Chauncey, Jr. Published in 1990 by Penguin Books USA Inc. Reprinted with permission.

Excerpt from *Conduct Unbecoming: Gays and Lesbians in the U.S. Military,* copyright © 1993 by Randy Shilts. Reprinted with permission of St. Martin's Press, Inc., New York.

Excerpts from *Eleanor Roosevelt: Volume One, 1884–1933,* by Blanche Weisen Cook. Copyright © 1992 by Blanche Weisen Cook. Used by permission of Viking Penguin, a division of Penguin Books USA Inc.

Excerpt from *Coming Out Under Fire: The History of Gay Men and Women in World War Two,* by Allan Bérubé. Copyright © 1990 by Allan Bérubé. Reprinted and abridged with permission of The Free Press, a division of MacMillan, Inc.

Excerpt from *Stonewall,* by Martin Duberman. Copyright © 1993 by Martin Duberman. Used by permission of Dutton Signet, a division of Penguin Books USA Inc.

Excerpt from *Out in the World,* by Neil Miller. Copyright © 1992 by Neil Miller. Reprinted by permission of Random House, Inc.

"Gay Millions: China's Silent Minority," by Lena H. Sun; "One Man's Story: 'What We Just Did, Is This Homosexuality?" by Lena H. Sun; copyright © 1992 by the *Washington Post.* Reprinted with permission.

"Tapioca Tapestry," by Pat Bond, from *Long Time Passing: Lives of Older Lesbians,* edited by Marcy Adelman, published by Alyson Publications, Inc. Copyright © 1986 by the Estate of Pat Bond. Reprinted by permission of the editor.

"If You Live, You're Going to Get Old," by Alma Adams, from *Long Time Passing: Lives of Older Lesbians,* edited by Marcy Adelman, published by Alyson Publications, Inc. Copyright © 1986 by Alma Adams. Reprinted by permission of the editor.

"A Free Spirit," by Barbara Tymbios, from *Long Time Passing: Lives of Older Lesbians,* edited by Marcy Adelman, published by Alyson Publications, Inc. Copyright © 1986 by the Estate of Barbara Tymbios. Reprinted by permission of the editor.

"Not Always a Bed of Roses," by Wilma and Roberta, from *Long Time Passing: Lives of Older Lesbians,* edited by Marcy Adelman, published by Alyson Publications, Inc. Copyright © 1986 by Wilma and Roberta. Reprinted by permission of the editor.

"A Charmed and Lucky Life," by Dr. Eileen, from *Long Time Passing: Lives of Older Lesbians,* edited by Marcy Adelman, published by Alyson Publications, Inc. Copyright © 1986 by Dr. Eileen. Reprinted by permission of the editor.

Excerpts from *Ulrichs: The Life and Works of Karl Heinrich Ulrichs, Pioneer of the Modern Gay Movement,* by Hubert Kennedy. Copyright © 1988 by Hubert Kennedy. Reprinted by permission of Alyson Publications, Inc.

Excerpts from *The Men with the Pink Triangle,* by Heinz Heger. Copyright © 1980 by Merlin-Verlag, Hamburg, Germany. Reprinted by permission of Alyson Publications, Inc.

Excerpts from *The Trouble with Harry Hay: Founder of the Modern Gay Movement,* by Stuart Timmons. Copyright © 1990 by Stuart Timmons. Reprinted by permission of Alyson Publications, Inc.

"In My Own Space," by Calvin Glenn, from *Brother to Brother: New Writings by Black Gay Men,* edited by Essex Hemphill, published by Alyson Publications, Inc. Copyright © 1990 by Calvin Glenn. Reprinted by permission of the author.

"They Aren't That Primitive Back Home," by Kim, from *A Lotus of Another Color: An Unfolding of the South Asian Gay and Lesbian Experience,* edited by Rakesh Ratti. Copyright © 1993 by Kim. Reprinted by permission of Alyson Publications, Inc.

"Breaking Silence," by Sharmeen Islam, from *A Lotus of Another Color: An Unfolding of the South Asian Gay and Lesbian Experience,* edited by Rakesh Ratti. Copyright © 1993 by Sharmeen Islam. Reprinted by permission of Alyson Publications, Inc.

INTRODUCTION

"Why teach gay and lesbian history?"

When I have spoken to my fellow teachers of the need to teach this subject, these are often the first words out of their mouths. In a culture that does not like to talk about homosexuality at all, the whole idea of discussing the gay and lesbian past in classes such as U.S. History is profoundly unsettling for some teachers. After I had proposed a course on gay history at my school, one of my colleagues wrote me to make his feelings clear. There simply wasn't much gay history, he said. It wasn't an important subject, and he couldn't see any reason to offer such a class.

I have to admit to being taken aback by the ignorance and insensitivity of my colleague's response. Leaving aside his insensitivity for a moment, my colleague's response simply revealed his own failure to keep up with current historical research. Indeed, as lesbian and gay studies has emerged as a discipline over the last two decades, its dramatic discoveries have shown it to be one of the most exciting fields in contemporary historical scholarship. Unfortunately, most of this dialogue has been within the university setting, meaning few high school teachers or students have had a chance to benefit from this work. This book is intended to give those of us in high schools a glimpse into this growing area of study. The breadth of the selections in this brief reader alone should dispel any lingering notions that there is no "gay history."

In order to help readers understand the insensitivity of my colleague's response (which will need no explanation to those readers who are themselves gay or lesbian), I need to describe an experience I had while researching this book. To make this experience understandable, I will need to share a bit of my own story.

I was born in 1963. I grew up in rural North Carolina, and realized in grade school that I was gay. I felt absolutely alone. I had no one to talk to, didn't know any openly gay people, and saw few representations of gays in the media of the 1970s. I imagined gay people were a tiny, tiny minority, who had been and would always be despised for their "perversion." Not once in high school did I ever learn a single thing about homosexuality or gay people. I couldn't imagine a happy life as a gay man. So I withdrew from my peers and used alcohol and drugs to try to dull the pain of my isolation. Eventually, at age seventeen I tried to kill myself, like one out of every three gay teens. I saw nothing in my past, my present, or (it seemed) my future suggesting that things would ever get any better.

I survived this suicide attempt, thanks to the alert actions of a friend. Shortly thereafter I left to attend college in an urban center with a substantial gay population. There I learned that I could be a happy person and be gay. I was fortunate enough to meet someone with whom I wanted to share my life, and have even brought him back to North Carolina to spend Thanksgiving with me and my family. I have discovered there are gay people in my old hometown, gay people who only recently became visible. However, there was still no history for me to feel a part of there and, as the black nationalist Marcus Garvey once said, "A people without history is like a tree without roots."

As I was researching this book, I learned of a magazine called *One*. This was America's first gay magazine, beginning publication in 1953, ten years before I was born. This fact in itself was exciting — imagine, there were gay people fighting for my rights and writing articles about their struggle a decade before I was even on the planet!

I decided to read some *One* magazines, to get a sense of what the concerns, problems, and hopes of these people were. I decided that reading the letters to the editor might be the most useful way of gaining this understanding. The letters are unsigned, as it was too risky in the McCarthy era for most people to reveal any sympathy for gays. Instead, they simply list the hometown of the writer. As I worked my way through the magazines, I picked up the October 1954 issue, and saw a letter that read:

> I will always remain willing to support, in my small way, any effort to reduce intolerance toward a minority group in the United States. Intolerance is basically as un-American as Communism. I realize the road ahead of us is long and difficult, but that part of the road already traveled has been pretty tough, too.

The first thing that struck me was how prophetic the last line was for gay people. Indeed, we have traveled a tough road, but looking back over our past to see how far we have come can inspire us to continue the difficult work we still need to do to gain full equality. But it was the signature below it that stopped me dead in my tracks. In bold print letters, it was signed *Winston-Salem, North Carolina.*

I grew up five miles from Winston-Salem, North Carolina.

At first I was literally too shocked to respond. This magazine had, after all, been printed nearly a decade before my birth, and a quarter-century before my teenaged suicide attempt. I couldn't quite believe what I had just read.

Soon, two emotions came to me. One was a sense of elation. Finally, I had found my past. I had known of the tolerance extended toward gay people in antiquity and in non-Western societies; I had known of gay liberation movements in Germany, England, and in American cities in the earlier part of the twentieth century; I had even become aware of gay groups in contemporary Winston-Salem, North Carolina. But I had never known that there had been gay people in my hometown fighting for their rights years before I was born. For the first time, I looked into a historical document and saw someone like me.

A second emotion followed closely on the heels of the first. I was angry. How was it, I thought, that this history existed, and no one had ever shared it with me? I thought back over my twelve years in North Carolina public schools and my four years at Harvard University, sixteen years when I never once learned anything in a classroom about gay people or gay history, and I was filled with rage. Denying me that history had nearly cost me my life, for gay invisibility had helped create the feelings of isolation that made me want to end it all.

Maybe if I had known that there were people like me in Winston-Salem even before I was born, I might have felt a little better about myself, and not spent so many years in self-hatred and self-destruction. Maybe if someone had taught me this "unimportant" piece of history, I would have made it through school a little more easily. Maybe if someone had taught this "unimportant" history to my straight brothers and my straight classmates, they wouldn't have called me "faggot" and we could have been friends. Maybe if someone had thought this history was important, my life could have been very different.

So, why teach gay history?

There are two main reasons. First, we, as teachers, must teach gay history because it is intellectually dishonest not to do so. There is a substantial gay history that we are just beginning to understand, thanks to the efforts of some remarkable scholars. Just as the curriculum has been revised to reflect the contributions of under-represented groups such as African-Americans and women to our civilization, so must it be revised to tell the story of gay and lesbian people. Not to do so is simply a distortion of the historical record.

More importantly, though, teaching such history may help our students to create a better society. Orwell wrote that "those who control the present, control the past; those who control the past, control the future." When we who teach in the present choose to leave out the gay and lesbian past, we are helping to ensure that homophobia and heterosexism are a part of our future. If our students, both gay and straight, graduate high school with no sense of gay people and where we have come from, then they will be less equipped to deal with the gay people they will encounter in their futures. If we can further their understanding of gay people through our teaching, the epidemic of suicide, gay-bashing, and discrimination that plagues our society may be lessened. If we do not teach about this past, there is little hope that this plague will begin to die out.

Why teach gay history, indeed. I'm glad to finally have the chance to answer that question with this book.

A note on the format of this book

This book is meant for two audiences. The first is the general public who might wish to learn something about gay history. At this time, there are few books on gay history aimed at a general, rather than an academic, readership. This book attempts to make the recent discoveries in gay history accessible to those of us who are not professional historians.

The second group is high school and college teachers and students. Numerous teachers have expressed an interest in teaching about gay history, but they have lacked the materials to do so. Readings in this book have been chosen to fill this gap.

Each chapter begins with an introduction that sets the historical context for the reading selections. The readings themselves include both primary and secondary sources, with readability for high school students being a primary consideration. In some cases, the limited amount of scholarship has meant that selections chosen are still quite academic in tone, and teachers should preview them in order to determine whether or not the selections are suitable for their students.

Readings are followed by questions and activities, addressed directly to students, to help incorporate the readings into class. Teachers will want to choose among these in planning their own lessons, or they can substitute their own ideas. These activities are not meant to be the only ways of using the book in a class, nor must they all be used. Teachers are encouraged to pick and choose, tailoring their activities to the needs of their students. I would welcome hearing about any new activities teachers develop, or any ones I have offered that were particularly effective or ineffective, for use in future revisions of the book. A special appendix has "Notes for Teachers" on issues that might arise when using specific chapters.

I see this book as the beginning of a conversation. It does not pretend to be "all you ever wanted to know about gay history." I am well aware that it is weighted toward the experience of white gay men; that's where most scholarship has been done. Numerous topics still need to be addressed. I hope to look back one day when manybooks like this have been published and smile at the shortcomings of this work. I hope it helps to begin the long-overdue process of developing the materials we teachers need to teach lesbian and gay history. As a historian, I feel the excitement of a new beginning, but I look forward to the day when books such as this will be commonplace.

PART 1

Homosexuals before "Homosexuality"

Looking at "Gay" People in Pre-Modern Societies

INTRODUCTION

How can there be homosexuals before there is "homosexuality"? The question seems to contradict itself.

In order to answer this, we must first look at the debates taking place among historians who study the lesbian and gay past. As with all fields, gay and lesbian studies is filled with people who interpret the same things in very different ways. This is the stuff of historiography. Basically, it's why we don't simply write one history book and put it on the shelf, updating it every ten years or so. We not only find new materials all the time, we also debate what both the new and the old materials actually mean.

In the case of gay and lesbian studies, the debate breaks down into two camps. Both are studying people in the past who loved members of their own sex, but each has a very different opinion on how this experience should be interpreted. On one side are those called "essentialists." Essentialists argue that there have always been "gay people," individuals whose identity was based on their attraction to members of their own sex. "Gay history," then, is "a history of changing attitudes toward an unchanging 'gay people.'" If we look back into the past, essentialists argue, we will always find gay people, who defined themselves by their sexual attraction. What will change is the attitudes of others toward people who defined themselves this way.[1] A person whose work has been categorized as "essentialist" is Yale historian John Boswell, the author of Reading 2-A.

"Social constructionists" disagree. They argue that, while there have always been people who loved members of their own sex, these people did not always "construct" their identities around this. They did not necessarily see themselves as members of a separate group because of their sexuality. In fact, the types of "groups" based on sexuality, constructionists say, have not always broken down into a "gay or straight" split. "Homosexuality," an identity based on exclusive attraction to members of one's own sex, is of fairly recent origin, they argue, pointing out that the actual word "homosexual" was not even invented until 1869.[2] While there may have been people who had and acted upon the feelings we today call "homosexual," constructionists say that it is historically inaccurate to call them "gay," since this is a modern concept that those people themselves did not have. Rather than imposing our modern-day definitions upon them, we must instead try to understand how they thought of themselves. A classic example of this type of analysis is found in Reading 4-A, Professor Walter Williams's analysis of the Native American "berdache" custom.

Because it is so different from our understanding of sexuality today, the constructionist argument can be hard to grasp, especially when applied to unfamiliar people in a faraway time. A simpler analogy might make things clearer. There are people in America today who find themselves overwhelmingly, perhaps exclusively, attracted to people with blond hair. They constitute a minority, as most people can be attracted to people with a variety of hair colors. We do not, at the current time, make a big deal out of this. We do not label these people "blonders," categorizing them based on their sexual attraction to blonds. We do not attribute personality traits to them because of this attraction. They, undoubtedly, do not "construct" their identities on this basis of this attraction. Perhaps in future times, however, this specific difference will become an important one. Historians may then look back, find comments from our time like "Blondes have more fun," and conclude that "blonders" of our time were attracted to this advantaged, glamorous minority. Such sayings may even be seen as evidence of the existence of "blonders" — after all, people wouldn't have said such things if there wasn't a group of people who were exclusively attracted to blonds, would they?

Social constructionists say that it has been the same in the past with those attracted to the same sex. Certainly we can look back and find evidence of same-sex love, in every time period and in every culture. But, social constructionists argue, we must try to look at this evidence as if we were living in that time period and culture. We must try to understand how the people of those times understood same-sex love, and not insist that they thought the same way we do today. To do so would be acting in a "presentist" manner, using standards of the present time as if they are "universal" and apply to all people in all times.

The readings in this section present a variety of interpretations of people whom we would call "homosexual" or "bisexual" today.

Drawn from a variety of cultures and time periods, they show how sexual categories are "constructed" differently throughout history. They reveal that there have always been people who loved members of their own sex; they also reveal that such people have not always been a despised minority, but have actually been tolerated or even honored at times. Through reading about them, we gain a new understanding of both sexuality and the history of those who love members of their own sex.

CHAPTER 1

Understanding Heterosexism and Homophobia

INTRODUCTION

This reader cannot begin right away with gay and lesbian history. The level of misunderstanding, ignorance, and prejudice surrounding the issue of homosexuality in American society is such that we must first establish a framework for discussion. This will allow us to focus on the history and not be blocked from seeing it by our own preconceptions about homosexuality and gay people.

First, we must begin with some definitions to help give us a common language:

- **Sexual orientation** is the "deep-seated direction of one's sexual attraction."
- **Homosexuals** are those whose sexual orientation is toward the same sex.
- **Heterosexuals** are those whose orientation is toward the other sex.
- **Bisexuals** are those whose orientation is toward both sexes.
- **Sexual identity** refers to how one defines one's sexuality and how one is perceived by others.
- **Gays** is a slang term for those who accept and define their identities as homosexual.
- **Straights** is a slang term for those who accept and define their identities as heterosexual.
- **Heterosexism** is a belief that heterosexuality is superior to other sexualities and involves an active promotion of it as *the* desired way of life.
- **Homophobia** is prejudice against gay people.
- **Unearned privilege** refers to privileges or advantages that one gets just because one belongs to a valued group in society, not because of individual efforts which "earned" them, but simply because of involuntary membership in a privileged group.

The readings in this chapter are designed to explain these concepts of sexual orientation and identity, and the prejudices that surround them. In Reading 1-A, a "heterosexual questionnaire" is offered for readers to complete, in order to illustrate the "unearned privilege" that accompanies heterosexuality in a heterosexist society. In Reading 1-B, a comparison is made between sexual orientation and "handedness," raising interesting parallels between the two. Both documents help to show "heterosexism" and how it pervades our thinking about sexual difference. Their inclusion is designed to help us break out of a limiting view of sexuality that blocks the empathy, understanding, and analysis upon which a true understanding of history must be based.

READING 1-A

A Questionnaire

1. What do you think caused your heterosexuality?

2. When and how did you first decide you were heterosexual?

3. Is it possible heterosexuality is a phase you will grow out of?

4. Is it possible you are heterosexual because you fear the same sex?

5. If you have never slept with someone of the same sex, how do you know you wouldn't prefer that? Is it possible you merely need a good gay experience?

6. To whom have you disclosed your heterosexuality? How did they react?

7. Heterosexuality isn't offensive as long as you leave others alone. Why, however, do so many heterosexuals try to seduce others into their orientation?

8. Most child molesters are heterosexual. Do you consider it safe to expose your children to heterosexuals? Heterosexual teachers particularly?

9. Why are heterosexuals so blatant, always making a spectacle of their heterosexuality? Why can't they just be who they are and not flaunt their sexuality by kissing in public, wearing wedding rings, etc.?

10. How can you have a truly satisfying relationship with someone of the opposite sex, given the obvious physical and emotional differences?

11. Heterosexual marriage has total societal support, yet over half of all heterosexuals who marry this year will divorce. Why are there so few successful heterosexual relationships?

12. Given the problems heterosexuals face, would you want your children to be heterosexual? Would you consider aversion therapy to try to change them?

READING 1-B

"A Discussion about Difference: The Left-Hand Analogy"

from *Looking at Gay and Lesbian Life,*
by Warren J. Blumenfeld and Diane Raymond

What do left-handedness and homosexuality have in common? This prologue explores some of the similarities which do in fact exist between the two. Though comparing handedness and sexual orientation might seem akin to comparing artichokes and jet planes, as we do so, striking connections appear. Although this analogy is in no way meant to imply any statistical correlation between left-handedness and homosexuality, it does aim to show how society transforms the meanings of what appear to be value-neutral personal characteristics into morally significant facts.

Every analogy attempts to make a point. Whether one does so successfully depends on how much the items being compared really resemble each other. This one suggests that there are crucial ways in which handedness and sexual orientation are similar. What follows here is a thumbnail sketch of some of those similarities, themes which will be addressed in greater depth throughout this book.

It is estimated that one out of every ten people is left-handed. In fact, this statistic probably holds true for all places and all times. That means there are approximately 25 million left-handed people in the United States alone; and, in a classroom of, say, thirty, at least three people are probably left-handed. Amazingly enough, the statistics are virtually the same for people who act on same-sex attractions.

Left-handed people have existed throughout all ages in all cultures, in all races, all social classes, and in every country. Even the earliest cave-drawings show left-handed figures. Similarly, same-sex acts have probably always existed. Even some of our most ancient literary fragments contain references to love between members of the same sex.

Who is left-handed and lesbian and gay?

Though it may seem obvious, it is not always easy to determine who is left-handed. Some people, for example, use different hands for different activities. Former President Gerald Ford uses his left hand to write while sitting and his right hand to write on blackboards while standing. Some people can successfully manage with either hand. In fact, it is probably true that most people aren't exclusively right-handed or left-handed. We usually, however, define our handedness in terms of whichever hand we use the most, especially in writing. Nevertheless, people in general exhibit a great variety of hand skills which covers a broad continuum between exclusive left-handedness and exclusive right-handedness.

The same difficulty exists when we try to apply labels referring to sexual orientation. Some people very early in their lives develop an awareness and acceptance of their attractions to members of their own sex. Others, though, may reach this stage later in life. Some people may be attracted to both sexes, defining themselves as "bisexual." In fact, it is probably true that most people aren't exclusively heterosexual or homosexual. Most of us, however, define our sexuality by the sex with which we feel more comfortable and to which we experience the stronger attraction. Nevertheless, people's sexuality is fairly flexible, covering a broad continuum between exclusive homosexuality and exclusive heterosexuality.

So far, these facts might seem interesting, but not particularly noteworthy. But for those who are left-handed or lesbian or gay, it might be comforting to know that they are not alone. And for the majority, right-handed people and heterosexuals, it might be worth considering that not everyone is the same. What "righties" usually take for granted — cutting with scissors, working with most tools, even writing from left to right — often involves awkward adjustment for "lefties." Similarly, what "straights" usually take for granted — holding hands in public, going to school dances, introducing girlfriends or boyfriends to parents — also often involves awkward adjustments for lesbians and gays.

Prejudice and discrimination

Though you might not think your friend or mother or classmate is all that weird because she or he is left-handed, such tolerance has not always been the case. In fact, for centuries, left-handed people have been viewed with scorn and even, at times, with fear.

Such scorn was often justified with references to religious texts such as the Bible. Both the Old and New Testaments consider "the left" to be the domain of the Devil, whereas "the right" is the domain of God. For this reason, Jesus told his followers to "not let thy left hand know what thy right hand doeth." (Matthew 6:3) Jesus also describes God's process for separating good from evil in the Last Judgment: "...the King [shall] say unto them on His right hand, 'Come, ye blessed of my Father, inherit the Kingdom prepared for you from the foundation of the world...' Then shall He say unto them on the left hand, 'Depart from me, ye cursed, into everlasting fire, prepared for the devil and his angels...'" (Matthew 25: 32-41)

Early Christians applied these categories so strictly that they even held that the saints, while still infants, were so holy that they would not suck from the left breasts of their mothers!

It is not only the Bible that condemns left-handedness. This was also the case in some ancient societies. The ancient Greeks and Romans shared this attitude. For example, the philosopher Pythagoras argued that left-handedness was synonymous with "dissolution" and evil, and Aristotle described good as "what is on the right, above, and in front, and bad what is on the left, below, and behind." (Fincher, p. 33) The Romans further reinforced these beliefs by standardizing the right-handed handshake, and in Western countries alphabets favor right-handed people in being written from left to right.

Later, in the Middle Ages, left-handed people were sometimes accused of being witches or sorcerers. The present-day wedding custom of joining right hands and placing the gold ring on the third finger of the left hand began with the superstition that doing so would absorb the evil inherent in the left hand.

Though few people today condemn left-handedness, lesbians and gays continue to be feared and excluded. Such treatment is also often justified with references to religious texts such as the Bible.

Though there is great disagreement over the interpretations of certain passages in the Bible, it is difficult to find anything positive in passages like the following: "If a man also lie with mankind, as he lieth with a woman, both of them have committed an abomination: they shall surely be put to death; their blood shall be upon them." (Leviticus 20:13)

Early Christians expanded this to include women when St. Paul condemned women "who did change the natural use into that which is against nature." (Romans 1:26)

Though homosexual relations were condoned for some males in Classical Greece, the Romans, beginning around the 4th century C.E. (Common Era), prescribed the death penalty for male homosexual behavior. Though sentences were rarely carried out, these laws were later used as the foundation for both Canon Law (the law of the Catholic Church) and many civil laws throughout Europe. During the High Middle Ages, beginning in the late 12th century, a number of governments punished people accused of same-sex eroticism with banishment, mutilation, and death by fire. People discovered engaging in same-sex acts were sometimes accused of being witches or sorcerers. In fact, the present-day term *faggot* is said by many to come from the practice of capturing gay men and tying them together as if they were a bundle (or "faggot") of wood to ignite as kindling over which a woman suspected of being a "witch" would be burned at the stake. Homosexuality was a crime punishable by death in colonial America, and in England until 1861. Following the American Revolution, Thomas Jefferson proposed that the penalty be reduced from death to castration. In the United States today, the Supreme Court has ruled that laws which prohibit private, consensual, adult sexual acts commonly associated with homosexuality are constitutional.

Even our terminology often reflects such biases. Words like *sinister* in Latin and *gauche* in French suggest a moral evil or physical awkwardness associated with left-handedness. (Note that their opposites, *dexter* in Latin and *droit* in French, mean "skillful," "artful," "clever," "correct," or "lawful.") In fact, the English word *left* comes from an old Dutch word (*lyft*) meaning "weak" or "broken," whereas *right* derives from an Anglo-Saxon word (*riht*) meaning "straight," "erect," or "just." The word "ambidextrous" literally means "being right-handed on both sides." Phrases like "left-handed compliment" are insults to left-handed people.

Correspondingly, there exists a heterosexual bias in the language we use. There are no common words like *husband* or *wife* that refer to same-sex partners. And words like *bachelor* and *spinster* often inaccurately label gay men and lesbians regardless of their relationship status. If a gay person is involved in a media story, newspapers, or the evening news commonly use phrases like "avowed homosexual" or "homosexual affair"; in contrast, no equivalent terminology is used to define the sexuality of a heterosexual person.

All right, you might respond, but what does this have to do with the treatment of left-handed people and lesbians and gays today? Regarding left-handers, most tools and utensils and most packaging of products are designed for the ease of right-handed people. These include phonograph arms, power saws, corkscrews, sewing machines, and even gum wrappers. Left-handed pilots are not allowed to sit on the right side of the cockpit to reach the controls in the center, even though to do so would make it easier for them.

In the case of lesbians and gays, most laws and ordinances are made to protect the rights of heterosexuals, and, in most states in the United States, these protections do not extend to gays and lesbians. Homosexual relationships do not have legal status. No state recognizes lesbian and gay marriages, people can be denied employment and housing in most areas simply because they happen to be lesbian or gay, and gays and lesbians are often prevented from serving as adoptive or foster parents.

No one really knows why a little more strength in one hand over the other or preference for one sex over the other has been the basis of wide-scale persecution of a minority group of human beings.

How did such social preferences arise? Some people argue that the preference for right-handedness began with the military. If all soldiers were right-handed, they would all pass to the right of their enemy, keeping the enemy on their left side, where they held their shields, and enabling them to maintain a uniform defensive posture. This practice then extended to the rules of the road, except in countries such as England, where they drive on the left side of the road. But even there, the practice was established from a right-handed preference. Knights on horseback would keep their opponents to their right with their lances while jousting.

It is possible that the emphasis on heterosexuality began with the early Hebrews, who were under pressure from competing faiths and cultures. Male homosexuality was a religious practice of the holy men of the Canaanite cults and it was an accepted activity in the early years of the Greek empire. In order to insure the survival of the Jewish faith, condemnations of many of the beliefs and practices of their neighbors, including that of homosexuality, were used to emphasize the differences between the Hebrews and their competition. Also, because their numbers were constantly depleted by drought, disease, and warfare with their neighbors, the early Hebrews placed restrictions on homosexual behavior to promote an increase in their birthrate.

Nowadays, we tend to think of these practices as "natural" and to overlook their origin in history and social necessity. Thus, what began as human diversity has been translated into moral pronouncements of all sorts.

Causes: Biology? Environment?

Any difference from the norm gets more attention from researchers. This is certainly the case with left-handedness and homosexuality. Few ask what causes right-handedness or hand orientation in general, or heterosexuality or sexual orientation in general.

Some theorists believe that the cause of left-handedness is biological, citing evidence that left-handed people are dominated by the right side (hemisphere) of the brain. Some researchers, though, dispute this view, arguing that the correlation does not hold true in many cases.

There is also evidence to suggest that left-handedness may be genetic — that it is inherited — since there is a higher statistical probability that two left-handed persons will have a left-handed child. Others maintain that left-handedness is a result of an imbalance in the mother's hormones while the fetus is developing *in utero*. Some theorists have suggested that a distinct preference for one side over the other is shown as early as the second day of life.

Some social scientists argue that left-handedness is environmentally determined and may be a form of mimicking or copying of the behavior of another left-handed family member by the developing child. And some people argue that left-handedness is a choice as opposed to being biologically determined, while others maintain that hand orientation is influenced by both heredity and environment, citing possible genetic factors that are then modified by cultural influences. Some others say that left-handedness is pathological, a result of trauma to the brain or stress to the mother during pregnancy.

Likewise, some people believe that the cause of homosexuality is biological, that some people are born with this orientation. Some researchers suggest that homosexuality is genetic, that there is a gay or lesbian gene. Others maintain that homosexuality is the result of a hormonal imbalance in the fetus of the pregnant woman. Some theorists have suggested that sexual orientation towards one's own sex over the other sex is determined as early as the fourth or fifth year of life.

Some researchers posit that homosexuality is environmentally determined as a result of certain family constellations. Some, though, argue that homosexuality is simply a choice a person makes, while others maintain that sexuality is influenced by both heredity and environment, citing possible genetic factors that are then modified by cultural influences. Still others say that homosexuality is a physical defect, perhaps a result of injury to the fetus or stress to the pregnant woman.

The fact remains that no one knows for sure the causal factors in the development of handedness or sexual orientation. The evidence that does exist tends to be inconsistent and often contradictory. It is therefore likely that there is no unitary explanation that applies in every instance.

Stereotypes abound in reference to both left-handed people and people with same-sex attractions. Left-handers are often labeled, for example, as willful or stubborn. Gays and lesbians are termed immature or sexually insatiable. Often, people have the notion that all left-handers are controlled by the right side of the brain, making them more visually oriented and artistic, while being less verbal and less inclined to grasp abstract concepts than right-handed people. In addition, some people even think that lefties are at a greater risk of committing criminal offenses. Likewise, some people have the notion that all gay men are overly effeminate and prey on young children, and lesbians are man-haters who secretly want to be men.

Is it natural?

No one really knows why hand preference or sexual preference occurs. In nature, four-legged creatures do not seem to show a preference for a side. And more animals seem to have developed "bilaterally," meaning that they have matching equal pairs which may be used interchangeably. There seems to be no solid evidence to support the idea of an animal preference of either the right or the left side, except for a few species of animals and plants, and sometimes a few individuals of different species. The honeysuckle is one of the few plants that twines to the left. The morning glory twines to the right, and others twist either way depending on other variables. Gorillas seem to exhibit a slight left-handed bias. But why humans prefer one side over the other remains a mystery even today. And, in the universe overall, there seems to be no common law for inanimate objects in terms of motion or favoring sides.

With respect to sexuality, many varieties of insects and reptiles, almost every species of mammal, and many types of birds engage in some form of homosexual behavior both in the wild and in captivity. Also, in some cultures, homosexual activity not only exists but is often encouraged. For example, the Azande and Mossi people of the Sudan in Africa and various tribes in New Guinea consider same-sex relations to be the norm. Adult lesbian relationships are quite common among the Azande, the Nupe, the Haussa, and the Nyakyusa people of Africa, as are adolescent lesbian activities among the Dahomeyan, the !Kung, and Australian aborigines.

Overall, there seems to be no common law for the attraction of inanimate objects, though some people have postulated that only opposites attract. Though this may hold true for positive and negative electric charges, this theory is contradicted time and time again. For example, in metallurgy, various metals which vary slightly chemically combine with little difficulty to form strong and stable unions. In addition, the concept of opposites is a subjective one, and males and females actually have quite a lot in common.

Why does this matter anyway? Well, it matters to some who believe that certain kinds of differences are innately unnatural. This attitude has led many theorists to propose strategies for changing an exhibited hand or sexual preference. They have urged parents to encourage young children to emphasize their right hands, especially in writing. In some schools, teachers have even tied the youngsters' left hands behind their backs or made them sit on their left hands to promote use of the right hand. Even noted baby doctor Benjamin Spock once urged mothers to discourage the use of the left hand in their infants. This treatment often results in emotional outbursts, speech impairments such as stuttering, reading problems, and other learning disabilities. And some "lefties" have tried to conceal their orientation, to "pass" as right-handed in order to fit in with the dominant majority group.

Homosexuals have also been coerced into changing their sexuality. "Experts" have urged parents to encourage young children to manifest behaviors and engage in activities which are considered "appropriate" to their sex. Schools have traditionally withheld teaching about the positive contributions made by lesbians and gays in all areas of society. Most sex education either omits any mention of alternatives to heterosexuality or presents homosexuality as a form of deviance to be avoided. This often results, for those who are not heterosexual, in self-hatred and isolation. Like lefties, some gays and lesbians have tried to conceal their orientation, hoping to "pass" as heterosexual in order to be accepted by the majority.

These kinds of treatments have prompted some people to question the underlying assumptions of the superiority of the majority group. Some lefties have maintained that they are the same as righties and that there are as many different kinds of left-handed people as there are right. Similarly, some lesbians and gays have maintained that they too are the same as heterosexuals and that there are as many different kinds of homosexual people as there are heterosexuals — but that certain types tend to be more visible because they fit into our expectations.

Others, however, have maintained that "being different" endows its possessors with exceptional qualities such as intuitiveness, creativity, and the like. In actuality, there seem to be some areas in which left-handed people do seem to have an advantage. Neurologists have shown that left-handed people adjust more readily to underwater vision, giving them an advantage in swimming. In the sports of baseball and tennis there is a significantly higher percentage of left-handed players. For instance, 40 percent of the top tennis professionals are left-handed, and 32 percent of all major-league batters, 30 percent of pitchers, and 48 percent of all those who play first base are left-handed. In fact, the term "southpaw" was coined to describe left-handed pitchers. In a typical major-league ballpark they pitch from east to west with their south, or left arm (home plate being located to the west to keep the sun out of the batter's eyes).

Gay and lesbian people may also have certain advantages. For example, they are generally less bound to gender-based role expectations within a relationship, they don't constantly have to worry about birth control, and by not being fully accepted within society, they may be more tolerant of difference and so can objectively critique their cultures.

Politics

In a world which ignores or hinders expressions of diversity, some people are pushing for rights of minority groups. Many political activists reject mere "tolerance," maintaining that such an attribute promotes invisibility and continues the discriminatory treatment of these groups. Some activists are demanding that society make more physical accommodations to left-handed people and reject all prejudices that prevent full support for the left-hander. Gay and lesbian activists, in like fashion, are demanding that society grant equality of treatment and an end to oppressive laws that prevent full inclusion of lesbians and gays. An early left-hand activist of sorts was Michelangelo, himself a left-hander, who bucked convention in his Sistine Chapel mural by portraying God as granting the gift of life through Adam's left hand. Gay and lesbian rights activities date back to the late 19th century in Germany, with calls for progressive law reform and public education. More recently, some individuals have created organizations such as the National League of Left-Handers and the National Gay and Lesbian Task Force to provide resources, support networks, and social settings for others like themselves. Some businesses which cater to the needs of left-handed people and gays and lesbians have come into being.

Minority advocates sometimes cite the examples of famous members of their group throughout history. Famous "lefties" include: Alexander the Great, Judy Garland, Gerald Ford, Marilyn Monroe, Leonardo da Vinci, Betty Grable, Ringo Starr, Casey Stengel, Rock Hudson, Ben Franklin, Harpo Marx, Carol Burnett, Raphael, Paul McCartney, Robert Redford, King George VI, Jimi Hendrix, Michael Landon, Babe Ruth, Charlie Chaplin, Mark Spitz, Ryan O'Neal, Cole Porter, Paul Williams, Cloris Leachman, Pablo Picasso, Michelangelo, Charlemagne, Kim Novak, Peter Fonda, Lou Gehrig, Rex Harrison, Dick Van Dyke, Arnold Palmer, Ted Williams, Stan Musial, Dick Smothers, Lord Nelson, Richard Dreyfuss, Clarence Darrow, Lefty Gomez, Herbert Hoover, Marcel Marceau, Edward R. Murrow, Anthony Newley, Warren Spahn, Henry Wallace, Queen Victoria, Paul Klee, Caroline Kennedy, and Lewis Carroll.

The list of famous people who have had important same-sex relationships throughout history is also impressive: Socrates, Sappho, Alexander the Great, Julius Caesar, King Richard II, Pope Julius III, Francis Bacon, Queen Christina, Leonardo da Vinci, Gertrude Stein, Alice B. Toklas, King James I, Hans Christian Anderson, Virginia Woolf, Walt Whitman, Dag Hammarskjöld, Bessie Smith, Michelangelo, Herman Melville, Willa Cather, Colette, Rock Hudson, Janis Joplin, Henry David Thoreau, Margaret Fuller, Alexander Hamilton, Montezuma II, Pope Sixtus IV, Plato, Natalie Clifford Barney, W.H. Auden, Bill Tilden, T.E. Lawrence, John Maynard Keynes, Marcel Proust, Vita Sackville-West, Sophocles, Aristotle, Kate Millett, King Edward II, Barney Frank, Radclyffe Hall, Leonard Bernstein, Renee Vivien, and Montgomery Clift. (Bullough; Haeberle; Katz; Klaich; Walker; Wallechinsky)

Regardless of the diversity of political views among left-handed people, and among lesbians and gays, there seems to be agreement that there must be greater awareness of the needs of these minorities. Authors have formulated credos to help solidify these political movements. Here are excerpts from two of these essays. From "A Left-Handed Manifesto":

> Be it resolved that all left-thinking citizens, mindful that their Birthleft has been denied them, shall henceforth stand up for their lefts. We call upon each one of them to support this Bill of Lefts, and specifically to buy left — purchase only left-handed products ... Act left — don't knuckle under! You've made enough adjustments ... Remember! There are at least 25 million left-handers in America. Singly, they can do nothing, but united they can change the world. (DeKay)

From "A Gay Manifesto":

> Where once there was frustration, alienation, and cynicism, there are new characteristics among us. We are full of love for each other and are showing it; we are full of anger at what has been done to us. And as we recall all our self-censorships and repression for so many years, a reservoir of tears pours out of our eyes. And we are euphoric, high, with the initial flourish of a movement. (Wittman)

IMPORTANT TERMS

sexual orientation	bisexual	heterosexism
sexual identity	gay	unearned privilege
homosexual	straight	
heterosexual	homophobia	

QUESTIONS/ACTIVITIES

1. In 5–10 minutes, complete as much of Reading 1-A as you can. After finishing, summarize your reaction to the questionnaire in a word or phrase. Make a list of these reactions on the board. Are there themes or common patterns in the reactions of the class?

2. Professor Peggy McIntosh of Wellesley College has come up with the concept of "unearned privilege," meaning people born into certain groups gain all sorts of advantages right away that they did nothing to deserve. Examples of this include: that white people can go into the vast majority of hair salons or barber shops and not have to worry about whether or not the person working there will know how to cut their hair; that men can walk down most nighttime streets without worrying about being sexually assaulted; that Christians can expect to see programs in December that reflect their religious tradition, and can count on having that day off.

After dividing your class in half, complete an overnight research project: have half look for concrete examples of "unearned privilege" for right-handers, the other look for unearned privilege for heterosexuals. Compile lists on the board the next day, and make generalizations based upon these specific instances.

3. If you are straight, how would your reactions change if gays were 90 percent of society and you had to answer the questions in Reading 1-A?

4. Rewrite 1-A to substitute homosexual for heterosexual. Divide the class in half: have one group research any evidence (from science, their own experience, etc.) that can be used to answer questions for heterosexuals, and have one do the same for homosexuals. What happens when you compare results?

5. How much of the analogy used in Reading 1-B seems realistic? How much does not seem realistic? Why? Be sure to provide evidence for the answers you give.

6. Interview either a left-handed or a gay person after Reading 1-B to see if the experiences of these individuals reflect the reading.

7. In order to further explore how people in your class have experienced oppression, have the entire class list any characteristics for which people have suffered discrimination (race, gender, height, intelligence, looks, etc.). List these on the board. Form groups with at least one other person who has shared this experience. If no one else has shared the exact experience, try to join with someone who has had some type of similar experience. Each group should answer three questions:

- What was bad about this experience?
- What is good about being a member of this group?
- What would you want people who aren't members of this group to know about you?

Have groups report back. You may not ask questions or debate whether or not someone should feel this way; this is their experience, and others may not devalue it — only they are the experts on their experience. Keep lists (on the board, on paper) to look for common themes that accompany oppression. Keep these as a reference: what do people who suffer from different forms of oppression have in common in their experiences, both positive and negative?

8. Watch the film *A Class Divided*. This film depicts the experiments of an Iowa elementary school teacher who had her students engage in an exercise where favoritism was based on eye color. What happens when we arbitrarily favor people with certain characteristics?

CHAPTER 2

The Greco-Roman World: Acceptance and Assimilation

INTRODUCTION

> [T]he original human nature was not like the present, but different. The sexes were not two as they are now, but originally three in number; there was man, woman, and the union of the two, ... [of which] the word "Androgynous" is only preserved ... the primeval man was round, his back and sides forming a circle; and he had four hands and four feet, one head with two faces .. He could walk upright as men do now, and he could also roll over and over at a great pace ... Terrible was their might and strength ... and they made an attack upon the gods...
>
> [Zeus] said, "Methinks I have a plan which will humble their pride and improve their manners; ... I shall cut them in two ... [and] they shall walk upright on two legs..."
>
> Each of us when separated [because of Zeus' action] ... is always looking for his other half. Men who are a section of that double nature which was once called Androgynous are lovers of women ... the women who are a section of the woman do not care for men, but have female attachments ... they who are a section of the male follow the male ... they hang about men and embrace them, and they are the best of boys and youths, because they have the most manly nature...[1]

This excerpt from Plato's *Symposium* introduces us to the very different views about same-sex love that were held in the classical ages of Greece and Rome. Few topics have drawn so much interest from gay scholars and the debate on this subject has been intense.[2] Although interpretations vary, one thing seems certain: As is demonstrated by Plato's story, attraction between members of the same sex in ancient Greece and Rome was not seen as "wrong," as it would be in later European societies. It was, in fact, seen as natural, and in some cases was not only tolerated but actually accepted and approved.

The historian whose work pioneered this field is Yale professor John Boswell. Reading 2-A is taken from his 1980 book, *Christianity, Social Tolerance, and Homosexuality: Gay People in Western Europe from the Beginning of the Christian Era to the Fourteenth Century.* Boswell's argument is straightforward: in ancient and early medieval Europe, those people who loved members of their own sex were not persecuted but were often influential, respected, and accepted. He presents vast amounts of evidence of same-sex love that was celebrated and admired by the poets and philosophers of that period. For those who believe that today's standards are "right" and that people have always thought the way we do now, Boswell's book is incredible. He shows that homophobia is not the "norm" in Western history but is instead a relatively recent invention, breaking with a tradition of tolerance that existed for centuries. His impressive scholarship, involving analysis of primary documents in many languages, has established him as one of the leading historians working today.

Since 1980, Boswell's interpretation has been challenged by other historians known as "social constructionists" (described in the introduction to Part One). They agree that some types of same-sex love were accepted as "normal" in ancient societies. However, they argue that calling these people "gay," as Boswell does, is inappropriate. Their studies maintain that a Greek adult male citizen chose among a variety of partners from both genders during his life. Our modern terms "gay" and "straight," implying exclusive attraction to one gender, would not have made sense to the ancient Greeks. Either would have been seen as "abnormal." As historian Eva Cantarella put it:

> For the Greeks and Romans..., homosexuality was not an exclusive choice. Loving another man was not an option falling outside the norm. It was just one part of the experience of life: ... during one's lifetime this would alternate and interweave (sometimes simultaneously) with the love of a woman.[3]

These scholars describe the following pattern for Greek men's sexual lives: a period as a young man when a Greek citizen could take an adult male lover; then, when of marriageable age, he would take a female wife; and, during his married life, he would choose sexual partners in addition to his wife (including younger men, freeborn adult women, or slaves of either gender) without risking scorn or ridicule. This was so accepted that many of the Greeks we admire today, including Socrates, Plato, and Alexander the Great, all loved members of their own sex.[4] Given this pattern, constructionists say, terms like "gay" and "straight" are just not very useful. Few individuals would fall into those categories, and virtually all would be confused by labeling people in this way.

Largely absent from this picture are women. To understand this, we must remember that both Greece and Rome were societies with vast inequalities. They were dominated by adult male citizens, whom all others (women, younger men, and slaves of both genders) had to obey. Women could never become citizens and have the privileges that went along with this position. Virtually all of the writings of the time concerned the lives of male citizens, leaving us few records of women's lives. Within the limited records we do have, the number dealing with love between women is small indeed. As Eva Cantarella explains:

> [L]ove between women ... was of no interest to the city ... [it] remained something of which only women continued to speak. Thus, sadly, we know little or nothing of how they experienced it, what space it occupied in their lives, what effects it had on their emotional life and its consequences on their attitude to men.[5]

Sappho, the noted poet, is in fact the only ancient female writer whose work addressing love between women has survived to the present day.[6] We simply do not have enough records to study women who loved other women in the same depth as we can men who loved other men.

Our understanding of same-sex love in the ancient world will always remain limited, due to the lack of records of women's lives. We will also continue to see historians debate how to interpret the subject. Despite these uncertainties, the research into sexuality in the Greco-Roman world has made one thing quite clear: those societies, which generally are considered the foundations of Western civilization, did not share today's homophobic attitudes toward same-sex love. John Boswell's account of Roman attitudes in Reading 2-A shows us just how different their thoughts on this subject were from ours today.

READING 2-A

Imperial Rome

from *Christianity, Social Tolerance, and Homosexuality,*
by John Boswell

[E]arly imperial Rome may be viewed as the "base period" for social tolerance of gayness in the West. Neither the Roman religion nor Roman law recognized homosexual eroticism as different from — much less inferior to — heterosexual eroticism. Prejudices affecting heterosexual behavior, roles, or decorum generally affected all persons uniformly. Roman society almost unanimously assumed that adult males would be capable of, if not interested in, sexual relations with both sexes. It is extremely difficult to convey to modern audiences the absolute indifference of most Latin authors to the question of gender ... Martial insists to his "wife" that both homosexual and heterosexual outlets are necessary and that neither can replace the other ("You use your part, let the boys use theirs,") but generally betrays complete indifference as to the gender of the object of his affections. Of some fifty-five love letters by Philostratus, twenty-three are to males, thirty to females; the two groups are so similar in tone that some manuscripts reverse the genders of the addressees.

Most imperial discussions of love juxtapose gay and nongay passions as equal sides of the same coin.

> Zeus came as an eagle to god-like Ganymede [a male], as a swan came he to the fair-haired mother of Helen.
> So there is no comparison between the two things; one person likes one, another likes the other; I like both.

Nor were there any exaggerated claims made for homosexual passion: it was not imagined to be the only form of noble love, and its adherents were not thought to possess any special genius.

This is certainly not to imply that there were no sexual prejudices or taboos in Roman society but simply that none was directly related to homosexual relations as a class...

Many Roman writers stigmatize behavior which they consider inappropriate to the gender of the party under discussion, but such characterizations must be read with caution. Sexual-object choice is almost never the issue. Words translated as "effeminacy" imply "unmanliness" in the sense of weakness or self-indulgence rather than gender roles or sexual behavior ... gender-related concepts of decorum and behavior were, as in most cultures, dependent on cultural variables. New styles of clothing were often derogated as "effeminate," as were habits of grooming which were novel or extravagant. Such charges were levelled at obviously heterosexual persons as well as apparently gay ones, and it is clear that the stigma had no relation to sexual preference.

On the other hand, a few writers do mock behavior which is strikingly like the inversion of gender expectations one occasionally encounters in modern gay subcultures. Martial, for instance, describes a lesbian who can outdrink and outeat any man, plays at male sports, wrestles, can lift heavier weights than a man, and who "puts it to" eleven girls a day. Lucian portrays Megilla as shaving her head and boasting that she "is a man in every way."...

Romans made strenuous efforts to protect free-born children from sexual abuse. Since homosexuality and heterosexuality were generally regarded as equal alternatives, this concern applied to both male and female offspring ... Horace praised his father for having protected him as a boy from "losing his virtue or even being suspected of it"; but when he grew up he frankly declared himself a lover of both boys and girls. It is likely that "boy" and "girl" in such cases should not be taken in too literal a sense; in terms of sexual adulthood persons were still classed as "boys" by Roman writers when they were serving in the Roman army. What is probably intended by "boy" in such cases is a suggestion of youthful beauty rather than chronological minority. Writers of other nationalities specifically criticize Roman men for limiting their eroticism to older youths.

The rather sensational sexuality of the Empire also obscures a deeper and more spiritual love between persons of the same sex which was equally common. This love is celebrated along with bawdier elements throughout Latin literature and finds a place in historical accounts as well. Whether or not one would consider Encolpius and Giton in the *Satyricon* models of faithful affection, there could hardly be more romantic accounts of love than those represented between homosexual lovers by Ovid or Vergil; and Horace and even the racy Catullus penned lines of deep feeling. Martial does not seem to have had one lover, but a number of his epigrams evince deep sensibility to spiritual love (esp. 1, 46, 88), and he suggests in 10.20 that it was a boyhood lover who drew him back to Spain after living in Rome for many years.

By the time of the early Empire the stereotyped roles of "lover" and "beloved" no longer seem to be the only model for homosexual lovers, and even emperors abandoned traditional sexual roles for more reciprocal erotic relations. Many homosexual relationships were permanent and exclusive. Among the lower classes informal unions like that of Giton and Encolpius may have predominated, but marriages between males or between females were legal and familiar among upper classes. Even under the Republic, as has been noted, Cicero regarded the younger Curio's relationship with another man as a marriage, and by the time of the early Empire references to gay marriages are commonplace. The biographer of Elagabalus maintains that after the emperor's marriage to an athlete from Smyrna, any male who wished to advance at the imperial court either had to have a husband or pretend that he did. Martial and Juvenal both mention public ceremonies involving the families, dowries, and legal niceties. It is not clear that only aristocrats were involved: a cornet player is mentioned by Juvenal. Martial points out (11.42) that both men involved in one ceremony were thoroughly masculine ("The bearded Callistratus married the rugged Afer") and that the marriage took place under the same law which regulated marriage between men and women.

[The emperor] Nero married two men in succession, both in public ceremonies with the ritual appropriate to legal marriage. At least one of these unions was recognized by Greeks and Romans, and the spouse was accorded the honors of an empress. (Suetonius reports a popular joke of the day to the effect that if Nero's father had married that sort of wife, the world would have been a happier place: *Nero* 28-29.) One of the men, Sporus, accompanied Nero to public functions, where the emperor would embrace him affectionately. He remained with Nero throughout his reign and stood by him as he died.

Accounts of lesbian love do not survive from Rome on the same scale as male homosexual passions. This is rather obviously due to the fact that almost all Roman writers were male; if they were gay, they wrote of men as lovers; if not, of women. There may also, however, have been some legal ambiguity about lesbianism as a form of adultery on the part of married women: both the Elder Seneca and Martial refer to lesbian activities as adultery, the former suggesting that the death penalty was appropriate when the two were discovered in the act by a husband. Ovid tells a story of erotic love between two women, but one is thought to be a man by the other and is eventually transformed into a male by the gods (*Metamorphoses* 9.666-797). It is striking that Ovid has this character expiate on the extreme oddness of lesbian passions, whereas he appears to regard homosexual love between males as perfectly normal (e.g. 10.78-215). (On the other hand, the moral prejudices evinced in the *Metamorphoses* are often simply rhetorical.)

Lucian (and his audience?) evinced less surprise and greater familiarity with female homosexuality in the fifth of his *Dialogues of the Courtesans,* where a woman from Lesbos is pictured as having fallen in love with and seduced Leaena, another of the characters in the dialogue. The other speaker, Clonarium, has heard that in Lesbos there are many such women (5.2), but the phenomenon is clearly not geographically limited: the woman in question, Megilla, is married to a woman from Corinth (5.3). Leaena is somewhat embarrassed about the whole thing and refers to it as "bizarre" (5.1), although she is apparently living with Megilla (and her wife?) at the time of the discussion. Clonarium, on the other hand, is fascinated and cannot pry enough details from her reticent friend.

Lucian's own attitude may account for the very stereotypical picture of Megilla, who seems quite male-oriented, although it is possible that gay women in the Empire did sometimes adopt stereotypically opposite-gender behavior in a way that gay men did not. The evidence of literature written by and for males is poor grounds for conjecture on this point...

Probably the most famous pair of lovers in the Roman world were [the emperor] Hadrian and Antinous. Hadrian (ruled 117–38) was the most outstanding of the "five good emperors"; his rule was peaceful and productive, and he was the first emperor since Tiberius to retire in peace rather than succumb to assassination or death in battle. He appears to have been exclusively gay.

Little is known of Antinous, the young Greek with whom Hadrian fell deeply in love, except that the affection the emperor displayed toward him excited wonder and admiration even in the passion-sodden early Empire. Antinous was drowned while crossing the Nile with Hadrian in 130 [C.E.]. The emperor was heartbroken and wept "like a woman."

Hadrian had Antinous deified and established an oracle in his name at Mantinea, with yearly mysteries and a festival every four years. Games were established in his name at Athens, Eleusis, and

Argos and were still being celebrated more than 200 years after his death. The emperor also founded a city on the Nile (halfway between Memphis and Thebes) to honor him and had great roads built to it to ensure it would thrive. Dio Cassius relates that Hadrian erected statues in honor of Antinous "throughout the entire world" and his image survives today in Hellenistic sculpture, architecture, painting, coinage, and literature: "The loftiest and most typical development of the Hadrianic period was the creation of the character of Antinous."

The enormous appeal of the love between Hadrian and Antinous may have been due in some part to the prevalence of same-sex couples in popular romantic literature of the time. Everywhere in the fiction of the Empire — from lyric poetry to popular novels — gay couples and their love appear on a completely equal footing with their heterosexual counterparts...

In Plutarch's *Amatorius* a handsome young man is being courted by males and females; his mother leaves the decision about whether he should marry to his older cousin and "the most responsible of his lovers." *The Affairs of the Heart,* like the other dialogues of the time, constantly juxtaposes love for "women at their fairest and young men in the flower of manhood" as two sides of the same coin.

In *Clitophon and Leucippe,* a novel read not only by Romans of the third century but by Christian monks for centuries thereafter, homosexual and heterosexual romantic love appear as absolutely indistinguishable except for the accident of gender. A heterosexual male goes to his older gay cousin for advice on love; the cousin helps him escape with the woman he loves; three men meeting on a ship are all bereft halves of star-crossed couples: two have tragically lost male lovers and one a female. When Charicles is killed riding a horse given him by his lover, Clinias, a servant of the family rushes immediately to inform Clinias of the former's death, and Charicles' father and lover weep together over his bier. Nor are such relations portrayed as unique to the upper class; in Hellenistic romances gay affections are felt by pirates and brigands as much as by aristocrats and philosophers.

Greek literature of the Empire was doubtless the product of the educated urban elite and was constructed as escapist fantasy: its particulars can hardly be invoked as historical evidence. But novels of this sort addressed to the general reading public were the closest ancient parallel to popular literature; the fact that permanent and exclusive homosexual relationships appear in them without any suggestion of oddity and are considered only as interesting as heterosexual relationships speaks eloquently of the climate of opinion in Mediterranean cities in the centuries following the birth of Christ.

Roman society is universally regarded the cultural matrix of western Europe; almost every aspect of culture and social organization among the peoples who used the ruins of its Empire as the foundations of new societies shows Roman influence or inspiration. This dependence makes it all the more odd that there could be such enormous difference between Romans and their heirs on matters as basic as sexuality and tolerance.

The common impression that Roman society was characterized by loveless hedonism, moral anarchy, and utter lack of restraint is as false as the sweeping derogations of whole people; it is the result of extrapolations from literature dealing with the sensational rather than typical behavior, which was calculated to shock or titillate Romans themselves. Most citizens of Roman cities appear to have been as sensitive to issues and feelings of love, fidelity, and familial devotion as people before or after them, and Roman society as a whole entertained a complex set of moral and civil strictures regarding sexuality and its use.

But Roman society was strikingly different from the nations which eventually grew out of it in that none of its laws, strictures, or taboos regulating love or sexuality was intended to penalize gay people or their sexuality; and intolerance on this issue was rare to the point of insignificance in its great urban centers. Gay people were in a strict sense a minority, but neither they nor their contemporaries regarded their inclinations as harmful, bizarre, immoral, or threatening, and they were fully integrated into Roman life and culture at every level.

AFTERWORD

After Reading 2-A, an immediate question emerges: What happened? How did the societies that came after Rome develop such homophobic attitudes, given the tolerance that seemed to exist during Roman times? Once again, we wade into the middle of a debate between historians when we try to answer this question, and cannot yet provide a sure answer.

To begin, we must return to the last years of the Roman Empire. Some historians trace the development of homophobia in the West from the time when Christianity was adopted by the Romans. They point out that the fourth-century emperor Constantine, one of the first Roman emperors to convert to Christianity, was also the one who put forth the first sweeping laws against same-sex activity in the empire (laws that set criminal punishments for passive adult male partners in same-sex acts). This began a series of increasingly strict laws that were put into place over the next two centuries. Finally, laws were put forth by sixth-century Byzantine emperor Justinian condemning to death all who engaged in same-sex relationships.[7]

Readers should remember that, during the fourth century, the Roman Empire was divided into two empires, a Western one with a capital at Rome and an Eastern one with a capital at Constantinople, now Istanbul in modern-day Turkey. The Western Roman Empire came to an end in 476 C.E. when Germanic peoples captured Rome, but the Eastern Empire, then called the Byzantine Empire, continued to exist until the fifteenth century. The Byzantine emperor Justinian actually succeeded in recapturing Rome from the Germans in the sixth century and was briefly able to restore the empire to a position similar to what it had held before the fall of Rome in 476.

Other historians, among them John Boswell, disagree with dating Western homophobia from the time of the early Christians. In fact, Boswell argues that these homophobic laws were put forth by nonreligious civil authorities and did not originate in the Christian Church. Justinian's code was largely forgotten when the Byzantines were driven out of western Europe after his death, and the first western European laws penalizing homosexual acts with death were not passed until 1280.[8] In the years between these legal changes, Boswell shows people known to love members of their own sex were accepted in medieval times and even rose to high offices within the Church.[9] He writes that:

> Around 1100, the efforts of prominent churchmen liked and respected by the pope could not prevent the election and consecration as bishop of a person well-known to be leading an actively gay life-style, and much of the popular literature of the day — often written by bishops and priests — dealt with gay love, gay life-styles, and a distinct gay subculture.[10]

Instead, Boswell argues that changing political conditions in the late Middle Ages are responsible for the birth of widespread homophobia. The twelfth through fourteenth centuries in Europe saw secular leaders begin to expand their power and break free of the control of the pope and the Catholic Church. The feudal system, where authority was held by local nobles, was replaced by more complex political systems, where many smaller states were brought together into larger ones ruled by a single monarch. These states would eventually evolve into today's modern European nations. The new leaders, however, needed to find a way to win the loyalty of the people who, after all, had no reason to follow them. To rally support, these new leaders began to persecute minorities such as gays, Jews, and "witches." Such groups were portrayed as a "them" against whom the monarch could protect "us," thus giving the average person a reason to want to be loyal to the new leader. Crusades against Islamic "infidels" began, "pogroms" against Jews were initiated, and burning of witches became common. Similarly, new laws and restrictions on same-sex love ended the period of tolerance that had prevailed before, as Boswell explains:

> During the 200 years from 1150 to 1350, homosexual behavior appears to have changed, in the eyes of the public, from the personal preference of a prosperous minority ... to a dangerous, antisocial, and severely sinful aberration ... By 1300, not only had overtly gay literature all but vanished from the face of Europe, but a single homosexual act was enough to ... — in many places — ... merit the death penalty.[11]

With the coming of bubonic plague and the "Black Death" to Europe in the fourteenth century (during which one-third of the continent's population died), this suspicion of "them" only grew larger. Certainly *someone* must be responsible for this dreadful catastrophe, people thought. Political leaders found it much easier to blame minorities than to risk seeing themselves become the object of the people's anger over the disastrous events of the time.[12]

Whether homophobia began in the late Roman Empire because of the introduction of Christianity, or became widespread in the late Middle Ages for political reasons, one thing remains clear: Biblical scriptures were used to justify persecution of those who loved members of their own sex. The Christian concept of what was sexually "natural" was drastically different from the Greco-Roman one. As we saw in the reading from Plato at the beginning of this chapter, same-sex attraction was seen by the ancient Greeks as being just as "natural" as attraction to the other sex. Christians, however, consistently referred to same-sex love as a "crime against nature," arguing that only heterosexual love was "natural." This notion replaced the older one, and served as the justification for persecution of homosexual acts. As historian Eva Cantarella writes:

> Christianity ... introduced the principle of "naturalness," which was exclusive to heterosexual intercourse ... It was necessary to ensure that all those who abandoned themselves to practices "against nature" should be severely punished ... The concept of nature had changed ... the only act "according to nature" was heterosexual intercourse.[13]

This hostility toward same-sex love became the dominant way of thinking in Western society, and has remained so up to the present day. The Greco-Roman tradition of tolerance and acceptance became a thing of the past, all but forgotten until recent times.

IMPORTANT TERMS

social constructionists   Hadrian and Antinous   "natural" sexuality

QUESTIONS/ACTIVITIES

1. What evidence or examples does Boswell present for his argument? Underline each one you can find. Does this present enough support to make his thesis convincing, in your opinion?

2. What biases did the Romans have toward sexuality? What ones did they seem to lack?

3. How were women who loved women regarded? Where is the evidence drawn from on this subject? How might the source of the evidence be biased, and how might that contribute to the image we have today?

4. Boswell goes into great depth with the example of Hadrian and Antinous. What does their relationship show us?

5. Cite as many examples as you can find about how the Roman view of same-sex love was different from the dominant one in our society today.

6. Why is Boswell's account historically important? If his interpretation is correct, how does it affect our view of homophobia today? If the "founders" of Western civilization held these attitudes, what should that mean for us today?

6. Why does the debate over when homophobia began in Western culture, discussed in the afterword, matter? Take one of the two major positions (either dating it from the beginning of Christianity or from the late Middle Ages) and explain the impact this interpretation would have. If we think of homophobia beginning when your interpretation says it does, how does our view of it change?

7. The concept of "natural" is key to the debate over homosexuality. What arguments do those who argue that it is natural present? What arguments do those who say it is unnatural present? Should the debate matter at all, in your opinion?

8. Imagine a conversation between a person from the Greco-Roman time and a later-period Christian who believes that same-sex love is sinful and unnatural. What would they say to one another?

CHAPTER 3

Love of the "Cut Sleeve" in Ancient China

INTRODUCTION

Europeans who visited China in ancient and medieval times were amazed by its sophistication and culture, which was far beyond that of their homeland at the time. Most Europeans simply could not believe the stories of their fellow countrymen who returned from China, telling of its wealth and splendor. Individuals such as Marco Polo, the thirteenth-century Italian traveler, were thought to be telling something like fairy tales when they spoke of China. Possessor of the world's oldest continuous cultural tradition, China prospered for centuries while Europe dwelled in a "Dark Age" after the fall of Rome.

While filled with admiration for most of China's civilization, European visitors were horrified by one aspect of it: its tolerance of gays. The sixteenth-century European Galeote Periera remarked, in an account otherwise admiring of the Chinese, that "the greatest fault we do find [among the Chinese] is sodomy, a vice very common among the meaner sort, and nothing strange among the best."[1] Indeed, open homosexuality had deep roots in China, with the first written references to it being found in the sixth century B.C.E.[2] An entire literature of love stories and folk tales had grown up around it, prompting European visitors to puzzle over how a people so "civilized" could tolerate such an "abominable vice."[3]

To understand the role of same-sex love in ancient Chinese society, we must first look at how they thought about the family. Chinese civilization was based on the teachings of Confucius, whose central idea was "filial piety" (loyalty to the father). Proper behavior involved following what one's ancestors had done in the past, and the individual's primary responsibility was to better the position of his family so his ancestors would look back fondly on him. Marriage, then, was not for love, but to make advantageous alliances for the family.

Since marriage did not necessarily have a romantic or sexual side, the Chinese developed a very different idea about sexual relations than the Western model of monogamy. Marriage was just a "duty" for men, and therefore it was not seen as the only sexual outlet. "Pleasure" could be sought outside the marriage, as this was not what marriage was for in the first place.[4] Sexual pleasure could involve women, men, or both. As one historian puts it, "[H]omosexuality seems to have been considered simply part of the broad range of sexual expression,"[5] rather than an "abominable vice" different from other forms of sexuality.

As is true of the ancient Greco-Roman civilization, existing records of same-sex love in China are almost entirely about men. Writing was a privilege reserved for (upper-class) men, meaning that few women were able to record their experiences for us to read today. Women were expected to follow the Confucian "Three Submissions": as a young girl, a female should submit to her father; as an adult woman, to her husband; and as a widow, to her son. They were largely confined to the home, so women attracted to other women had fewer chances to act on their desires than did men in the same situation. As is the case in much of history, lesbians are nearly invisible in Chinese documentary records.[6]

The opposite is the case for men who loved other men. A literary tradition of writing about these loves developed from the sixth century B.C.E. on, leaving many documents for present-day historians to explore. In Reading 3-A, we learn about a short period in a tradition that spanned two millennia, the Han dynasty (206 B.C.E. to 220 C.E.). During this period, the Chinese developed the word *duanxiu,* one of their most popular terms referring to same-sex love. In this excerpt from Bret Hinsch's groundbreaking study, we see how same-sex love was easily accepted among the Chinese elite of that time.

READING 3-A

Imperial China

from *Passions of the Cut Sleeve: The Male Homosexual Tradition in China,* by Bret Hinsch

Between the collapse of the Zhou and the founding of the Han dynasty in 206 B.C., China underwent political upheavals as painful as they were decisive. An onslaught of armies from the state of Qin finally swept away the decayed Zhou dynasty. For the first time, all under heaven bowed before a single powerful ruler. But the Qin proved to be intolerable masters. Grandiose public works projects sent multitudes into forced labor, while those still at home chafed under a draconian rule of law. Books were burned and wise men were buried alive. The universal unpopularity of the Qin brought the dynasty down after just one generation. It took subsequent Han rulers decades to reunite and rebuild the devastated nation.

Although the traumatic change from Zhou to Han brought enormous political ferment, it does not seem to have significantly altered the patterns of sexual relations among the social elite. Throughout the dynasty, historical records speak openly of the bisexuality of numerous Han emperors. These inexhaustible monarchs retained large harems of wives and concubines while also indulging in regular trysts with male favorites. Although heterosexual intercourse was vital to the continuation of the dynasty, their homosexual liaisons were purely voluntary. The choice of the half-eaten peach [another term referring to same-sex love] by these emperors, together with the frank and straightforward manner in which contemporaneous sources recorded their loves, leaves no possible conclusion except that, like their Zhou predecessors, the social elite of the Han continued to include homosexuality as an accepted part of sexual life.

Like those of the Zhou, the vast majority of Han records concern the lives of rulers. Consequently, our view of homosexuality during the Han pertains almost exclusively to the male loves of the emperors. Just as Edward Gibbon observed that all but one of the first fourteen emperors of Rome were either bisexual or exclusively homosexual, for two centuries at the height of the Han China was ruled by ten openly bisexual emperors. We can better comprehend the extent of homosexuality at the Han court when we consider the emperors together with a few of their more important favorites:

Emperor	Reign	Male Favorite(s)
Gao	206–195 B.C.	Jiru
Hui	194–188 B.C.	Hongru
Wen	179–157 B.C.	Deng Tong, Zhao Tan, Beigong Bozi
Jing	156–141 B.C.	Zhou Ren
Wu	140-87 B.C.	Han Yan, Han Yuc, Li Yannian
Zhao	86–74 B.C.	Jin Shang
Xuan	73–49 B.C.	Zang Pengzu
Yuan	48–33 B.C.	Hong Gong, Shi Xian
Cheng	32–7 B.C.	Zhang Fang, Chunyu Zhang
Ai	6 B.C.–A.D. 1	Dong Xian

All of these attributions are made in the official histories of the period, the *Memoirs of the Historian (Shi ji)* by Sima Qian and the *Records of the Han (Han shu)* by Ban Gu, both respected works that include lengthy chapters describing in detail the biographies of the emperors' male favorites.

These histories convey a detailed picture of an imperial court at which male favorites of the emperor had enormous prominence. In many ways, homosexuality became a central feature of early court life. Grand Historian Sima Qian attested to thc power of imperial favorites in his introduction to the biographies of these influential men:

> Those who served the ruler and succeeded in delighting his ears and eyes, those who caught their lord's fancy and won his favor and intimacy, did so not only through the power of lust and love; each had certain abilities in which he excelled. Thus I made the Biographies of the Emperors' Male Favorites.
>
> The proverb says "No amount of toiling in the fields can compare to a spell of good weather; no amount of faithful service can be compared to being liked by your superiors." This is no idle saying. Yet it is not women alone who can use their looks to attract the eyes of the ruler; courtiers and eunuchs can play at the game as well. Many were the men of ancient times who gained favor this way.

The first of the Han rulers was Emperor Gao, more commonly known as Gaozu. He and his heir, Emperor Hui, started the Han custom of emperors favoring officials willing to employ their sexual talents:

> When the Han arose, Emperor Gaozu, for all his coarseness and blunt manners, was won by the charms of a young boy named Ji,

> and Emperor Hui had a boy favorite named Hong. Neither Ji nor Hong had any particular talent or ability; both won prominence simply through their looks and graces. Day and night they were by the ruler's side, and all the high ministers were obliged to apply to them when they wished to speak to the emperor.

The men each ruler loved subsequently rose to lofty official ranks. These favorites accrued extraordinary privileges owing to their unique intimacy with the emperor and exercised even greater power by helping to determine who else could have access to the human hub of the Han cosmos.

...The celebrated love of the Han Emperor Ai for his beloved Dong Xian exemplified the privileges a devoted imperial patron could bestow, as well as the political ramifications this kind of relationship could entail. The following passage summarizes the account of his life in *Records of the Han.*

> Dong Xian's father, a respected censor, appointed Dong Xian to be a retainer to the Emperor Ai. He was a person whose beauty incited admiration. Emperor Ai gazed at him and spoke of Dong Xian's deportment and appearance. The emperor asked, "What about this retainer Dong Xian?" Because of this Dong Xian spoke with the Emperor. Thus began his favor.
>
> Dong Xian's favor and love increased daily. He held high office and each year was granted ten thousand piculs of grain. His honors alarmed the court.
>
> Dong Xian's nature was always gentle, affable, and flattering. He was good at seducing by holding fast. Every time he was granted a leave of absence he turned it down. Instead he remained constantly at the palace studying medicine. The emperor found it difficult to make Dong Xian return home. He summoned Dong Xian's wife and, like an official, she took up residence in a government estate. The emperor also summoned Dong Xian's sons and daughters, finding them to be bright and well mannered.
>
> The Emperor ennobled Dong Xian's father as the marquis of Guannei, with an attendant fief. Dong Xian became the marquis of Gao'an. These fiefs were each worth two thousand piculs of grain annually. Everyone in Dong Xian's household, down to his slaves, received grants from the emperor. The prime minister repeatedly remonstrated that because of Dong Xian the regulations of the state were in chaos.

Dong Xian's powers and privileges were extraordinary. Their sheer numbers and repetitiveness make it needless to recount them all here. His biography enumerates the highest offices and titles attainable, the greatest of which he received at the age of twenty-two. He was even entrusted with the construction of the emperor's tomb, a duty of the greatest ritual importance and solemnity. Dong Xian's power was such that he was even able to help block one of the most important land reform proposals of the Han, since any such restrictions would have had the most effect on the wealthiest subjects of the realm, such as himself.

During a feast, a visiting chieftain from the northern nomads remarked on the incongruous youth of such a mighty official. The emperor explained that Dong Xian was a sage, which accounted for his early attainments. At this, the chieftain rose and bowed to the youthful prodigy, congratulating his hosts on the good fortune of having a flesh-and-blood sage in their midst. Of course, the real reason for Dong Xian's rank was just the opposite of sagacity. Sexual favor along with a privileged background better explain how someone might attain the pinnacle of worldly success at an age so young that it would even warrant comment from foreign visitors.

Dong Xian's family also received extraordinary benefits from his favor. Father, father-in-law, brother, and grandson all received office and privilege. We should not be surprised at the emperor's willingness to reward the family of a beloved. The practice directly parallels the custom of choosing important officials from the families of imperial consorts. Treating a favorite's family with the same esteem accorded the families of favored concubines further indicates the similarities between male homosexuality and heterosexual concubinage in early China.

Before his death, Emperor Ai openly suggested handing over his empire to Dong Xian. The imperial counselors quickly dismissed this possibility. Even so, on his deathbed, lacking both sons and a designated heir, Ai handed over the imperial seals to Dong Xian and declared him Emperor. In doing so he appealed to the ancient precedent of the mythical Yao's abdication in favor of Shun instead of handing the throne over to his son. Such a tenuous pretense to legitimacy did not impress Dong Xian's many political enemies. He was forced to commit suicide, and the usurper Wang Mang placed a child on the throne, through whom he ruled. Eventually Wang Mang did away with the child emperor and ruled in his own right.

Since Ai was the last adult emperor of the Western Han, his failed attempt to hand over his title to his male lover doomed the dynasty. The bond between emperor and favorite was strong, but not strong enough to overcome the traditions of succession. With no successful opponent to counter Wang Mang, the Western Han dynasty came to an end...

Han authors did not portray favorites as stereotypically effete or effeminate, despite the attention men at court gave to outward ornamentation. Emperor Wu and Han Yan typify Han ideas of ruler and favorite:

> Han Yan was an illegitimate grandson of Han Tuidang, the Marquis of Gonggao. When the present emperor was still king of Jiaodong, he and Yan studied writing together and the two grew very fond of each other. Later, after the emperor was appointed heir apparent, he became more and more friendly with Yan. Yan was skillful at riding and archery and was also very good at ingratiating himself with the emperor. He was well versed in the fighting techniques of the barbarians and therefore, after the emperor came to the throne and began making plans to open attacks on the Xiongnu, he treated Yan with even greater respect and honor. Yan had soon advanced to the rank of superior lord and received as many gifts from the ruler as Deng Tong had in his days of honor.
>
> At this time Yan was constantly by the emperor's side, both day and night. Once the emperor's younger brother Liu Fei, the king of Jiangdu, who had come to court to pay his respects, received permission from the emperor to accompany him on a hunt in the Shanglin Park. The order had already been given to clear the roads for the imperial carriage, but the emperor was not yet ready to depart, and so he sent Yan ahead in one of his attendant carriages, accompanied by fifty or a hundred riders, to gallop through the park and observe the game. The king of Jiangdu, seeing the party approaching in the distance, supposed it was the emperor and ordered his own attendants off the road while he himself knelt down by the side of the road to greet the emperor. Yan, however, raced by without even noticing him, and after he had passed, when the king of Jiangdu realized his error, he was enraged and went to the empress dowager in tears. "I beg to return to the kingdom which has been granted to me and become a bodyguard in the palace," he said. "Perhaps then I may be accorded as much honor as Han Yan!"

> From this time on the empress dowager bore a grudge against Yan.
>
> Because he attended the emperor, Han Yan was allowed to come and go in the women's quarters of the palace and did not have to observe the customary prohibitions against entering them. Some time later, it was reported to the empress dowager that Yan had had an illicit affair with one of the women there. She was furious and immediately sent a messenger ordering him to take his life. Although the emperor attempted to make apologies for him, he was able to do nothing to change the order, and in the end Yan was forced to die.

Traditional historians regarded Emperor Wu as a quintessentially masculine emperor. His name itself means "martial," and he spent his long reign subjugating the surrounding non-Chinese people. Wu garnered fame as both a warrior and a hunter. His beloved shared these interests. In addition to being both literate and intelligent, Han Yan enjoyed stereotypically masculine pursuits, including riding, archery, and warfare. In this sense he epitomized the masculine virtue valued by the aristocracy since the Shang dynasty. Although many court officials pursued vain stylishness in their attempts to gain favor, Han Yan and Emperor Wu's intimacy conformed to the earlier Zhou-dynasty conception of close friends and even lovers as not different from other men in their behavior...

Within marriage, the husband held supreme authority. Prior to the Han, a man could even legally kill his own son, and traces of this life-and-death authority remained even during the Han. A woman would not dare to question her husband on the vital question of his sexuality or object when her husband sought others, such as concubines, for sexual companionship. In fact, jealousy was one of the seven reasons for which a husband could divorce a wife. This recognition of polygamy as an unquestioned Han custom sanctioned male promiscuity. Wives were legally required to acquiesce to their husbands' demands for alternate sexual partners, among whom were other men. By denying wives any say in their sex lives, married men could favor the half-eaten peach [another phrase associated with same-sex love] at will. The government did not interfere with the sexual status quo because it left most moral questions regarding the household to be resolved within the household itself — which in a patriarchal society meant that decisions regarding sexual morality inevitably favored male interests. The very organization of the Han household therefore facilitated the acceptance of male homosexuality.

This atmosphere of openness allowed further development of an emerging sense of homosexual tradition, taking many of its most moving accounts from Han historical literature. The Han tradition finds its greatest exemplar in the famous tale of the Emperor Ai and his favorite Dong Xian. As Ban Gu succinctly observed, "By nature Emperor Ai did not care for women," and the genuine tenderness he felt for his beloved Dong Xian captivated the popular imagination. This short passage describing his love is the most influential in the Chinese homosexual tradition:

> Emperor Ai was sleeping in the daytime with Dong Xian stretched out across his sleeve. When the emperor wanted to get up, Dong Xian was still asleep. Because he did not want to disturb him, the emperor cut off his own sleeve and got up. His love and thoughtfulness went this far!

Just as Mizi Xia gave a homosexual connotation to the term "eating peaches," so did the image of a cut sleeve come to signify the devotion of Emperor Ai to Dong Xian and, broadly, male homosexual love. All of Ai's courtiers "imitated the cut sleeve, also calling it the chopped sleeve," as a tribute to the love shared by their emperor and Dong. The tender power of this image — an array of opulent courtiers fastidiously dressed in colorful silk tunics, each missing a single sleeve — guaranteed the moment would continue to burn in the imaginations of readers for almost twenty centuries.

The terse account of the cut sleeve became absorbed into a tradition of recorded homosexuality that must have seemed ancient even to Emperor Ai. Men in dynastic history did not feel alone in having affectionate feelings for other men. The complete integration of homosexuality into early Chinese court life, as reported in *Memoirs of the Historian* and *Records of the Han,* was alluded to repeatedly in later literature and gave men of subsequent ages a means for situating their desires within an ancient tradition. By seeing their feelings as passions of the "cut sleeve," they gained a consciousness of the place of male love in their society.

The dramatic ascendance of Dong Xian almost to the imperial throne marks a high point in the Chinese homosexual tradition and in the influence of homosexuality over Chinese society. Not only was male love accepted, but it permeated the fabric of upper-class life. From the vital concerns of politics to the frivolous world of men's fashion, homosexuality played an important role. This sway over elite society was most pronounced at the height of the Western Han, when homosexuality occupied an esteemed and powerful place in court life. Still, the patterns and images of homosexuality formed during the Zhou and brought to fruition during the Han became even more elaborated under subsequent dynasties.

AFTERWORD

Readers may wonder what became of these attitudes in China, particularly if they are familiar with contemporary homophobic attitudes there (see Chapter 16).

The male homosexual tradition in China lasted until fairly recent times. Sodomy was made a crime only in 1740, much later than in Europe.[7] These laws were proclaimed by the Qing dynasty, which came to power in China in the mid-1600s. Invaders from the outlying province of Manchuria (hence their nickname as the "Manchus"), the Qing seized power from a weak Ming dynasty. The Qing saw the Ming as being too self-indulgent and given over to pleasures of the flesh, and felt that this was the source of their weakness. To make sure that the same thing did not happen to them, the Qing sought to "clean up" China. One item that needed to be "cleaned up" was the homosexual tradition, which by that time had become widespread in popular literature. Since it was foreign to the Qing (who, after all, did not come from central China and were not ethnically Chinese), the homosexual tradition was seen as part of the weakness of the Ming period. The Qing thus put forth the first laws against it in Chinese history, and proceeded to destroy many historical records of same-sex love.[8]

Western influences, arriving in the nineteenth century, added to this homophobia. The Industrial Revolution made Europe much stronger than China by the 1800s. Following its defeat in the Opium War (1839–1842) with Great Britain, China suffered a series of humiliations at the hands of different European nations against which it was unable to defend itself. Eager to return China to the position it had once held as the world's strongest society, many

Chinese decided that ideas from the West, such as industrialization, democracy, and Marxism, were the way to restore China's greatness. One import was Western homophobia. As Hinsch writes, "In importing Western sexual morality, however, the Chinese also imported Western intolerance of homosexuality."[9] The victory of the Chinese Communists in 1949 helped increase this intolerance. Communism preached that homosexuality was a "bourgeois decadence" that would cease to exist when the perfect society had been created.[10] Thus, the current rulers of China feel that stamping out homosexuality is their duty and actively persecute gay people. Chapter 16 addresses the current situation there. Only recent scholarship, such as that of Hinsch, has brought the Chinese tradition of tolerance of gays to light.

IMPORTANT TERMS

Confucius
filial piety
duty vs. pleasure
duanxiu (passion of the cut sleeve)
Han dynasty

QUESTIONS/ACTIVITIES

1. Underline Hinsch's evidence. What are his sources? Who is speaking? What advantages or disadvantages do they present as sources for information? Are they reliable as a way of understanding gays in ancient China? Can we make generalizations about a society's attitudes from what goes on with its leaders and their lives?

2. What motivated the same-sex activities in the stories? Choose an individual and list all the motivations he may have had to take a same-sex lover.

3. What personal qualities are valued in these stories? Are the stories focused on the sexuality or the character of the individuals involved?

4. Rewrite one of the stories, substituting a female lover for a male one. Does this significantly change the tone of the story? Why or why not?

5. How do others seem to regard the homosexuality of the individuals depicted in the stories? Are their reactions positive, negative, or both? What seems to motivate their reactions? Are they "homophobic" reactions?

6. What factors allowed men in the stories to engage in these activities? Why might women not have been able to do so?

7. Would you say that this is an “essentialist” or a “constructionist” interpretation? Why?

8. Compare this with Reading 16-B: how have things changed in China?

CHAPTER 4

The Celebration of Difference: The Institution of the Berdache among Native Americans

INTRODUCTION

When Europeans arrived in the Western Hemisphere in the late fifteenth century, they encountered an incredible diversity of societies among those already living here, people they called "Indians." Ranging from settled societies with cities of over one hundred thousand (as with the Aztecs of Mexico) to small bands of hunter-gatherer peoples, Native Americans often confused and frightened the Europeans, who found their cultures at times alien and offensive. The cultural conflict that resulted still continues to some extent, with Native Americans struggling to hold onto their traditions in the face of an outside people who historically have labeled those traditions "backwards" or even "evil."

Europeans found few Native American cultural traditions as startling as that which became known as the "berdache." Existing in over 150 North American tribes,[1] "berdaches" were men who took the social roles of women. They often wore women's clothes and at times took male spouses. Early explorers were shocked to discover this practice. Spanish explorer Cabeza da Vaca, in his account of his captivity among Florida's Indians from 1528 to 1533, wrote, "During the time I was thus among these people I saw a devilish thing, and it is that I saw one man married to another ... they go about dressed as women, and do women's tasks..."[2] French explorer Jacques LeMoyne confirmed da Vaca's discoveries in his 1564 trip, writing, "Hermaphrodites ... are quite common in these parts."[3]

Even more baffling to Europeans than the existence of berdaches were Indian attitudes toward them: in some places, Indians seemed to approve of and celebrate these people! Seventeenth-century French explorer Jacques Marquette reported from his 1673–1677 voyage down the Mississippi that "they [berdaches] are summoned to the Councils, and nothing can be decided without their advice. Finally, through their profession of leading an Extraordinary life, they pass ... for persons of Consequence."[4] Nineteenth-century American artist George Catlin found that the Sioux, Sacs, and Foxes of the Plains even had a special dance celebrating the berdache,[5] and anthropologist Mathilde Coxe Stevenson reported that We'wha, a Zuni berdache, was "the strongest character and the most intelligent of the Zuni tribe."[6]

Europeans were so dumfounded by this practice that at first they did not know what to call these people. Some early observers assumed that, since berdaches had male appearance but wore women's clothes, they must be "hermaphrodites," individuals who possessed the genitalia of both sexes. Others decided that these must be "sodomites," those who engaged in same-sex sexual activities. Since they dressed in women's clothes, they must be passive "sodomites." The French word "berdache," which referred to passive homosexual partners, became the most-used name for these Indians. It is still used today to describe this custom.7

Whatever term they used (hermaphrodite, berdache, or another), most Europeans came to a quick conclusion about this custom: it was an "abominable sin." As early as the seventeenth century, historical records show berdaches being put to death for their "sin." Spanish explorer Vasco Nunez de Balboa "put a large number of them to death by setting wild dogs upon them."[8] Spanish priest Francisco de Pareja developed special questions to be asked during confession of suspected berdaches, to help them to be "saved."[9] Franciscan missionary Francisco Palou summed up the dominant attitude in 1777 when he said, "The abominable vice will be eliminated ... for the glory of God and the benefit of those poor ignorants."[10]

Historians have had trouble uncovering accurate information about the berdache. Influenced by their religious beliefs, early explorers judged the berdaches harshly, making their accounts of them questionable. Native Americans themselves, aware of how Europeans have interfered with their culture throughout history, have often been reluctant to share information on customs such as berdachism of which they knew whites disapproved. Only in recent years, when more open-minded historians have approached the subject, have accounts of berdachism that are based on accurate information emerged.

The premier historian in this field is Professor Walter Williams of the University of Southern California. In his groundbreaking study *The Spirit and the Flesh: Sexual Diversity in American Indian Culture,* Williams used both historical documents and first-person interviews with Native Americans to shed new light on the subject. He explained that berdaches were not hermaphrodites, nor were they "gay" people, i.e., people whose identity was based on being attracted to their own sex. Rather, he explains that the berdache is a "male who does not fill a society's standard male role ... They are not seen as men, but they are not seen as women either. They occupy an alternative gender role that is a mixture of diverse [male and female] elements."[11] Berdaches were occasionally scorned but more often celebrated, and they existed in a tremendous range of Native American tribes across the entire North American continent. In Reading 4-A, Williams explains the special "calling" that berdaches were seen to have experienced that destined them to take this role. Having received an unusual calling, berdaches were seen as gifted holders of a special vision that could be used to benefit all of the tribe. By helping us to comprehend the custom of the berdache, Williams helps us to understand what early Europeans could not: how a role that would have been so shameful among the Europeans of that time could have been regarded so positively by Native Americans.

READING 4-A

The Berdache

from *The Spirit and the Flesh,*
by Walter Williams

The emphasis of American Indian religions, then, is on the spiritual nature of all things. To understand the physical world, one must appreciate the underlying spiritual essence. Then one can begin to see that the physical is only a faint shadow, a partial reflection, of a supernatural and extrarational world. By the Indian view, everything that exists is spiritual. Every object — plants, rocks, water, air, the moon, animals, humans, the earth itself — has a spirit. The spirit of one thing (including a human) is not superior to the spirit of any other. Such a view promotes a sophisticated ecological awareness of the place that humans have in the larger environment. The function of religion is not to try to condemn or change what exists, but to accept the realities of the world and to appreciate their contributions to life. Everything that exists has a purpose.

...The physical aspects of a thing or a person, after all, are not nearly as important as its spirit. American Indians use the concept of a person's *spirit* in the way that other Americans use the concept of a person's *character*. Consequently, physical hermaphroditism is not necessary for the idea of gender mixing. A person's character, their spiritual essence, is the crucial thing.

The Berdache's Spirit

Individuals who are physically normal might have the spirit of the other sex, might range somewhere between the two sexes, or might have a spirit that is distinct from either women or men. Whatever category they fall into, they are seen as being different from men. They are accepted spiritually as "Not Man." Whichever option is chosen, Indian religions offer spiritual explanations. Among the Arapahoes of the Plains, berdaches are called *haxu'xan* and are seen to be that way as a result of a supernatural gift from birds or animals. Arapaho mythology recounts the story of Nih'a'ca, the first *haxu'xan*. He pretended to be a woman and married the mountain lion, a symbol for masculinity. The myth, as recorded by ethnographer Alfred Kroeber around 1900, recounted that "these people had the natural desire to become women, and as they grew up gradually became women. They gave up the desires of men. They were married to men. They had miraculous power and could do supernatural things. For instance, it was one of them that first made an intoxicant from rainwater." Besides the theme of inventiveness, similar to the Navajo creation story, the berdache role is seen as a product of a "natural desire." Berdaches "gradually became women," which underscores the notion of a woman as a social category rather than as a fixed biological entity. Physical biological sex is less important in gender classification than a person's desire — one's spirit.

The myths contain no prescriptions for trying to change berdaches who are acting out desires of their heart. Like many other cultures' myths, the Zuni origin myths simply sanction the idea that gender can be transformed independently of having biological sex. Indeed, myths warn of dire consequences when interference with such a transformation is attempted. Prince Alexander Maximillian of the German state of Wied, traveling in the northern Plains in the 1830s, heard a myth about a warrior who once tried to force a berdache to avoid women's clothing. The berdache resisted, and the warrior shot him with an arrow. Immediately the berdache disappeared, and the warrior saw only a pile of stones with his arrow in them. Since then, the story concluded, no intelligent person would try to coerce a berdache. Making the point even more directly, a Mandan myth told of an Indian who tried to force *mihdacke* (berdaches) to give up their distinctive dress and status, which led the spirits to punish many people with death. After that, no Mandans interfered with berdaches.

With this kind of attitude, reinforced by myth and history, the aboriginal view accepts human diversity. The creation story of the Mohave of the Colorado River Valley speaks of a time when people were not sexually differentiated. From this perspective, it is easy to accept that certain individuals might combine elements of masculinity and femininity. A respected Mohave elder, speaking in the 1930s, stated this viewpoint simply: "From the very beginning of the world it was meant that there should be [berdaches], just as it was instituted that there should be shamans. They were intended for that purpose."

This elder also explained that a child's tendencies to become a berdache are apparent early, by about age nine to twelve, before the child reaches puberty: "That is the time when young persons become initiated to the functions of their sex ... None but young people will become berdaches as a rule." Many tribes have a public ceremony that acknowledges the acceptance of berdache status. A Mohave shaman related the ceremony for his tribe: "When the child was about ten years old his relatives would begin discussing his strange ways. Some of them disliked it, but the more intelligent began envisaging an initiation ceremony." The relatives prepare for the ceremony without letting the boy know of it. It is meant to take him by surprise, to be both an initiation and a test of his true inclinations. People from various settlements are invited to attend. The family wants the community to see it and become accustomed to seeing the boy as an *alyha*.

One the day of the ceremony, the shaman explained, the boy is led into a circle: "If the boy showed a willingness to remain standing in the circle, exposed to the public eye, it was almost certain that he would go through with the ceremony. The singer, hidden behind the crowd, began singing the songs. As soon as the sound reached the boy he began to dance as women do." If the boy is unwilling to assume *alyha* status, he would refuse to dance. But if his character — his spirit — is *alyha,* "the song goes right to his heart and he will dance with much intensity. He cannot help it. After the fourth song he is proclaimed." After the ceremony, the boy is carefully bathed and receives a woman's skirt. He is then led back to the dance ground, dressed as an *alyha,* and announces his new feminine name to the crowd. After that he would resent being called by his old male name.

Among the Yuman tribes of the Southwest, the transformation is marked by a social gathering, in which the berdaches prepare a meal for the friends of the family. Ethnographer Ruth Underhill, doing fieldwork among the Papago Indians in the 1930s, wrote that berdaches were common among the Papago Indians, and were usually publicly acknowledged during childhood. She recounted that a boy's parents would test him if they noticed that he preferred female pursuits. The regular pattern, mentioned by many of Underhill's Papago informants, was to build a small brush enclosure in which they placed a man's bow and arrows, and also a woman's basket. At the appointed time the boy was brought to the enclosure as the adults watched from outside. Once he was inside, the adults "set fire to the enclosure. They watched what he took with him as he ran out and if it was the basketry materials, they reconciled themselves to his being a berdache."

What is important to recognize in all of these practices is that the assumption of a berdache role was not forced on the boy by others. While adults might have their suspicions, it was only when the child made the proper move that he was considered a berdache. By doing woman's dancing, preparing a meal, or taking the woman's basket he was making an important symbolic gesture. Indian children were not stupid, and they knew the implications of these ceremonies beforehand. A boy in the enclosure could have left without taking anything, or could have taken both the man's and the woman's tools. With the community standing by watching, he was well aware that his choice would mark his assumption of berdache status. Rather than being seen as an involuntary test of his reflexes, this ceremony may be interpreted as a definite statement by the child on the berdache role.

Indians do not see the assumption of berdache status, however, as a free will choice on the part of the boy. People felt that the boy was acting out his basic nature. The Lakota shaman Lame Deer explained:

> They were not like other men, but the Great Spirit made them *winktes* and we accepted them as such ... We think if a woman has two little ones growing inside her, if she is going to have twins, sometimes instead of giving birth to two babies they have formed up in her womb into just one, into a half-man/half-woman kind of being ... To us a man is what nature, or his dreams, make him. We accept him for what he wants to be. That's up to him.

...

It is in this context that I later understood one of my earliest fieldwork experiences in the northern Plains. When I first began doing research on the Omaha reservation I interviewed two Omaha men in their twenties, and I asked them to define *mexoga* [berdache]. They laughed and said it was "like a faggot." Their joking manner at first led me to believe that they were typical homophobes. But after seeing that I was approaching the subject in a serious manner, they went on to say: "Indians accept it, and don't condemn it like white people do. I don't care what reservation you go to, you always find one among every group of Indians." It soon became obvious that these men simply accepted it as part of life, nothing to get upset about. In fact, they later took me to meet a *mexoga,* and they treated him in a most respectful manner. Anther Omaha man refers to a *mexoga,* saying "People leave him alone and don't tease him. He is an oddball, but that is his right. We respect a man for what he is."

While there might be joking or ridicule, it never went beyond that. The literature does not show instances where a berdache was physically attacked because of his differences. As Terry Calling Eagle states, "*Winktes* are not hurt, because if someone did that something bad happens to them." Again, it is the spiritual element that protects the berdache...

Double Vision and Prophecy

The berdache receives respect partly as a result of being a mediator. Somewhere between the status of men and women, berdaches not only mediate between the sexes but also between the psychic and the physical — between the spirit and the flesh. Since they mix the characteristics of both men and women, they possess the visions of both. They have double vision, with the ability to see more clearly than a single gender perspective can provide. This is why they are often referred to as "seer," one whose eyes can see beyond the blinders that restrict the average person. Viewing things from outside the usual perspective, they are able to achieve a creative and objective viewpoint that is seldom available to ordinary people. By the Indian view, someone who is different offers advantages to society precisely because he or she is freed from the restriction of the usual. It is a different window from which to view the world.

With this different perspective, this double vision, berdaches see themselves as unique. Jerry Baldy, a Hupa, expresses this idea about his childhood: "I knew I was different, being so attracted to men and being effeminate, but there was something else different about me beyond all that. I always wanted to explore the unknown." Likewise, Michael One Feather, a Lakota *winkte,* specifies his differentness in growing up: "I always knew I had a different concept from what everybody else had. Of things, of life; how I saw things. Most people didn't see the way I saw. What I would call a way of looking at things. My ideas were always spectacular — overshooting, you know, and overachieving. I always had to do something more, to do it my way, based on my different view."

Since they have such vision, many cultures found that berdaches can also see into the future. As a consequence, they are respected as prophets. Winnebago berdaches were noted for their ability to foretell future events. A Lakota berdache explains that a shaman helped to interpret his dreams: "He respected me, and said I could foretell the future. Since then I often have predicted things that would happen. For example, one time I had a feeling that a specific relative would die, and then later I found out that that relative did die suddenly with no warning right at the time I was having my vision. People realize that I am a seer."

In 1971 the Sioux shaman Lame Deer interviewed a berdache: "He told me that a *winkte* has a gift of prophesy and that he himself could predict the weather ... He told a woman she would live to be eighty years old, and she gave him a fine pair of moccasins for that. He told me that if nature puts a burden on a man by making him different, it also gives him a power." It is this power, based on the spiritual origins of berdachism and in the context of ceremonial leadership, in which the respected status of the berdache is rooted. Proceeding from the view that a person's different character is a reflection of his or her closeness to the spiritual, berdaches are often associated with shamanism and sacredness. Such spiritual abilities mean that berdaches may take on specific ceremonial tasks that are recognized specifically as their own. Whether in blessing ceremonies, providing lucky names, offering spiritual protection, or predicting the future, berdaches are often both respected and feared for their qualities of strength and power. They utilize their strength to be of social benefit to others, in particular to their own family.

IMPORTANT TERMS

sex	berdache	"spirit" (Indian conception of)
gender	hermaphrodite	

QUESTIONS/ACTIVITIES

1. Underline all pieces of evidence Williams presents. What are his sources? Who is speaking? Does this evidence support the points he claims it supports?

2. Write a paragraph explaining why the Indians accepted berdachism.

3. Analyze the specific rituals connected to the berdache. What happens during them? What do they seem to mean?

4. Contrast Indian notions of what makes a person the way they are ("spirit") with today's concepts: are they more alike or more different?

5. Imagine that you are a European explorer and a Native American berdache in the sixteenth century who have just met. Write a dialogue between the two, or write an "internal monologue" of what they each might be thinking about the other.

6. Examine the link between gender roles and homophobia. Boys who "act like girls" are often called "faggots," while girls who are too aggressive may be labeled "butches" or "dykes." What would Indians think about this kind of labeling?

7. Williams writes that the "specialness" of berdaches, the fact that they were not "normal," was why they were cherished by their fellow tribespeople. Research how people who are not "normal" are regarded in your school and community. Categories could include modes of dress, hairstyle, talents, or others. Do we value or devalue such individuals? Why?

CHAPTER 5

"Passing Women" in Early Modern America

INTRODUCTION

As we have seen in Chapters 2 and 3, historians face an easier task recovering the history of men than that of women. This is largely because much of what we are able to learn is based on written records. Men usually had greater access to education than women did, meaning that fewer women were able to record their lives. Since men did most of the writing, they recorded what was of interest to them. This often did not include women, who were seen as "unimportant." In addition, the types of activities that were judged "worthy" of recording, such as politics, have usually been the province of men, so historic records of women's lives can be scarce indeed.

If all women are generally "hidden from history," lesbians are among the most hidden women of all. There are many reasons. First, sexuality in general was often not deemed "appropriate" for recording, so we have few records of any sort on sexual history. Among the most "inappropriate" were same-sex activities, further reducing our number of sources. Moreover, those who were doing the recording were usually men, so what they did write down was generally about their own same-sex encounters, not those of lesbians. And, finally, Western society has generally denied the fact that women are sexual beings, especially without the presence of men. This belief was so strong that many early laws condemning same-sex activities did not even mention women, as the (male) lawmakers could not even conceive of such activity.[1] "Lesbian invisibility" was born.

Given these obstacles, how do we know anything at all about lesbians? First, we do have some writings of women who loved women. These are often open to disputed interpretation, as we will see in the next chapter when we look at the life of Eleanor Roosevelt. A second source is in the records of women who somehow "broke the rules" and came to the attention of men in positions of power, such as political leaders, legal authorities, or medical personnel. We know, for instance, that women were prosecuted for "sodomitical" acts in the British North American colonies as early as 1642, telling us that women who loved women did indeed exist from the beginning of American history.[2] These prosecutions also present problems for the historian, however. "Rule-breakers" of any sort are not typical of their group, and it is dangerous to make generalizations about an entire population from the actions of a few unusual individuals. Nevertheless, by revealing what was forbidden by society, these "rule-breakers" do show us what was acceptable and what was unacceptable for women to do in a given time period.

A fascinating group of female "rule-breakers" were those we call "passing women." "Passing" is a phenomenon often seen in history, when individuals from an oppressed group pretend to be members of the dominant group in order to escape discrimination. In the days of segregation, light-skinned African-Americans often used their paler complexions to get jobs or buy homes in neighborhoods open only to whites. During the Holocaust, some Jews saved their lives by "passing" as Christians. And throughout history, some individual women have "passed" as men in order to gain some of the "unearned privileges" men receive.[3]

Reading 5-A examines the phenomenon of "passing women" in late-nineteenth- and early-twentieth-century America. As the reading shows, these women "passed" for different reasons. It would be incorrect to label all of these women "lesbians," as some of them "passed" for reasons other than their sexuality. Some, however, did take female spouses, suggesting that perhaps love played a role in their decision to "pass." Although their lives were very different from the ordinary women of their time, these "passing women" offer us a fascinating glimpse into the forces that shaped the economic, political, social, and sexual destinies of women before the emergence of the modern feminist and lesbian and gay liberation movements.

READING 5-A

"She Even Chewed Tobacco"
by the San Francisco Lesbian and Gay History Project

from *Hidden from History: Reclaiming the Gay and Lesbian Past,* edited by Martin Duberman, Martha Vicinus, and George Chauncey, Jr.

Over the past fifteen years, feminist research has done much to dispel the stereotypes of life in Victorian America. One contribution to this revision is the study of women who dressed as men, worked for men's wages, courted and married women they loved, and even voted. "Passing women" succeeded in hiding their identities from most of the world and claimed economic and political privilege enjoyed by men. As Jonathan Katz has written, they not only cross-dressed, but cross-worked and cross-spoke. American newspapers headlined their stories — "Poses, Undetected, 60 Years as a Man," "A Gay Deceiver of the Feminine Gender," and "Death Proves Married 'Man' a Woman" — announcing to readers the shocking discovery of these women's deceptions. These reports, which appeared more frequently after 1850, provide our most visible evidence of a larger social phenomenon in which many American women chose to abandon constraining feminine roles and to pass as men. To call these women "lesbians" is historically inaccurate, but many actively pursued — and won — the women they loved.

Since Biblical times some women have attempted to pass as men, and they have been severely punished if they were discovered. And yet they took the risks, for reasons we can as yet only guess. Pictures and ballads show that women dressed as soldiers and sailors to fight in wars, to join a lover, or to see the world. Mary Read and Anne Bonney, who were convicted of piracy in 1720, dressed as men. Dr. James Barry, the most famous British woman to go to war, rose to become Inspector-General of army hospitals. Deborah Sampson fought with the Fourth Massachusetts Regiment during the American Revolution, and hundreds of other women soldiers have been identified in later wars.

In a fund-raising autobiography, written in 1855, Lucy Ann Lobdell, of rural New York State, explained her decision to pass as one of economic necessity: "I made up my mind to dress in men's attire to seek labor, as I was used to men's work and only got a dollar per week, and I was capable of doing men's work and getting men's wages. I resolved to try to get work away, among strangers."

The courageous woman who could pass not only earned more money for the same work; they could also open bank accounts, write checks, own houses and property and vote in local and national elections. In New York City, Murray Hall, a woman who posed as a man for twenty-five years, became an influential politician in the Tammany Hall Democratic machine during the 1880s and 1890s. She married other women twice; both marriages broke up because Hall was "too attentive to other women." Hall kept her identity a secret. Even though she had breast cancer, she refused to see a doctor for fear he would expose her, and eventually one did. Indeed, we know of many passing women because they were exposed to the press by doctors.

Whatever their motives for passing — to earn a decent wage, to marry women, or to enjoy political rights — all passing women were in constant danger of exposure, arrest, and incarceration in a jail or insane asylum. At the very least they risked fines or imprisonment (and consequent loss of work) for wearing male attire. To avoid exposure, passing women had to be physically strong, confident in the streets, and know how to flirt with women! A newspaper account of "Bill," a Missouri laborer who became the local secretary of the International Brotherhood of Boilermakers, typified a successful passing woman: "She drank, she swore, she courted girls, she worked as hard as her fellows, she fished and camped, she even chewed tobacco."

The women who passed often had a clear sense of the political implications of their decision. An American woman, Cora Anderson, passed as Ralph Kerwinnieo for thirteen years. When she was arrested in Milwaukee in 1914 for "disorderly conduct," she defended herself:

> Do you blame me for wanting to be a man, free to live life in a man-made world? ... In the future centuries, it is probable that woman will be owner of her own body and the custodian of her own soul. [But] the well-cared for woman [now] is a parasite, and the woman who must work is a slave ... Do you blame me for hating to resume again a woman's clothing and just belong? Is it any wonder that I determined to become a member of the privileged sex, if possible?

Throughout the United States, nineteenth-century newspapers reported on women who passed as men, but the history of the San

Francisco Bay area includes several especially well-documented cases. The city's rapid growth after the Gold Rush (from three hundred inhabitants in 1847 to thirty thousand in 1850) brought opportunities for many single men — and women. The free and easy atmosphere of the city seems to have encouraged many women to wear men's clothing...

The most notorious passing woman in San Francisco was Jeanne Bonnet. Born in Paris in 1849, she moved to San Francisco with her family as part of the French Theatrical Troupe. Soon Jeanne was in trouble, possibly for petty thievery. She was committed to the Industrial School, San Francisco's first reformatory. Newspaper reports condemned her unfeminine behavior:

> By the time she was 15, Jeanne Bonnet evinced a disposition to go it alone, spurning the advice of relatives and friends and hastening down the broad road to moral destruction. She became imbued with the spirit of heroism and cursed the day she was born a female instead of a male.

Upon release from the reformatory Jeanne organized a gang of boy thieves. Her illegal acts, the newspapers claimed, were "seldom equalled by even the most daring men of her class for the boldness of execution." One reporter described her as a "man-hater" with "short cropped hair, an unwomanly voice, and a masculine face which harmonized excellently with her customary suit of boys' clothes, including a jaunty hat which she wore with all the grace of an experienced hoodlum." Although arrested over twenty times for "wearing male attire," Jeanne Bonnet refused to pay her fine and often went to jail, declaring, "The police might arrest me as often as they wish — I will never discard male attire as long as I live."

In 1875, when Jeanne was twenty-six, she began visiting San Francisco brothels. She organized an all-woman gang with members from the brothels. These women swore off prostitution, had nothing to do with men, and supported themselves by petty thievery and shoplifting. Jeanne's special friend, and probably her lover, was gang member Blanche Buneau. Blanche had arrived in San Francisco from Paris in 1875 with a man named Arthur Deneve, who had been living off her earnings as a prostitute. Jeanne persuaded Blanche to leave him. She resolved to "step in between as many women of Blanche's character and men of Deneve's stripe as she possibly could and cause a separation." Jeanne's life was threatened and she was physically attacked many times by pimps, who were furious at her for stealing away the prostitutes they considered their own property. Jeanne's life came to an abrupt end at the San Miguel Saloon, some four miles outside San Francisco. She had gone there on September 14, 1876, to spend the night with Blanche. Lying in bed, waiting for Blanche, she was shot through the window and killed. The murder was never solved.

In 1895 the police near San Jose, California, arrested businessman Milton Matson for passing bad checks. Discovered to be, in reality, Luisa Matson, she insisted, "I have no reason whatever for wearing this garb except monetary matters." Yet, reporters learned, Matson was engaged to a San Francisco schoolteacher, Helen Fairweather. After her release from jail, Matson secretly moved to San Francisco and became S.B. Matson, a man who worked in the San Francisco Public Library. Eleven years later, in 1906, Matson lost her job and home in the fire following the earthquake. She moved to a permanent refugee settlement called Point Lobos, and was rediscovered when she died of a stroke. Letters from "Helen" revealed that Helen Fairweather was still a part of Matson's life, although Fairweather denied continuing their friendship.

In August 1897, the police in Stockton, California, briefly held a twenty-year-old woman for masquerading in men's clothing. She claimed to have lost her speech in an accident, but she wrote out her story for police and reporters, explaining that although her neighbors called her Jack, her real name was Babe Bean. Bean lived on a houseboat, or ark, on McLeod's Lake, near Stockton. She wore a blue suit, white silk shirt, large shoes, and a hat pulled over her eyes. "I have been wearing men's clothing off and on for five years," she wrote, "for as a man, I can travel freely, feel protected and find work." She refused to reveal her family origins, but, she claimed, they were one of the best in the land:

> I loved my mother with all my life, but I feared even to talk to her at times, lest my rough manner might offend her. From a tomboy full of ambitions, I was made into a sad and thoughtful woman. I commenced to be rebellious. My mother feared for my future, and thought that nothing but a convent would save me, and there I remained. How I yearned for that freedom I dreamed of and how often I wished I could enjoy the liberty that the world sees fit to allow a boy.

At fifteen she decided to marry her brother's best friend in order to escape the convent and see the world. Within a few months she divorced her husband and set out on her own, passing as a man. She lived for four years in the mountains, on city streets, and in hobo camps.

The people of Stockton became fascinated with Babe Bean, the ark dweller in a man's attire, and they began to treat her with affectionate curiosity. For months her every movement made front-page news in the Stockton papers, and stories of the "Trousered Puzzle" reached San Francisco and Boston papers. The Stockton Bachelor's Club made Babe Bean an honorary member and the guest of honor at a dinner. She was hired by the Stockton *Evening Mail* as a reporter and assigned to cover the Baby Show at the San Joaquin County Fair.

But all was not well. The "Girls of Stockton" spitefully wrote to the newspaper:

> What puzzles us girls is why Babe Bean should be allowed to dress in that way, while if any of the rest of us wanted to walk out in that kind of costume for a change, we would be arrested quicker than quick. There used to be a law against females dressing like a male human being, but it seems not to apply to Babe Bean. If Babe Bean is a girl, and continues to dress in boys' clothing, the rest of us ought to have the same privilege, and we are going to do it. Some fine evening, there are going to be about twenty-five young women on the streets of Stockton, all dressed in men's clothing and we're going to the ark and get Babe Bean and duck her in McLeod's Lake till she cries, "Nuff." Then she can talk if she wants to.

Babe Bean replied to this attack with characteristic aplomb. "It is your privilege to dress as you see fit, whether it is after the fashion of Venus or after the fashion of Babe Bean. I wish to state that boys' clothes are still selling in Stockton at reduced prices. You are quite welcome to that information." She also added that she was quite capable of defending herself. Another more supportive letter appeared, declaring, "I do not know Babe Bean, but she is a woman, and I do not think it is a woman's place to injure a sister because she does not happen to live just as we do; and if she wants to wear men's clothes and have sixteen pockets, it is none of our business."

In 1898 war was declared between the United States and Spain, and front-page articles about Babe Bean were replaced by accounts of Stockton's recruits leaving for Cuba or the Philippines. Babe Bean disappeared from Stockton, but a small man named Jack Garland served as a lieutenant during the Spanish-American War. He later moved to San Francisco, where in 1906, he served as a male nurse during the earthquake and fire, and provided emergency care for the homeless. For the next thirty years Jack Garland lived in San Francisco rooming houses and acted as a kind of free-lance social worker, aiding homeless and hungry people. He was affectionately known as "Uncle Jack" by those who knew and loved him. On September 18, 1936, this "little man with the big heart" collapsed and was taken to a hospital, where attendants did not at first realize that he was really a woman. His death revealed not only his true sex, but also his true identity. The sixty-six-year-old "Uncle Jack," alias Babe Bean, had once been Elvira Virginia Mugarrieta, the daughter of José Marcos Mugarrieta, who had founded the Mexican consulate in San Francisco; her mother, Eliza Alice Garland, was said to be the daughter of a Louisiana Supreme Court Justice.

By the time Jack Garland/Babe Bean died, the world had changed enormously for women. The vote had been won; educational opportunities had been increased; the professions had admitted a few determined women; and women were visible in a variety of new jobs. In 1903, a group of at least ten women passed as men and worked for the New York Central Railway in Buffalo, New York. They were porters (most likely black women), train agents, "switchmen," and cooks. A reporter claimed that these women "often met together and made themselves not a little merry over the success of their transference from one class of humanity to another." During the Depression of the 1930s, women hoboes sometimes passed as men. In the meantime, passing women sought companionship with other women, and even married them. In 1925, for example, the marriage of "Peter" Stratford and Elizabeth Rowland made headlines.

After 1920 women who occasionally wore men's clothing and those who passed as men began to socialize more openly in cafés and night clubs. In Chicago two night clubs, the Roselle Club, run by Eleanor Shelly, and the Twelve-thirty Club, run by Becky Blumfield, were closed by the police during the 1930s because "women in male attire were nightly patrons of the places." Many of the couples who frequented these clubs had been married to each other by a black minister on Chicago's South Side. In San Francisco, lesbians met at Mona's, where, it was said, "Girls will be boys." The growing subculture marked a change from the earlier passing woman, who seemed to be a loner, wary of doctors, police, and reporters.

Public attitudes toward passing women also changed in the early twentieth century, imposing stricter penalties on cross-dressing. In addition to the older, legal sanctions against passing, new medical and psychiatric theories labelled these women as "sexual deviants." Some doctors described passing women as typical of all lesbians. "The female invert," wrote an American doctor in 1915, "likes to ... dress herself entirely in men's attire and disguise her identity. She further prefers the occupations of men." Psychologists labelled these new passing women as inverts, tribadists, sapphists, men-women, he-shes, gyanders, femino-sexuals, uraniads, delusional masculinity, and women who suffered from viraginous disorders.

But passing women had already developed a more positive language to describe their own emerging lesbian identities. In the 1870s the word "dike" referred to a man who was all dressed up, or "diked out," perhaps for a night on the town. By 1900 the word "bulldyker" had come into use in the red-light district of Philadelphia to mean lesbian lovers. And, in 1935, black blues singer Bessie Jackson recorded a song called "B-D Woman," meaning "Bulldagger Woman," which described lesbians who adopted a masculine style. It describes the oppression and celebrates the economic independence and rebellious spirit shared by generations of women who passed as men:

Comin a time, B-D women ain't gonna need no men.
The way they treat us is a low down and dirty shame.

B-D women, they can lay their claim,
They can lay that jive just like a natural man.

B-D women, you know they sure is rough,
They all drink plenty whiskey and they sure can strut their stuff.

B-D women, you know they work and make their dough,
And when they get ready to spend it they know just where to go.

The tradition of passing women, begun in the nineteenth century, lives on today, a small but important part of lesbian and women's history.

IMPORTANT TERMS

lesbian invisibility	sex (biological)
"passing"	gender (social)

QUESTIONS/ACTIVITIES

1. A film version of this article, which was originally a narrated slide presentation, is available from: Women Make Movies, 225 Lafayette St., New York, NY 10012. It includes photographs and drawings of nearly all individuals listed, bringing them to life in a way the written word cannot.

2. Break down the article by looking at each individual cited. Analyze the different reasons each tried to "pass" as a man. Then make generalizations about the incentives a woman of that time would have for seeking masculine status. Make a list of the "unearned privileges" (see Chapter 1) men had that these women wanted to gain.

3. What qualities do these "passing" women have that are considered "masculine"? Are these truly qualities of men? Could they be adopted by either gender?

4. Write a first-person explanation of why one of these women passed as a man, as if you were that person. Especially interesting might be ones from Babe Bean and Jeanne Bonnet, looking back over their experiences at the end of their lives.

5. Why would a lesbian of that time perhaps have found it easier to "pass" as a man than to be a woman-identified lesbian?

6. Find statistics today about earning differences between men and women, the number of men in executive positions and political office, and similar data. Are there still incentives for women to "pass" as men?

7. For extra credit, try to "pass" as the other gender in a setting where no one knows you (an all-boys school a friend attends, for instance). Report back on your experience: what did you learn?

8. Several films can be used to draw parallels or illustrate the phenomenon of "passing." The 1993 feature *The Ballad of Little Jo* is based on the life of an American woman who passed in the late-nineteenth-century West, while the 1992 feature *The Crying*

Game presents the story of a man passing as a woman. *Europa, Europa* depicts the true story of a Jewish boy who passed for Christian in order to survive the Holocaust. *Black Like Me,* both a book and a film, depicts the story of a white man and the lessons he learns when he passes for black (through the use of makeup) in the days of segregation.

CHAPTER 6

"Hidden from History": Understanding the Lives of Gay and Lesbian Individuals from the Past

INTRODUCTION

Recovering the past is never an easy task. It becomes even more difficult when we try to understand the life of an individual person, and more difficult still when the subject is that person's sexuality. It can be almost impossible if that person's sexuality was scorned by the society of the time in which he or she lived. For obvious reasons, people often felt they had to hide same-sex activities. Such activities leave no records behind unless the individuals involved chose to record them, and often this seemed like an unwise thing to do. People who loved members of their own sex frequently deleted this part of their lives from personal documents like diaries and letters, for fear that these documents might fall into the wrong hands. Historians seeking out "gay heroes" in the past thus face a difficult task: how do we recover these stories in the face of such obstacles?

In this chapter, we look at two case studies of writers who have tried to do so. In Reading 6-A, journalist Randy Shilts argues that Baron von Steuben, the man called the "Father of the American Army," was in fact gay, a thesis sure to be controversial given the recent debate over "gays in the military." In Reading 6-B, historian Blanche Weisen Cook looks at the life of one of the most prominent women in American history, First Lady Eleanor Roosevelt (1884–1962), the wife of four-term president Franklin Delano Roosevelt. Cook argues that Roosevelt had relationships with members of both genders, with this excerpt centering around her relationship with journalist Lorena Hickok. Reading 6-C presents excerpts from letters between Hickok and Roosevelt, allowing the reader to look at some of the primary source evidence upon which Cook's account is based. While reading, keep this question in mind: How would I write this if I were trying to address this subject?

READING 6-A

Two Officers

from *Conduct Unbecoming: Gays and Lesbians in the U.S. Military,* by Randy Shilts

Even before the armed forces of the United States were formally organized, gays were bearing arms for the yet unborn nation. The United States might never have become a nation, in fact, were it not for the services of one particular gay general in the first difficult years of the American Revolution.

In 1777, the rebellion was going badly. General George Washington made a dashing figure on horseback and was revered by his troops, but had little background in the art of military drills and training. Thirteen disparate and mutually suspicious colonies had contributed soldiers for what were, in effect, thirteen different armies. Though all fought under the fraying banner of the Continental Army, they were not yet one unified and disciplined force. The army desperately needed training and, in Paris, Benjamin Franklin plotted to provide the one man he believed could save them: Baron Friedrich Wilhelm Ludolf Gerhard Augustin von Steuben.

Steuben was the son of a Prussian military officer of high enough rank to be able to secure King Frederick William I as the godfather for the infant. At sixteen, young Steuben followed his father into the army, and distinguished himself in the Seven Years War, in which he was taken prisoner by the Russians. While a prisoner, history records, Steuben became a favorite of Czar Peter III and Peter's ambitious wife, who soon overthrew her husband and became Czarina Catherine the Great. After his release, Steuben was particularly a valuable aide to the greatest military genius of his era, King Frederick II of Prussia.

Steuben's acceptance into Frederick's all-male court was the first historical suggestion of his homosexuality. Frederick was Europe's most notorious gay ruler at the time and had been known as such since his youth. From his earliest days, Frederick had evinced an interest in poetry, music, and art that enraged his overbearing, militaristic father. When he had attempted to escape his father's beatings by running off to England with his lover, Lieutenant Hans Hermann von Katte, the son of an important Prussian general, King Frederick William had both his son and his lover court-martialed and sentenced to death. The king ordered a scaffold erected outside his son's prison cell, and guards forced the crown prince to watch while an executioner chopped off his lover's head. Frederick blew the lieutenant a kiss and shouted his oath of love as the executioner's sword fell. Ultimately, the king granted his son clemency and sent a soldier to be his valet, but those two also apparently became lovers. Once Frederick became king, he banished women from his palace and surrounded himself not only with handsome soldiers and pages but with the greatest cultural figures of his day, most notably Voltaire.

In the following years. Frederick turned to military matters and soon emerged as one of the most brilliant strategists in European history. His prowess transformed Prussia from a weak backwater to the strongest military power in Europe and made the Prussian army the most feared fighting machine on the Continent. The king also set about to formalize the instruction of his officers. He personally directed the military tutelage of thirteen handpicked officers, among them Steuben. His education, at the forerunner of the famous Kriegs Academie, made Steuben a charter member of the "Great General Staff" and perfected his military skills. In 1763, for reasons never made public, Steuben abruptly left the Prussian service and spent the next years as a chief minister for the prince of Hohenzollern-Hechingen, who named him a baron in 1771.

Benjamin Franklin was convinced that the Prussian penchant for order and discipline was precisely what the American forces needed to prevail in their uphill fight against the well-trained British army. His first meeting with Steuben in Paris, however, proved unsuccessful. The Continental Congress was already bridling at having two generals of foreign birth, Lafayette and De Kalb, and were reluctant to commission a third, so Franklin could not guarantee Steuben a commission in the Continental Army, or even a salary. Steuben could accept that; when Franklin indicated that the Americans could not even pay travel expenses across the Atlantic, however, Steuben declined Franklin's entreaties and instead took a position with another royal family in Baden. But as he was returning to Germany, he heard news that sent him back for another meeting with Franklin.

The identity of the author of the crucial letter was later lost to history, but it is known that it arrived at the desk of the prince of Hohenzollern-Hechingen in August 1777. "It has come to me from different sources that M. de Steuben is accused of having taken familiarities with young boys which the law forbids and punishes severely," the letter said. The dispatch further noted that "the clergy ... intend to prosecute him by law as soon as he may establish himself anywhere." That Steuben would be hounded for homosexuality during the reign of Frederick was no small irony, as was noted even by his contemporaries. A newspaper article in 1796 commented, the "abominable rumor which accused Steuben of a crime the suspicion of which, at another more exalted court of that time (as formerly among the Greeks) would hardly have aroused such attention." Still, the impending scandal forced Steuben out of Europe. As his biographer, John McAuley Palmer, wrote, "Whether it is true or false, it is certain that the charge was made and that it was a final determining influence in sending Steuben to America."

The scandal that exiled Steuben did not receive broad circulation in Europe until more than a decade after the Revolutionary War, and it is unlikely the Americans knew of them when Franklin negotiated an arrangement with Steuben. The French government secretly agreed that it would compensate Steuben for his services if the Continental Congress did not.

There remained the delicate test of promoting the baron to the Americans. Though Steuben had risen only to the rank of captain in the Prussian army, Franklin did not think this position grand enough to impress the Continental Congress, so he spread word that Steuben was a lieutenant general. Silas Deane, who served with Franklin as a Colonial commissioner to France, wrote Congress that Steuben had left behind the "certificates of service" that attested to his status as a lieutenant general when he left Germany, and that it would take too long to retrieve them. But, Deane said, he had seen the certificates himself and could attest to Steuben's credentials. Never one to question his own importance, Steuben went along with the ruse, although keeping the stories about his past straight would cause him no small amount of difficulty in his later life. Before leaving France, Steuben had Parisian designers sew a set of impressive-looking uniforms that were largely of his own invention. If he were going to be a lieutenant general, he wanted to look the part.

When Steuben arrived in America, it was in the company of a handsome seventeen-year-old French nobleman who served as his secretary and translator. The pair was entertained by Governor John Hancock in Boston and was immediately the toast of the revolutionary leadership. With his long, thin patrician nose and erect bearing, the forty-seven-year-old Steuben looked like everything a European military genius was supposed to be. He also had a self-deprecating wit that charmed even the most skeptical colonist. To the Continental Congress, Steuben suggested that he be paid only if he actually helped the Americans win some battles, a proposal the cash-strapped Congress enthusiastically accepted.

Great expectations greeted Steuben when he arrived at George Washington's encampment in Valley Forge on February 23, 1778, in the last months of the Continental Army's most bitter winter. The American cause was imperiled. The British occupied Philadelphia, and the Americans had sustained losses at Brandywine and Germantown. The colonists' lines of supply were ravaged, and the army was scarcely clothed and even less disciplined. Washington asked Steuben to review his troops and offer his frank suggestions for improvement. Communication was difficult; Steuben's teenage protégé quickly proved so ignorant of military ways that he was an inept interpreter, so Washington assigned Steuben two French-speaking colonels from his own staff, twenty-year-old Alexander Hamilton and twenty-four-year-old John Laurens.

The assignment was uniquely appropriate. Hamilton was Washington's most trusted aide and Laurens was the son of Henry Laurens, president of the Continental Congress. The pair was inseparable, to the point that some later historians have surmised they were lovers. Their letters to each other swore undying love and included numerous double entendres, such as Hamilton's complaining that during a separation their written correspondence was "the only kind of intercourse now in my power." (Laurens was later killed in a minor skirmish with the British.) At Valley Forge, both Laurens and Hamilton became close friends of Steuben and his most effusive admirers.

After his review of Washington's troops, Steuben was discouraged. There was no uniformity among the regiments. Some drilled in the French style, others in the English, others in the Prussian. He set about writing a drill book. Every day, he issued new chapters in French, which were translated and then laboriously hand-copied for each brigade and regiment and company in the Army. Once the first chapter was completed, General Washington ordered one hundred top soldiers selected from fourteen infantry brigades to form a model training brigade.

The first uniform drills of the Continental Army began on the morning of March 19, 1778. Steuben led them himself. Though he knew no English, he had memorized the words for each drill and shouted the orders — load musket, fix bayonet, and charge — eliminating the Prussian flourishes so the American Army would use the minimum number of motions.

The fact that Steuben led the drills himself greatly impressed the enlisted men, since American officers, like their English counterparts, did not perform such menial tasks. When the training went poorly, Steuben swore in both French and Prussian, with frequent "goddams," the only English oath he knew. He asked his translator to put the better profanities in English for the benefit of the troops. All this made Steuben immensely popular. This was no effete European adventurer, but a military man who was going to win battles.

Three days after the first drills were performed in what would become the United States Army, General Washington was impressed enough that he ordered Steuben's training to be extended to his entire command. No general in the Continental Army would do any more drills, he added, until they had Steuben's specific instructions. Two days later, the whole army at Valley Forge was training under Steuben's guidance. Members of the model brigade became drill masters who trained other drill masters as they had been trained. Five weeks after the first drill, Washington appointed Steuben the first Inspector General of the Army. Six days after that, Congress commissioned him a major general at a salary of $166.67 a month. A year later, Congress enacted Steuben's "Regulations for the Order and Discipline of the Troops of the United States." In 1780, he received his coveted field command, and was a division commander in the war's final siege at Yorktown.

His impact on the Revolutionary cause was incalculable. Some historians have counted Steuben, along with General Washington, as one of the only two men whose services were "indispensable" to the success of the Revolution. When the American cause was won at Yorktown and Washington issued his congratulatory order, Steuben was one of only three commanders he singled out for praise. In 1783, General Washington's last official act as Commander in Chief of the Continental Army was to write a letter thanking Steuben. As Colonel Hamilton later wrote, "Tis unquestionably to his efforts we are indebted for the introduction of discipline in the Army."

The acceptance of General Steuben and his contributions to the fledgling American military did not mean there was even tacit acceptance of homosexuality. On March 11, 1778, just sixteen days after Steuben arrived at Valley Forge, drums and fifes assembled on the Grand Parade in the brisk morning air to conclude the punishment ordered by a general court-martial and approved by General Washington himself. On that morning, Lieutenant Gotthold Frederick Enslin became the first known soldier to be dismissed from the U.S. military for homosexuality.

Enslin had arrived in the United States on September 30, 1774, aboard the ship *Union,* which had sailed from Rotterdam to Philadelphia. He was in his late twenties or early thirties. He arrived alone, according to the ship's records, suggesting that he was single. Three years later he enlisted in the Continental Army; within a few months, he was serving as an officer in Lieutenant Colonel William Malcolm's regiment.

Though little is known of Enslin's earlier life, the exacting penmanship he used on his company's muster sheets and his command of the English language indicate that he was an educated man of some financial means. The Continental Army preferred its officers to be educated and able to provide their own supplies.

Under the bunking arrangements at Valley Forge, enlisted men lived in communal barracks while officers resided in small cabins with officers of similar rank. It was in Enslin's cabin that Ensign Anthony Maxwell apparently discovered the lieutenant with Private John Monhart. Maxwell reported this to his commanding officer, Lieutenant Colonel Aaron Burr. Enslin responded that Maxwell was lying in an attempt to impugn his character.

On February 27, 1778, the company commander being in New York, Burr presided first at a court-martial of Ensign Maxwell, charged with "propagating a scandalous report prejudicial to the character of Lieutenant Enslin." In his orderly book, Burr later wrote, "The court after mature deliberation upon the evidence produced could not find Ensign Maxwell had published any report prejudicial to the character of Lt. Enslin further than the strict line of his duty required and do therefore acquit him of the charge."

Eleven days later, on March 10, Burr presided over Enslin's court-martial, in which the lieutenant was found guilty of sodomy and perjury, the latter presumably stemming from his charges against Maxwell. According to General Washington's general order of March 14, Enslin was "...to be dismiss'd with Infamy. His Excellency the Commander in Chief approves the sentence and with Abhorrence and Detestation of such Infamous Crimes orders Lieutt. Enslin to be drummed out of Camp tomorrow morning by all the Drummers and Fifers in the Army never to return; The Drummers and Fifers to attend on the Grand Parade at Guard mounting for that Purpose."

Drumming a soldier out of the Army was a dramatic event in those times. According to custom, an officer's sword was broken in half over the head of the disgraced soldier, while drummers played a very slow tattoo. So did Lieutenant Enslin leave the Continental Army on that cold morning in March, trudging alone on the deeply rutted and muddy road out of Valley Forge, not far from where Major General von Steuben was shouting orders in broken English.

Some observers have suggested that Enslin's sentence is evidence that Washington held a lenient view of homosexuality, since such transgressions could have been punishable by imprisonment or even death in the conventions of the day. (Thomas Jefferson demonstrated his liberalism by proposing a year earlier that sodomy be punished by castration instead of death in the new penal code that would replace Virginia's Colonial charter.) This, however, remains speculation.

Editor's note: *Von Steuben retired to upstate New York after the Revolution, living off a pension granted him by the grateful young United States for his services during the war. He died in 1794 at the age of sixty-two. In his will, he left his estate to two of his young captains, whom he referred to as his "adopted sons." Near his grave is a plaque with the inscription "Indispensable to the Cause of American Independence."*[1]

READING 6-B

Eleanor Roosevelt

from *Eleanor Roosevelt (Volume One, 1884-1933),*
by Blanche Weisen Cook

Editor's note: *In this reading, Blanche Weisen Cook examines the relationship between Eleanor Roosevelt and Lorena Hickok. Excerpting from Cook's voluminous work (Volume One alone is, with notes, nearly six hundred pages) is a difficult task, and runs the risk of taking material out of context. Consequently, two excerpts from different segments of the book are included. The first segment is taken from the Introduction (pp. 10–15). In it, Cook examines the overall context for a discussion of Eleanor Roosevelt's private life. She addresses the traditional reluctance of historians to deal with women's sexuality (especially lesbian sexuality), the contemporary attitudes toward this in Roosevelt's day, the circumstances of her individual life, and the problems with the existing historical records concerning the details of Roosevelt's life and relationship with Hickok. The second segment, taken from Chapter 20, "The First Lady's First Friend" (pp. 477–480), deals specifically with Lorena Hickok. In it, Cook addresses why individuals might be reluctant to accept the possibility that Hickok and Roosevelt were more than "just friends" and explains briefly why she herself believes they were.*

For background, readers should note that Hickok and Roosevelt first met in 1928. The intense period of their friendship began late in 1932, when Roosevelt was forty-eight and Hickok forty. They apparently wrote daily letters for a number of years. In the 1930s they took vacations together to New England, Canada, Puerto Rico, and the Virgin Islands, and Hickok dwelled primarily at the White House from 1940 until 1944. She moved to Hyde Park, the town in which Roosevelt lived, in 1954, co-authored a book with the former First Lady, and lived there until her death in 1964.[2]

1.

Now recently opened archives, ER's FBI and State Department documents, and access to the letters of long-ignored friends give us another set of facts for interpreting a woman's life. More than twenty years after her death, we discovered that for decades ER had had a very full private life that was well known to her husband, her mother-in-law, her children, and many of the scores of people who shared her intimate life and her public work.

If her heirs followed her lead and honored her discretionary code, they can hardly be faulted. But the continual, almost hysterical reactions to the intimate life revealed in her correspondence (a correspondence she carefully preserved for the historical record) suggests another pattern: Our generation is as prudish as our "Victorian" forebears when faced with the real lives of historically significant women...

Until recently, historians and literary analysts have preferred to see our great women writers and activists as asexual spinsters, odd gentlewomen who sublimated their lust in their various good works. But as we consider their true natures, we see that it was frequently their ability to express love and passion — and to surround themselves with like-minded women and men who offered support, strength, and emotional armor — that enabled them to achieve all that they did achieve. The fact is that our culture has sought to deny the truths and the complexities about women's passion because it is one of the great keys to women's power.

Born in 1884, ER reached adulthood long after Queen Victoria was dead. Nevertheless, all explanations of her life have continued to assure us that she was limited by her Victorian upbringing, confined by her Victorian sensibilities. Even in 1984, a contemporary historian assured us that ER was "imprisoned in the cage of her culture."

To "encage" Eleanor Roosevelt seems a remarkably limited reading of a woman's life. It is not simply the language one revolts against; it is the failure to consider a woman's wants and needs, including her range of choice and freedom to have, or not to have, sex; it is the failure to consider the nature of passions, lust, and love in a woman's life.

The "true" Victorian woman was assured to be virtuous, compliant, passive, dependent, and childlike. She was meant to have neither influence nor authority. For her, pursuing a college education was as dangerous as riding a bicycle, or a horse astride. Our culture's seemingly endless devotion to the Victorian woman is actually more about mindlessness than about sexlessness. The Victorian woman was, above all, deprived of the capacity for free thought and independence. A simple and compliant figure, she ran from ambition and refused the trappings of power.

Now nothing shatters the myth of the angel in the house, the fragrant spirit in the garden, so fundamentally as the appearance of the independently passionate woman, who chooses her mate, her partner, her lover, for reasons of her own, and according to the needs and wants of her own chemistry. The myths of Victorian prudery and purity have been history's most dependable means of social control. Class-bound and gender-related, obscured by privets and closets and vanishing documents, establishment lust has followed the dictates of establishment culture: traditionally for men only.

Eleanor Roosevelt has been a persistent victim of this effort at social control. Portrayed as a Victorian wife and mother, she has been rendered a saint without desire, an aristocratic lady without erotic imagination. We have even been told that she birthed six children because she knew nothing about the "facts" of life. But then we learn that she was a lifelong member of the Birth Control League. We have been told, over and over again, based exclusively on her daughter's casual observation, that ER considered "sex an ordeal to be borne." Beyond the fact that such a remark raises the question of FDR as a selfish and lazy lover, ER maintained a dedicated optimism concerning love: She encouraged the romances of her young friends and children, supported their divorces, provided safe havens for trysts and liaisons, and expresses relief when they stepped out of painful marriages and into new relationships. Not unlike her own mother-in-law, but with a vastly different emphasis, Eleanor Roosevelt could be quite meddlesome.

After a period of intense self-discovery, during World War I, ER forged for herself new and intimate friendships with two lesbian couples, Esther Lape and Elizabeth Read, and Nancy Cook and Marion Dickerman. Later her relationships with Earl Miller and Lorena Hickok were erotic and romantic, daring and tumultuous, though so many letters have been lost or destroyed that the full dimensions of her love will remain to some degree a mystery of interpretation. Most grievously, all of Earl Miller's long, daily letters written from 1928 until ER's death in 1962, have disappeared without a trace.

How, then, do we asses ER's intimate life? We begin by acknowledging that the disappearance of so many documents was not an accident, but rather a calculated denial of ER's passionate friendships. In the case of her demonstrated ardor for Lorena Hickok, the denials have been high-strung and voluble; and ER's love for her younger friend Earl Miller, which began when she was forty-five and he thirty-two, has been dismissed almost without hesitation.

And yet it is now clear that ER lived a life dedicated to passion and experience. After 1920 many of her closest friends were lesbian women. She honored their relationships, and their privacy. Women who love women, and women who love younger men, have understood for generations that it was necessary to hide their love, lest they be the target of slander and cruelty. For over a century, scandal and love have seemed so entwined that it has been merely polite to love in private. The romance of the closet, and the perspective of the fortress, become necessary barricades against bigotry and pain.

In the closet, romance between women developed its own ceremonies: coded words and costumes, pinky rings and pearls, lavender and violets. The closet allowed one to avoid embarrassed smiles, discomfort, a friend's disdain, a parent's shock, a child's confusion. For some the closet was lonely and disabling. For others it was entirely satisfying and intensely romantic — its very secrecy lent additional sparkle to the game of hearts. The romance of the closet had a life of its own.

Public women of Eleanor Roosevelt's generation, long protective of their private lives, see nothing particularly valuable about our insistence today on greater openness. I was told quite frankly during one interview: "I have been in the closet for sixty years; why the hell should I come out for you?" During another interview, a veteran British journalist exploded: "Listen, you young reporters are wrecking everything. We had much more fun before it all started coming out." Both women believed that hateful stereotypes followed in the wake of trivializing labels. Ultimately, they argued, the public woman, no matter how talented or independent, could not be free outside the closet, and the potential for scandal threatened work, publication, and influence.

Over the years, in Greenwich Village and at Val-Kill, Eleanor Roosevelt created homes of her own, with members of her chosen family, private and distinct, separate from her husband and children. Even as First Lady, ER established a hiding house in a brownstone walk-up that she rented from Esther Lape in Greenwich Village at 20 East 11th Street. Away from the glare of reporters and photographers, she stepped outside and moved beyond the exclusive circle of her heritage to find comfort, privacy, and satisfaction. In conventional terms, ER lived an outrageous life.

She never considered her friends or friendships secret or shameful. Her family and friends lived in one extended community. For decades, there was Eleanor's court and Franklin's court, which included Missy LeHand, his live-in secretary and companion. After ER's death, her friends might deny one another, in private or in print. But during her lifetime, they had to deal with one another. They sat across from one another at Christmas and Thanksgiving. They were invited to the same parties, and the same picnics.

Although ER never wrote a word for publication about the stirrings of her heart, she purposefully saved her entire correspondence with both Lorena Hickok and Esther Lape. After her death, Hickok and Lape sat around an open fire at Lape's Connecticut estate and spent hours burning letter after letter. To date, no correspondence between Esther Lape and her lifetime companion, Elizabeth Read, has been found. Although Lape agreed to be interviewed by an archivist for ER's oral-history project, she changed her mind and sealed her interview. After Hick's death, her sister burned another packet of letters found in her home. What is left is sufficient to detail a thirty-year friendship marked by the most intense ardor for at least six years, but what has been lost is immeasurable: not only the Lape letters, but ER's correspondence with Earl Miller and Nancy Cook; the letters between Nancy Cook and Marion Dickerman; and all of Caroline O'Day's correspondence, covering a lifetime of activism and three terms as a member of Congress at large.

With the documentary record in tatters, we cannot be certain about what ER felt or believed on subjects about which she remained forever elusive. We can only conclude, with Virginia Woolf: "When a subject is highly controversial — and any question about sex is that — one cannot hope to tell the truth. One can only show how one came to hold whatever opinion one does hold."

2.

For years — for decades, actually — neither Aunt Kassie nor anybody else outside the magic circle "found out" about Lorena Hickok. The fact of ER's closest woman friend during the White House years was erased, distorted, and demeaned. Even photographs of intimate family dinners were cropped before publication to delete Hick. When included, she was not identified. More recently, when identified, she was framed by the most insulting stereotypes.

Hateful stereotypes aside, attractiveness — that mysterious chemical element that draws one to another — is after all in the eyes of the beholder. To her detractors, Hick was "without sexual attraction. She was five foot eight but weighed almost two hundred pounds." She smoked cigars, cigarettes, and pipes. She acted and looked "like one of the boys ... In any case she was no vamp."...

Since friendship and love are rarely about straight teeth and bony clavicles, one must pause to ask how it has served history to caricature Lorena Hickok, and why she was for so long disregarded. Like the disappearance of ER's correspondence with Earl Miller, the answer in retrospect seems evident: Today, our generation continues to cringe and turn away from cross-class, cross-generational, or same-sex relationships. In this instance, however, both Eleanor Roosevelt and Lorena Hickok saved their correspondence, although Hickok typed, edited, and then burned the originals of ER's letters between 1932 and 1933, and many more of her own letters over the years. For all the deletions and restraint, the thousands of letters that remain are amorous and specific.

ER repeatedly ended her ten-, twelve-, fifteen-page daily letters with expressions of love and longing. There are few ambiguities in this correspondence, and a letter that was defined as "particularly susceptible to misinterpretation" reads: "I wish I could lie down beside you tonight and take you into my arms."

After a long separation, during which both ER and Hick counted the days until their reunion, Hick noted: "Only eight more days ... Funny how even the dearest face will fade away in time. Most clearly I remember your eyes, with a kind of teasing smile in them, and the feeling of that soft spot just north-east of the corner of your mouth against my lips..."

The fact is that ER and Hick were not involved in a schoolgirl "smash." They did not meet in a nineteenth-century storybook, or swoon unrequitedly on a nineteenth-century campus. They were neither saints nor adolescents. Nor were they virgins or mermaids. They were two adult women, in the prime of their lives, committed to working out a relationship under very difficult circumstances. They had each already lived several other lives. They knew the score. They appreciated the risks and the dangers. They had both experienced pain in loving. They never thought it would be easy or smooth. They gave each other pleasure and comfort, trust and love. They touched each other deeply, loved profoundly, and moved on. They sought to avoid gossip. And, for the most part, they succeeded. They wrote to each other exactly what they meant to write. Sigmund Freud notwithstanding: A cigar may not always be a cigar, but the "north-east corner of your mouth against my lips" is always the northeast corner.

The romantic and passionate friendship between ER and Hick was neither idyllic nor perfect. Actually, it was a very bumpy ride. It was simply there — inevitable and undeniable. Alone in a sea of unknown and uncontrollable events, they were drawn to each other. Theirs was a powerful attraction, in the beginning based on work and political interests. ER admired Hick's independence, her single-minded dedication as a journalist. They shared a world-view, and were ardently engaged by the political game.

Hick may have been "one of the boys," but she was no man-hater. Like Eleanor Roosevelt, she was a team player, content to work for and with men — although she consistently promoted the interests of women. If she was perceived to be a lesbian by those who knew her, FDR and Louis Howe nevertheless encouraged and appreciated her company and professional support. ER came to rely upon it.

In the fulfillment of their desire to be with each other, ER and Hick risked publicity, discovery, national scandal. Over the years, for three decades, they created a rare and loving friendship of absolute trust and amazing generosity. Their relationship passed through phases, some more distant than others. There were storms and hurt silences. But there was also laughter, pleasure, and respect.

READING 6-C

Excerpts from the Hickok-Roosevelt Correspondence

Editor's Note: *The documentary record of the Hickok-Roosevelt relationship is voluminous: The Franklin D. Roosevelt Library in Hyde Park holds eighteen boxes of letters, including 2,336 (!) from*

Roosevelt to Hickok and another 1,024 from Hickok to Roosevelt.[3] *When we take into account the fact that, as Cook explains, thousands more letters were destroyed, the true breadth of the evidence becomes daunting. Given the missing letters as well as the fact that Hickok edited many of hers before she died, it is clear that the letters present some real problems as historical evidence.*

Nevertheless, taking a look at this primary evidence is crucial if we are to judge the matter for ourselves. The excerpts below, while obviously only a tiny fragment of the entire correspondence, provide some of the crucial pieces of evidence in this historiographic debate. Reading them allows one to enter into the job of the professional historian, examining documents written by people long dead, and trying to decide exactly what they mean. Access to these allows the readers to make their own judgments on the nature of Hickok and Roosevelt's friendship.

March 5, 1933
Roosevelt to Hickok

"Hick, my dearest, I cannot go to bed tonight without a word to you. I felt as though a little part of me was leaving tonight. You have grown so much to be a part of my life that it is empty without you even though I'm busy every minute."[4]

March 6, 1933
Roosevelt to Hickok

"Hick darling, how good it was to hear your voice. It was so inadequate to try and tell you what it meant. Funny was that I couldn't say je t'aime et je t'adore as I longed to do, but always remember I am saying it, that I go to sleep thinking of you."[5]

March 7, 1933
Roosevelt to Hickok

"Hick darling ... Oh, I want to put my arms around you. I ache to hold you close. Your ring is a great comfort, I look at it and think she does love me or else I wouldn't be wearing it."[6]

March 8, 1933
Roosevelt to Hickok

"Just telephoned you. Oh! It is good to hear your voice, when it sounds right no one can make me so happy."[7]

March 9, 1933
Roosevelt to Hickok

"My pictures are nearly all up and I have you in my sitting room where I can look at you most of my waking hours! I can't kiss you so I kiss your picture good night and good morning!"[8]

March 10, 1933
Roosevelt to Hickok

"Hick, darling, remember one things always. No one else is just what you are to me. I'd rather be with you this minute than anyone else and yet I love many other people and some often can do things for me probably better than you could, but I never enjoyed being with anyone the way I enjoy being with you."[9]

March 11, 1933
Roosevelt to Hickok

"I couldn't bear to think of you crying yourself to sleep. Oh, how I wanted to put my arms around you instead of in spirit. I went and kissed your photograph instead. Oh, dear one, it is all the little things, tones in your voice, the feel of your hair, gestures, these are the things I think about and long for."[10]

Dec. 5, 1933
Hickok to Roosevelt

"I've been trying today to bring back your face — to remember just how you look... Most clearly I remember your eyes with a kind of teasing smile in them, and the feeling of that soft spot just northeast of the corner of your mouth against my lips: I wonder what we'll do when we meet — what we'll say. Well, I'm rather proud of us, aren't you? I think we've done rather well."[11]

Sept. 1, 1934
Roosevelt to Hickok

"I wish I could lie down beside you tonight and take you in my arms."[12]

QUESTIONS/ACTIVITIES

1. After finishing Reading 6-A, write down whether or not you are convinced by Shilts's account that von Steuben was indeed gay. Explain why or why not.

2. Underline every piece of evidence (every "fact") that Shilts presents in his account. How many of these relate directly to von Steuben's life? Is this enough evidence to support his argument that von Steuben was gay?

3. Why might there not be more evidence concerning von Steuben's life?

4. What obstacles does a historian confronting Eleanor Roosevelt's private life face?

5. Cook's account of Roosevelt's life raises a number of questions, among which are:

- According to Cook, what are the reasons that important parts of women's lives have been left out of history?
- What was a "Victorian" woman supposed to be like?
- What details about Roosevelt's life contrast with the "Victorian" image?
- Which characteristics of Hickok were attacked by contemporaries and historians? Why?
- What does Cook mean when she says, "A cigar may not always be a cigar, but the 'north-east corner of your mouth against my lips' is always the northeast corner"?

6. Cook asks, "How, then, do we assess ER's private life?" How does Cook do so? What approach does she take? What evidence does she use and how does she use it?

7. Do you agree with Cook's assessment that ER led an "outrageous life" for her time? What aspects of her life are "outrageous" for women of her day?

8. Divide the class into four groups (two supporting the historians' accounts, two attacking them), and have members of each group write letters to the editor after reading 6-A or 6-B. Be sure to explain your position with specific references from the accounts.

9. After reading 6-C, write down your opinion of what this evidence proves. Take a position, either pro or con, on whether or not this proves that Hickok and Roosevelt had a lesbian relationship. Either write accounts or do an in-class debate representing your position.

10. Cook quotes Virginia Woolf, who says, "When a subject is highly controversial, and any question about sex is that, one cannot hope

to tell the truth. One can only show how one came to hold whatever opinion one does hold." Take either Shilts or Cook, and explain how the author comes to hold the opinion he or she holds.

11. In your opinion, which is the better work of historical scholarship? Why?

12. Choose a prominent figure from today's world and try to "prove" his or her sexuality. Offer your "proof" to other students (either the whole class or in one-on-one discussion), allowing them to raise every objection they can to your evidence. How easy is it to "prove" a famous person's sexuality?

PART 2

The Emergence of the Modern Gay Movement

INTRODUCTION

The emergence of the modern gay and lesbian liberation movement is rooted in the dramatic changes that swept Western society in the eighteenth and nineteenth centuries. While some historians say that gays began to develop a "group consciousness" as early as the Renaissance,[1] it is not until the mid-nineteenth century that we begin to see gays organizing political groups. For this reason, many historians date the beginning of the gay movement to the mid-1800s.

To understand this, we have to first understand the times. In the 1700s and 1800s, both Europe and America experienced the Industrial Revolution. The rise of factories created new economic opportunities. Individuals, once dependent on their families to survive, could move to a city and get a job there. Personal freedom grew: individuals who felt oppressed in rural areas could just move to the city, where fewer people would be looking over their shoulders.

This was especially important for those attracted to members of their own sex. First, they were freed from the requirement to marry. It was now possible to live alone and survive, which couldn't be done in a rural area, as running a farm single-handedly wasn't practical. In addition, it was much more likely that you might meet someone like yourself, thanks to the large numbers of people concentrated in one place. Finally, it was more possible to "get away with" homosexual acts. While privacy was next to impossible in rural areas, where everyone knew each other, few people knew who you were in a city, and many of them didn't care what you did. The family, that traditional upholder of morality, was often far away, and it was possible to act on one's homosexual desires without worrying about the prying eyes of relatives.

Distinct "communities" of people attracted to the same sex began to emerge as they found one another in these cities. This development was documented in many writings of the time. As one visitor noted about the U.S. in 1915:

> The world of sexual inverts [a term for homosexuals] is, indeed, a large one in any American city, and it is a community distinctly

organized — words, customs, traditions of its own; every city has its numerous meeting-places: certain churches where inverts congregate; certain cafes well-known for the inverted nature of their patrons; certain streets where, at night, every fifth man is an invert. The inverts have their own "clubs," with nightly meetings...[2]

A community was being born.

This was regarded with dismay by many authorities of the time. They were confronted with a dilemma, however: How could sexual behavior be controlled in this new setting? In the past, religious authorities and the family played important roles in maintaining community standards. By the nineteenth century, however, many people were questioning the authority of religious leaders. As explained above, the family's ability to control its members was declining as opportunities to live away from home expanded. Believers in the old ways began to seek new means of "social control" to enforce their moral standards.[3]

Onto this scene came the new field of psychiatry. In the 1800s, science was taking the place of religion for many. In the age of Darwin, scientists were seen as having "the answers" for the strange new problems being created by modern society. Eager to prove their worth, psychiatrists, a subset of the new "medical profession," set out to look at social "ills" such as these new communities of people who loved the same sex. New vocabulary was invented to describe and categorize this behavior. This vocabulary helped make psychiatrists seem like specialists blessed with extraordinary knowledge not available to the average person, who should therefore trust these "experts," just as priests had once been trusted because of their special knowledge about religion. The term "homosexual" was invented by the Hungarian psychiatrist Benkert in 1869, and terms like "pervert" and "invert" came into use.[4] Soon medical texts were referring to these "homosexuals" as "sick" individuals who needed to be "cured." Same-sex love had been transformed from an "unnatural sin" to a "sickness." The new "scientific" terminology gave this judgment an authority that the older religious beliefs no longer held for many. These new authorities sought to maintain the same traditional homophobic moral standards, but now in the name of "health" rather than that of God.[5]

Another important shift took place in the way homosexuality was turned into an "illness" afflicting an entire group. As seen in the introduction to part one, earlier societies may have disapproved of same-sex love, but they did not classify individuals based on their sexual orientation. In early American society, for example, same-sex love was seen as a single, sinful act committed by an individual, for which repentance could be sought. After repentance, that individual could return to his or her previous position as a "normal" member of the community. The new medical authorities, however, changed this. One could be a "pervert" even if one had never even had sex. Rather than simply being a single wrongful action by a misguided individual, engaging in perverted acts or thoughts now made one a member of a new group, called "homosexuals" or "perverts" or "inverts." Psychiatry began to categorize people in ways previously unknown to those who disapproved of same-sex love, as historian Jonathan Katz explains:

> [E]motions were considered "perverted" by doctors whether or not they ever issued in ... [sexual] acts. "Sexual perversion" could lurk "latently" in the brain, even if never "overtly" expressed by the body; in the head it might be "conscious" or "unconscious." "Perversion" referred fundamentally to feeling; "inversion" was typically a "psycho-sexual condition" ... merely feeling "perverted" or "inverted" made one a "pervert" or an "invert." "Perverted" emotions determined "perverted being."[6]

This categorization by medical authorities actually helped the development of a gay "group consciousness" and a gay liberation movement. As Katz explains:

> The mutual association and new visibility of such persons in American cities, and their naming by the medical profession, made their group existence manifest [obvious] in a way it had not been earlier. By way of contrast, in the early [American] colonies, isolated enactors of sodomy did not perceive themselves, and were not seen, as members of a sodomitical collective [group].[7]

In the face of this persecution, and secure in the growing knowledge they were not alone, gays began to fight back. It is the story of this movement that is detailed in this section.

The story essentially begins in Germany, as shown in chapters 7 and 8, where the gay-rights movement reached its earliest heights. Germany, with its high rates of industrialization and urbanization, provided the basic conditions for the emergence of a gay subculture.

Its oppressive laws gave the members of that subculture the inspiration to come together and fight back. Their progress was brought to a tragic end by the Holocaust, in which gays were one of several groups, Jews being the main one, targeted by the Nazis.

The American gay-rights movement arose somewhat later. Few involved in it had any idea that a similar movement existed in Germany, and the early leaders basically began from scratch. Detailed in chapters 9 to 13, the American gay movement responded to the anti-gay persecution that became institutionalized during World War II and the McCarthy era. The first small groups, called the "homophile" movement, primarily urged gays to try to "fit in" to win acceptance. However, a new attitude emerged in the late sixties, inspired by the example of other civil rights movements of the era and by changes in youth attitudes. Preaching "Gay is Good," the sixties generation actively rejected the negative branding and harassment of gays by society. The turning point was the Stonewall Riots of 1969, when, in response to continual raids and harassment, gays battled police in the streets of New York. In the aftermath of Stonewall, a "gay liberation movement" grew. It rejected its homophile predecessor by calling on gays to fight back against, rather than fit into, society's standards.

The Stonewall Riots have traditionally been considered the beginning of the gay movement. Gay pride marches commemorate it in American cities each June, with hundreds of thousands of marchers, many of whom are completely unaware of the work for gay rights that preceded Stonewall. The readings in this chapter prove that a great deal went on "before Stonewall." It is an exciting story, as we see an entire movement being born and growing as an oppressed group begins to fight for its rights for the first time.

CHAPTER 7

Karl Heinrich Ulrichs and the Beginnings of Gay Consciousness

INTRODUCTION

The life and work of Karl Heinrich Ulrichs (1825–1895) is a fascinating, little-known chapter in gay history. Ulrichs is the first person who is known to have spoken in public on behalf of what we now know as "gay rights." The story of how he did this gives us insight into how the gay liberation movement came into being.

Karl Heinrich Ulrichs was born in 1825 in the state of Hanover in what is now Germany. He was aware of his attraction to other men from an early age. By the time of his young adulthood, Ulrichs had grown outraged by the legal persecutions attached to same-sex behavior. He resented the stress that such oppression produced, stress that often resulted in suicides and ruined lives. He resolved to take action to challenge these laws.

Ulrichs, however, faced an interesting problem. He was operating in a day when the words "homosexual" and "heterosexual" had not even been coined yet, and he literally had to invent a vocabulary to describe the people on whose behalf he was fighting. As described earlier, individual acts of same-sex love were punishable in the last century, but they did not mark the perpetrator as "different." They were merely singular crimes.

A similar situation exists with some "crimes" today. We do not, for example, always refer to people who get speeding tickets as "speeders" but see their offense as a single instance of breaking of the law. Likewise, until the late 1800s, people who loved the same sex were convicted of "sodomy" but not labeled forever as degenerate people. Nor had these people yet developed a "group consciousness."

Ulrichs, then, had to find a way to get people attracted to the same sex to be aware of themselves as a group, and to convince the public that this was a group being unfairly persecuted, not a series of individuals committing "crimes" that deserved punishment.

During the 1860s, Ulrichs developed a theory that explained his views. People we now call gay, he called "urnings." He argued that "urnings" composed a "third sex" who were naturally attracted to members of the same gender instead of the other gender. The word "natural" is key here, as it shifted the focus off the "unnatural" actions of "urnings" by claiming they were simply acting out their inborn nature, just as those people were who loved the other sex. If what "urnings" were doing was "natural" to them, they should not be persecuted for it, Ulrichs argued. Ulrichs even invented the word "urning," which derives from Greek mythology, so that "urnings" would have a name for themselves and understand that they were not alone.

Throughout the 1860s Ulrichs tried to spread his ideas and work for an end to the conditions oppressing him and his fellow "urnings." He wrote numerous pamphlets and distributed them widely to tell others of his theory. Finally, he decided that he must speak out publicly, and he found his ideal opportunity to do so at the Congress of German Jurists in 1867. Germany at this time was not a single nation but was divided into many small states, each with its own system of government and legal codes. This Congress was designed to try to create a single legal code for all the German states. Ulrichs hoped to persuade the Congress to repeal the anti-gay laws that existed in some German states (but not others) rather than include these in the new system of laws. His initial proposal was not even put on the agenda, and he petitioned for the opportunity to address the whole Congress in order to bring the matter up. His petition was granted and, in Reading 7-A, historian Hubert Kennedy presents an account of this first-ever public speech on behalf of the rights of gay people.[1]

READING 7-A

Ulrichs Speaks Out

excerpt from *Ulrichs: The Life and Works of Karl Heinrich Ulrichs, Pioneer of the Modern Gay Movement,* by Hubert Kennedy

The Congress of German Jurists met in Munich, 27–30 August 1867. Two years earlier Ulrichs had proposed the resolution ... asking for a revision of the German penal legislation regarding homosexual acts. This was rejected, as we have seen, by a deputation of the Congress as "not suitable to be considered by the Congress." Shortly before the Congress met, Ulrichs wrote the chairman, asking to speak in order "to read to the General Assembly and to lay before the chair a legal protest against the exclusion of an item from the agenda." This request was granted and his speech was scheduled for the closing General Assembly on Thursday, August 29.

Since Ulrichs did not have enough money to pay for the trip to Munich, he appealed to other Urnings for funds. These were forthcoming, so that he was able to set off for Munich. He was well aware of the unique and revolutionary nature of the action he planned. It was one thing to write, even passionately, about his subject in private. It was quite another to speak out in person before over five hundred people — many of them important and distinguished — and expose himself to their immediate reaction. It was no wonder he had second thoughts about it...

As he made his way to the Odeon ... Ulrichs was strengthened in his resolve by several thoughts. He knew that his distant comrades-in-nature were watching him: "Was I to answer their trust in me with cowardice?" he asked himself. He also recalled an Urning in Bremen who had been driven to suicide by the system the previous September. Finally, as he was walking to the Great Hall of the Odeon, where the session was to be held, he received a letter which reported that a "comrade" had voiced the opinion: "Numa [a pseudonym under which Ulrichs wrote] is afraid to do it!"

The doubts returned. A voice whispered in his ear: "There is still time, Numa, to keep silent. As for the request you have made to speak, you only have to quickly waive it. Then your heart can stop pounding!" But then another voice began to whisper, the voice of [Heinrich] Hössli [1784–1864, a Swiss intellectual whose writings against the oppression of homosexuals had inspired Ulrichs] with the words from the preface of his work:

> Two paths lie before me: to write this book and expose myself to persecution, or not to write it, but then be burdened to my grave with guilt ... And I wrote on, deliberately averting my eyes from those who are working for my downfall. I have no other choice between speaking and keeping silent. I tell myself: Speak and be judged!

Ulrichs wanted to be worthy of Hössli, and so he took his seat in the hall determined to openly bear witness to the suppressed rights of inborn nature...

[T]he assembly of more than five hundred German jurists, including elected representatives and a Bavarian prince, gave their full attention as Ulrichs mounted the steps of the speaker's platform "with my breast pounding" and began to read:

> Gentlemen! Already two years ago a proposal was regularly presented by two members of the Congress, Professor Dr. Tewes of Graz and myself, and I would like in a legal protest to complain that it was suppressed by our deputation, that is to say, it was excluded from the agenda as "not suitable to be considered by the Congress." I base my protest on material and formal ground.
>
> I. Material
>
> This proposal is directed toward a revision of the current penal law, in particular toward the final repeal of a special, unjust penal regulation that has come down to us from earlier centuries, toward the abolishing of the persecution of an innocent class of persons that is included in this penal regulation.
>
> ...Finally it is also a question, on a secondary level, of damning a continuing flood of suicides, and that of the most shocking kind.
>
> I believe that this is indeed a very worthy, serious, and important legal question, with which the Congress of German Jurists may quite suitably be called upon to be concerned.
>
> It is a question, gentlemen, of a class of persons that indeed in Germany is numbered in the thousands, a class of persons to which many of the greatest and noblest intellects of our and other nations have belonged...

At this point there were expressions of astonishment and scorn, and isolated cries of "Stop!"

> ...which class of persons is exposed to an undeserved legal persecution for no other reason...

Here there was a storm of "Stop! Stop!" from one side of the hall. The chairman wanted to put to a vote this loud call to stop. Ulrichs then said: "Under these circumstances I give up the floor and lay my protest on the table." From the other side of the hall there were now equally loud shouts of "No, no! Continue, continue!" Ulrichs then continued, pronouncing the following words with special emphasis:

> ...which class of persons is exposed to an undeserved legal persecution for no other reason than that mysteriously disposing creating nature has planted in them a sexual nature that is the opposite of that which in general is usual...

Now there was a roaring noise and tumultuous interruption, and an uncommon excitement in the assembly on the side from which the earlier cries to stop had come. The chairman spoke: "I request the speaker to use Latin in continuing!" At this point, however, Ulrichs laid his pages on the chairman's table and left the speaker's platform.

...An elderly man then took to the floor "to thank the deputation in the name of the assembly for having suppressed the proposal in the interest of morality." He, too, received shouts of approval. One can imagine how Ulrichs felt at this moment. Still, he was not personally insulted and so kept his seat for the remainder of the session. The chairman quickly moved on to other matters and the session soon ended.

The excitement did not die down so quickly, however, and Ulrichs heard some people asking others what it was all about. He could hear that the answers mostly hit the mark — with some exception. Some thought he wanted to give free rein to any kind of "crime of the flesh" whatever: incest, rape, adultery, etc. And two members even came up to him in the hall and accosted him with: "Ah, you were the speaker just now. Just tell us please what kind of race that is, which is exposed to such persecution?"

There were, however, those who felt Ulrichs had been unjustly treated and told him so. Judge Feuerbach from Stuttgart came up to say: "The assembly judged completely incompetently. They judged without knowing what it was about. I did not agree with them." And he added with perfect hindsight: "Your only mistake was in not sending us the proposal yourself."

Unheard by Ulrichs was the remark of another member: "My God! The man making that proposal puts himself under the greatest suspicion of being 'so' himself!"... [Ulrichs also made] the unexpected discovery that one of the members in his audience was also an Urning. He was a Bavarian judicial official, who apparently revealed himself to Ulrichs shortly afterwards, telling him how surprised and shaken he was by Ulrichs's speech.

Ulrichs would have no doubt have preferred to get away from it all at this point, but he was determined not to do anything that could be interpreted as weakness or shame. Consequently he attended the closing banquet that afternoon in the Crystal Palace ... and went on the outing to the Wurmsee the following day...

On both occasions Ulrichs noticed that there were some who avoided him. But he commented: "In contrast, however, was my satisfaction in having others freely and loyally join me in conversation."

AFTERWORD

Ulrichs's hopes to end the legal oppression of gays in Germany went unfulfilled. In 1871, four years after this speech, Germany was unified into a single nation by Prussia, and in 1872 the Prussian legal code became the legal system for all of Germany. It included Paragraph 175, a law which made homosexuality illegal throughout the entire German nation.

Ulrichs himself, undiscouraged by his poor reception at the 1867 Congress, continued his activism for many years. He was particularly outraged by police entrapment of gays who sought to meet other gays on the street, which ironically would be the same subject that inspired the first American gay-rights groups seventy-five years later (see Chapter 11). He continued to be concerned about the suicide issue, which remains a problem for young gays today (see Chapter 17). To try to bring about change, he began the first gay magazine in 1870 which, among other things, fought to legalize same-sex marriage, a position which only two nations — Norway and Denmark — have adopted as of this writing (see Chapter 16).

As all of this suggests, however, Ulrichs was a bit ahead of his time. He was unable to persuade enough other "urnings" to join him in his fight, and his magazine quickly went out of business due to financial problems. Ulrichs had long opposed Prussia's goal of controlling all of Germany (his home state of Hanover was a smaller, more liberal state than Prussia), and was very discouraged when the conservative Prussians succeeded in unifying all of Germany under their domination in 1871. He left Germany in 1880 and moved to Italy, where he died in 1895.

Ulrichs left a double legacy. First, he interested many of the members of the budding new science of psychiatry in the issue of same-sex attraction. He hoped to persuade them that this was "natural" and thereby win the help of the medical establishment for his fight. Among those he corresponded with were Karl Maria Kertbeny, who coined the term "homosexual," and Richard von Krafft-Ebing, who was recognized as one of the early "experts" on homosexuality. Unfortunately for Ulrichs, the psychiatric profession chose to view homosexuality as a "sickness" instead, a stance not repealed until 1973 in the U.S. when the American Psychiatric Association removed homosexuality from its list of "illnesses."

On the other hand, Ulrichs did inspire a whole new generation of gay activists who carried on his work. In particular, Magnus Hirschfeld (see Chapter 8) was directly inspired by him. Ulrichs's pioneering work served as the starting point for the German gay-rights movement, which was the world's largest in the early twentieth century. In his last years Ulrichs corresponded with other "urnings" around the world, even in English-speaking countries like Britain and the United States. His concept of gays as a "separate" people helped build the sense that gays were a "minority" group rather than a collection of individuals. This notion, picked up on by later activists, became the foundation of the gay liberation movement. Like many pioneers, Ulrichs did not live to see the fulfillment of his goals, but his crucial role in beginning the gay-rights movement is increasingly recognized by historians today.[2]

IMPORTANT TERMS

"group consciousness" urnings Paragraph 175

QUESTIONS/ACTIVITIES

1. What is a "minority"? What made Ulrichs begin to think of himself and fellow "urnings" as a "minority"?

2. Why did the delegates at the conventions have a hard time grasping this notion? Why did they lump "urnings" with those who commit incest, rape, and adultery rather than with groups like Jews?

3. The following first-person exercises can either be done in writing, acted out in small groups, or performed as skits in front of the class:

a. Imagine that you are Ulrichs and are trying to convince friends in Hanover to support your trip to the Congress in Munich by giving you the money to go. What reason(s) could you give your fellow "urnings" to justify the money?

b. Imagine you are Ulrichs's best friend and he has just confided in you his plan to go to the Congress in Munich. Try to talk him out of it, explaining the reason(s) such a speech would be a bad thing.

c. You are Ulrichs and it is the night before you are to speak. Make a "pro and con" list of the advantages and disadvantages of actually giving the speech the next day.

d. You are Ulrichs, and your name has just been called for you to speak. Write an "internal monologue" (in first person) about what is going through your mind as you make your way to the podium.

e. As Ulrichs, explain why you decided to continue to attend the Congress after you were shouted down, while also exploring how it might have felt to be there.

f. As Ulrichs, write down how you feel about this incident at the end of your life.

4. Debate the following proposition: "Karl Ulrichs achieved no significant changes during his life, and is thus not an important historical figure." What makes someone "important"? Why? How do we measure this? All of these questions will need to be addressed during the debate.

5. Write an obituary for Ulrichs in 1895. What would be different about how he was regarded when he died, and how historians regard him today?

6. Using documents from Chapter 14, imagine a dialogue between Ulrichs and a gay activist from the past decade. What similarities would still exist? What differences?

CHAPTER 8

Gays and the Holocaust

INTRODUCTION

Until recent years, little attention has been paid to the fate of gays during the Holocaust. This neglect has concealed the fact that gays were among the most viciously persecuted of Hitler's many victims, with thousands being interned and eventually dying in concentration camps. The failure to tell this story is partly a result of the homophobia of historians, but also because of the reluctance of gay survivors to come forward after the war to tell their stories. This unwillingness was because the laws that made homosexuality illegal (and led to the arrest of gays before the war) remained on the books afterwards.

Some gay concentration-camp inmates were actually transferred directly from camps to jails after they were "liberated," for they were still seen as "criminals." Incredibly enough, camps were not deemed "prisons," and those years spent in a concentration camp were not counted toward jail terms Germans received for violating the anti-gay law, Paragraph 175. So after the war, some homosexual camp inmates were sent to regular jails to complete their sentences.[1]

As convicted "criminals," gay survivors were also denied the financial payments made by the postwar German government to Holocaust victims, and gays were excluded from most Holocaust memorials. With few people willing to hear the stories of gay survivors, an important chapter of the Holocaust went unwritten for years. It was not until the 1970s that first-person accounts (such as the one excerpted here) and secondary surveys of the gay experience of the Holocaust became widely available.[2]

It is ironic that Germany was the scene of this massacre of gays. As we saw in the previous chapter, Germany could be considered the birthplace of the modern gay movement, thanks to the pioneering leadership of Karl Heinrich Ulrichs. In the decades prior to the Nazi takeover in 1933, the German gay-rights movement was the world's leader. Much of this was thanks to Magnus Hirschfeld (1868-1935), a Jewish gay man who was Ulrichs's intellectual and spiritual successor. Hirschfeld was inspired by Ulrichs's "third sex" theory and spent his entire adult life organizing to improve conditions for homosexuals. A remarkably productive writer (he produced over two hundred separate works),[3] Hirschfeld fought tirelessly for legal and social reform not only in Germany but also around the world. His motto, "Justice through Knowledge," reflected his belief that education would change the ignorance he felt was responsible for the oppression of gay people.[4]

Hirschfeld was considerably more successful than Ulrichs. In 1897 he founded the Scientific-Humanitarian Committee, with the goal of getting Paragraph 175, the law making homosexuality a crime, repealed. By 1898 he already had August Bebel, leader of Germany's largest political party (the Social Democrats), speaking out against Paragraph 175 on the floor of the Reichstag (Germany's parliament).[5] A petition drive for the repeal effort gathered six thousand signatures, including those of scientist Albert Einstein, and writers Thomas Mann and Hermann Hesse.[6]

Hirschfeld's work was derailed by the turmoil of World War I (1914–1918), but it regained momentum under the democratic "Weimar Republic" which governed Germany after the war. In 1919 Hirschfeld founded the Institute for Sex Research, which gathered scientific data on sexuality with the aim of providing accurate information on homosexuality.[7] In 1921 he organized the First Congress for Sexual Reform, which was attended by delegates from several countries. Out of this grew the World League for Sexual Reform, which claimed 130,000 members worldwide by the late twenties.[8] By decade's end, his work to repeal Paragraph 175 had moved further than ever before; after winning a crucial committee vote in the Reichstag (the German parliament) in 1929, it appeared that victory was at hand.[9]

Larger events, however, were to overtake the German gay-rights movement. Troubled by hyperinflation in the early twenties and the effects of the Great Depression in the 1930s, the German people blamed democracy and the Weimar Republic for their many problems. They turned to Adolf Hitler and his Nazi Party as the solution, and they elected him chancellor in 1933. This was the beginning of the end for Hirschfeld's movement.

The Nazis had long been vocal in their hatred of homosexuals. They viewed gays as part of the "rot" that had undermined Germany after the war. In 1928 the Nazi Party issued a statement on the Paragraph 175 repeal effort that made their views quite clear:

> ...[W]e reject you [homosexuals], as we reject anything that hurts our nation. Anyone who thinks of homosexual love is our enemy. We reject anything that emasculates our people and makes it a plaything for our enemies, for we know that life is a fight, and it is madness to think that men will ever embrace fraternally. Natural history teaches the opposite. Might makes right. The strong will always win over the weak. Let us see to it that we once again become strong! But this we can achieve in only one way — the German people must once again learn how to exercise discipline. We therefore reject any form of lewdness, especially homosexuality, because it robs us of our last chance to free our people from the bondage which now enslaves it.[10]

The Nazi Party sent Hirschfeld a telegram after his 1929 committee victory telling him "don't think that we Germans will allow these laws to stand for a single day after we come to power."[11]

The Nazis wasted little time in their efforts to make Germany "homorein" ("free of homosexuals") once they took power. On February 23, 1933, barely three weeks after Hitler became chancellor on January 30, gay-rights groups were banned. On May 6 the Institute for Sexual Research was destroyed by Nazi thugs.[12] (Hirschfeld was lecturing abroad at the time, and never returned to Germany; he died in France in 1935.)[13]

By 1934 the Gestapo was ordered to compile lists of homosexuals.[14] In 1935 Paragraph 175 was extended to cover not only those who actually had sex with someone of the same sex, but also those who merely thought about it. Authorities called this "contemplation of the desired object," and it allowed nearly anyone to be criminally charged.[15] After all, how can one prove that one isn't thinking about something? By 1938, it became legal to move those arrested under Paragraph 175 from regular jails to concentration camps. In 1940 the authorities were actually required to send those charged with violating this law to the camps.[16] The effort to exterminate gays was under way.

As is the case with Jews and the other groups victimized during the Holocaust, the exact number of gays who died is not easy to pin down. Around 50,000 convictions under Paragraph 175 took place, and apparently somewhere between 5,000 and 15,000 of those sent to concentration camps died.[17] (Readers should keep in mind the important distinction between extermination camps, which existed only to kill people and to which mainly Jews were sent, and concentration camps, where inmates were often used for labor and not killed immediately).

The 5,000–15,000 figure is considered the most conservative of estimates, however, and many put the death toll much higher. Tens of thousands undoubtedly shared experiences like those of Heinz Heger, the gay survivor from whose memoir Reading 8-A comes. Heger, imprisoned in camps for over six years, is the only gay survivor to have written a full-length account of his experiences there. At the opening of his narrative, he is living in Vienna, the capital of the independent German-speaking country of Austria, just before it was absorbed by Hitler in the "Anschluss" of 1938. His story of forced labor, degradation, and inhuman conditions helps us understand not only the experience of gays in the Holocaust but also the nature of this darkest chapter in human history.

READING 8-A

A Story of the Camps

excerpts from *The Men with the Pink Triangle,*
by Heinz Heger

Vienna, March 1939. I was 22 years old, a university student preparing for an academic career, a choice that met my parents' wishes as well as my own. Being little interested in politics, I was not a member of any Nazi student association, or any of the party's other organizations...

Ever since I was sixteen I knew I was more attracted to my own sex than I was to girls. At first I didn't think this was anything special, but when my schoolfriends began to get romantically involved with girls, while I was still stuck on another boy, I had to give some thought to what this meant...

At university I was able to get to know several students with similar views, or rather, feelings, to my own ... [A]t the end of 1938 I met the great love of my life.

Fred was the son of a high Nazi official from the Reich, two years older than I, and set on completing his study of medicine at the world-famous Vienna medical school. He was forceful but at the same time sensitive, and his masculine appearance, success in sport, and great knowledge made such an impression on me that I fell for him straight away. I must have pleased him too, I suppose, with my Viennese charm and temperament. I also had an athletic figure which he liked. We were very happy together, and made all kinds of plans for the future, believing we would never more be separated.

It was on Friday about 1 p.m. ... that I heard two rings at the door ... When I opened it I was surprised to see a man with a slouch hat and a leather coat. With the curt word "Gestapo," he handed me a card with a printed summons to appear for questioning at 2 p.m. at the Gestapo headquarters in the Hotel Metropol.

My mother and I were very upset, but I could only think it was something to do with something at the university, possibly a political investigation into a student who had fallen afoul of the Nazi student association...

My mother was still not satisfied and showed great concern. I, too, had a nervous feeling in my stomach, but then doesn't anyone in a time of dictatorship if they are called in by the secret police? ... My mother must have felt the same, for when I said goodbye to her she embraced my very warmly and repeated: "Be careful, child, be careful!"

Neither of us thought, however, that we would not meet again for six years, myself a human wreck, she a broken woman, tormented as to the fate of her son, and having had to face the contempt of neighbors and fellow-citizens ever since it was known her son was homosexual and had been sent to a concentration camp.

I never saw my father again. It was only after my liberation in 1945 that I learned from my mother how he had tried time and again to secure my release ... Because of these requests, but above all because his son was imprisoned for homosexuality, and this was incompatible with his official position [as a civil servant] under the Nazi regime, he was forced to retire on reduced pension in December 1940. He could no longer put up with the abuse he received, and in 1942 took his own life — filled with bitterness and grief for an age he could not fit into, filled with disappointment over all those friends who couldn't or wouldn't help him. He wrote a farewell letter to my mother, asking her forgiveness for having to leave her alone. My mother still has the letter today, and the last lines read: "And so I can no longer tolerate the scorn of my acquaintances and colleagues, and of our neighbors. It's just too much for me! Please forgive me again. God protect our son!"

At five to two I reached the Gestapo HQ ... I showed my summons, and an SS man took me to department IIs. We stopped outside a room with a large sign indicating the official within, until a secretary sitting in the antechamber, also in SS uniform, showed us in. "Your appointment, *Herr Doktor!"* The SS man handed in my card, clicked his heels, and vanished.

The doctor, in civilian clothes, but with the short, angular hair-cut and smooth-shaven face that immediately gave him away as a senior officer, sat behind an imposing desk piled up with files, all neatly arranged. He neither greeted nor even looked at me, but just carried on writing.

I stood and waited. Still nothing happened, for several minutes. The room was quite silent and I scarcely dared breath, while he steadily wrote on. The only sound was the scratch of his pen. I became more and more nervous, though I recognized the "softening up" tactic. Quite suddenly he laid down his pen and stared at me with cold grey eyes: "You are a queer, a homosexual, do you admit it?"

"No, no, it's not true," I stammered, almost stunned by his accusation, which was the last thing I expected. I had only thought of some political affair, perhaps to do with the university; now suddenly I found my well-kept secret was out.

"Don't you lie, you dirty queer!" he shouted angrily. "I have clear proof, look at this."

He took a postcard-sized photo from his drawer.

"Do you know him?"

His long hairy finger pointed at the picture. Of course I knew the photo. It was a snap someone had taken showing Fred and me with our arms in friendly fashion round each other's shoulders.

"Yes, that's my student friend Fred X."

"Indeed," he said calmly, yet unexpectedly quick: "You've done filthy things together, don't you admit it?" His voice was contemptuous, cold and cutting.

I just shook my head. I couldn't get a word out, it was as if a cord was tied round my neck. A whole world came tumbling down inside me, the world of friendship and love for Fred. Our plans for the future, to stay faithful together, and never to reveal our friendship to outsiders, all this seem betrayed. I was trembling with agitation, not only because of the "doctor's" examination, but also because our friendship was now revealed. The "doctor" took the picture and turned it over. On it read: "To my friend Fred in eternal love and deepest affection!" I knew as soon as he showed me the photo that it had my vow of love on the other side. I had given it to Fred for Christmas 1938...

"Is that your writing and your signature?"

I nodded, tears rising to my eyes.

"That's all, then," he said jovially and content, "sign here."

He handed me a half-written sheet, which I signed with trembling hand. The letters swam in front of my eyes, my tears now flowing openly. The SS man who had brought me here was now back in the room again.

"Take him away," said the "doctor," giving the SS man a slip of paper and bending over his files again, not deeming me worthy of further attention.

I was taken the same day to the police prison ... My pressing request was to telephone my mother to tell her where I had been taken, was met with the words: "She'll soon know you're not coming home again."

...I was locked into a cell designed for one person, although it already held two other occupants. My fellow-prisoners were criminals, one under investigation for housebreaking, the other for swindling widows on the lookout for a new husband...

When they found out I was "queer," as one of the policeman gleefully told them ... they then started to insult me and "the whole brood of queers" who ought to be exterminated. It was an unheard-of insult that the authorities should have put a sub-human such as this in the same cell with two relatively decent people. Even if they had come into conflict with the law, they were at least normal men and not moral degenerates. They were on quite a different level from homos, who should be classed as animals...

...I later had the misfortune to discover that it wasn't only these two gangsters who had that opinion, but almost all "normal" men. I still wonder today how this division between normal and abnormal is made. Is there a normal hunger and an abnormal one? A normal thirst and an abnormal one? Isn't hunger always hunger, and thirst thirst? What a hypocritical and illogical way of thinking!

Two weeks later, my trial already came up, justice showing an unusual haste in my case. Under paragraph 175 of the German criminal code, I was condemned by an Austrian court for homosexual behavior, and sentenced to six months' penal servitude...

On the day that my six months were up, and I should have been released, I was informed that the Central Security Department had demanded that I remain in custody ... for transit to a concentration camp.

This news was like a blow on the head, for I knew from other prisoners who had been sent back from concentration camp for trial that we "queers," just like the Jews, were tortured to death in the camps, and only rarely came out alive. At that time, however, I couldn't, or wouldn't, believe this. I thought it was exaggeration, designed to upset me. Unfortunately, it was only too true!

And what had I done to be sent off this way? What infamous crime or damage to the community? I had loved a friend of mine, a grown man of 24, not a child. I could find nothing dreadful or wrong in that.

What does it say about the world we live in, if an adult man is told how and whom he should love?...

By January 1940 the complement for the transport was made up, and we were taken to a camp...

To make my experience in concentration camp a bit more comprehensible, I should first of all describe how the camps were constructed and run...

The prisoners' uniforms were marked with a coloured cloth triangle to denote their offence or origin. Their prison number was sewn below the triangle. The triangle was about five centimetres across and placed point down, and was stitched onto the left breast of the jacket and the outside right trouser-leg.

The colors of the triangles were as follows:

yellow for Jews,
black for anti-socials,
red for politicals,
purple for Jehovah's Witnesses,
green for criminals,
blue for emigrants,
pink for homosexuals,
brown for gypsies.

The pink triangle, however, was about 2 or 3 centimetres larger than the others, so that we could be clearly recognized from a distance.

Jews, homosexuals, and gypsies, the yellow, pink, and brown triangles, were the prisoners who suffered the most frequently and most severely from the tortures and blows of the SS and the capos. They were described as the scum of humanity, who had no right to live on German soil and should be exterminated. Such were the oft-repeated words of the commandant and his SS subordinates. But the lowest of the low in this "scum" were we, the men with the pink triangle.

As soon as we were unloaded on the large, open parade-ground, some SS NCOs came along and attacked us with sticks. We had to form up in rows of five, and it took quite a while, and many blows and insults, before our terrified ranks were assembled. Then we had a roll call, having to step forward and repeat our name and offence, whereupon we were immediately handed over to our particular block leader.

When my name was called I stepped forward, gave my name, and mentioned paragraph 175. With the words, "You filthy queer, get over there...!" I received several kicks from behind and was kicked over to an SS sergeant who had charge of my block.

The first thing I got from him was a violent blow on my face that threw me to the ground. I pulled myself up and respectfully stood before him, whereupon he brought his knee up hard into my groin so that I doubled up in pain on the ground. Some prisoners who were on duty immediately called out to me:

"Stand up quick, otherwise he'll kick you to bits!"

My face still twisted, I stood up again in front of my block sergeant, who grinned at me and said:

"That was your entrance fee, you filthy Viennese swine, so that you know who your block leader is."

When the whole transport was divided up, there were about twenty men in our category. We were driven to our block at the double, interrupted by the commands: "Lie down! Stand up! Lie down, stand up!" and so on, from the block leader and some of his men, then having once again to form up in ranks of three. We then had to strip completely naked, lay our clothes on the ground in front of us, with shoes and socks on top, and wait — wait — wait.

It was January and a few degrees below zero, with an icy wind blowing through the camp, yet we were left naked and barefoot on the snow-covered ground, to stand and wait. An SS corporal in winter coat with fur collar strode through our ranks and struck now one of us, now another, with a horse-whip, crying: "This is so you don't make me feel cold, you filthy queers."...

Finally, after a terribly long time, we were allowed to march to the showers — still naked and barefoot. Our clothes, which had already had name tags put in, remained behind, and had vanished when we returned. We had to wash ourselves in cold water, and some of the new arrivals collapsed with cold and exhaustion. Only then did the camp doctor have the warm water turned on, so that we could thaw ourselves out. After the shower we were taken to the next room where we had to cut our hair, pubic hair included.

Finally we were taken, still naked — to the clothing stores, where we were given underwear and were "fitted" with prison clothing. This was distributed quite irrespective of size. The trousers I received were far too short, and came only just below my calves, the jacket was much too narrow and had too short sleeves. Only the coat fitted tolerably well, but by mere accident. The shoes were a little too big and smelled strongly of sweat, but they had leather soles, which made walking a lot easier than the wooden-soled shoes that many new arrivals had received. As far as clothing went, I didn't do too badly. Then we had to form up again outside our block and have its organization explained to us by the camp commander. Our block was occupied only by homosexuals, with about 250 men in each wing...

The windows had a centimetre of ice on them. Anyone found with his underclothes on in bed, or his hands under his blanket — there were checks almost every night — was taken outside and had several bowls of water poured over him before being left standing outside for a good hour. Only a few people survived this treatment. The least result was bronchitis, and it was rare for any gay person taken into sick-bay to come out alive...

We new arrivals were now assigned to our work, which was to keep the area around the block clean. That at least is what we were told by the NCO in charge. In reality, the purpose was to break the very last spark of independent spirit that might possibly remain in the new prisoners, by senseless yet very heavy labor, and to destroy the little human dignity that we still retained. This work continued until a new batch of pink-triangle prisoners were delivered to our block and we were replaced.

Our work, then, was as follows. In the morning we had to cart the snow outside our block from the left side of the road to the right side. In the afternoon we had to cart the same snow from the right side to the left. We didn't have barrows or shovels to perform this work either, that would have been far too simple for us "queers." No, our SS masters had thought up something better.

We had to put on our coats with the buttoned side backwards, and take the snow away in the container this provided. We had to shovel the snow with our hands — our bare hands, as we didn't have any gloves. We worked in teams of two. Twenty turns at shovelling the snow with our hands, then twenty turns carrying it away. And so right through to the evening, and all at the double!

This mental and bodily torment lasted six days, until at last new pink-triangle prisoners were delivered to our block and took over from us. Our hands were cracked all over and half frozen off, and we had become dumb and indifferent slaves of the SS.

I learned from prisoners who had already been in our block a good while that in summer similar work was done with earth and sand.

Above the gate of the prison camp, however, the "meaningful" Nazi slogan was written in big capitals:

"Freedom through work!"

After the infamous snow detachment, we new arrivals were transferred to the same work as the rest of our entire block: the clay-pit of the Klinker brick works. The clay-pit, known among us prisoners as the death-pit, was both famed and feared by all prisoners in all other concentration camps, as a factory of human destruction, and up until 1942 it was the "Auschwitz" for homosexuals...

Work in the clay-pit was the hardest it is possible to imagine, and exposed to all elements. Whether in summer, with the singeing heat, or in winter with biting frost and deep snow, a fixed daily number of carts filled with clay had to be pushed by hand up to the brick-making machines and their ovens, so that sufficient raw material was always available and production need not be interrupted. Since the clay-pit was quite deep, the stretch up which these carts had to be hand-pushed on rails to the plant was both very long and very steep. For half-starved prisoners covered with marl, this was a real Golgotha...

It happened very often that prisoners shoving a full cart uphill simply ran out of strength, and the cart slipped violently back down on them. If it could not be braked in time with wooden sticks, then it ran right back with full force into the cart below. Many prisoners were already so numbed and indifferent that they didn't even bother to jump out of the way when a full cart came roaring towards them. Then human bodies would fly through the air, and limbs be crushed to pulp, while the remaining prisoners only received more blows with the stick. The clay-pit thus took its daily toll of fatalities, both accident victims and those who simply succumbed to exhaustion. The death-pit richly deserved its name.

My dormitory, with 180 prisoners or more, contained the most varied collection of people. Unskilled workers and shop assistants, skilled tradesmen and independent craftsmen, musicians and artists, professors and clergy, even aristocratic landowners ... All of these otherwise decent people had been assembled here, in this melting pot of disgrace and torment, the "queer block" of a concentration camp, for extermination through back-breaking labor, hunger, and torture. None of them were child molesters, or had had sex with children or adolescents, as all of these had a green triangle. Were we with the pink triangle really outrageous criminals and degenerates, a menace to society?...

By now it was April, yet I was still alive, despite constant work in the clay-pit.

Though already weak in my body, my mind was still absolutely clear and alert. A necessary condition, if one was to remain alive in concentration camp and survive the incessant torment.

One day I was called out at morning parade and transferred to a different work detachment, assigned to build a new firing-range for the SS.

God, how happy I was to get out of the death-pit! ... My joy, unfortunately, was brief and soon cut short, for it turned out that I had only exchanged the frying pan for the fire. Once again, it was only homosexuals who were employed, plus a few Jews who never returned to the camp in the evening alive. I soon found out how in this unit too, no concern was shown for human life, particularly the lives of queers and Jews.

We had to carry earth and clay to build up a mound for the firing-range butts, to stand behind the target zone which was already installed. At first this went off quite smoothly; we carted our barrows and the earth slowly rose. But then, after only a few days, groups of SS men came to the firing range to start their firing practice, while we prisoners had to carry on emptying our barrows onto the mound. Naturally enough, we wanted to stop unloading when the shooting practice was going on, but the capos [camp officials] and the SS guards forced us to continue with blows and threats of a beating.

Then shots started to whip through our ranks, and several of my fellow-sufferers collapsed, some only wounded, but many killed. We soon found out that the SS far preferred to fire on us prisoners than they did at the proper targets, and had directly aimed at certain people pushing their barrows.

Every day, our group suffered some dead and wounded. We came to work each morning full of terror and dread, not knowing which of us were to meet our death, but sure that some or other of us would. We had become a sitting target for the SS, who greeted each direct hit with a shout of glee...

It must have been great sport for the SS, then, to use us pink-triangle prisoners as living targets. What a nice change for them, to have live human beings to play with!...

[On 15th May 1940, Heger was transferred to another camp called Flossenbürg, where he was assigned to work in a granite quarry.]

Just like the prison camp itself, the granite quarry was completely surrounded by barbed wire, and guarded outside and inside by SS sentries. No prisoner was permitted to get closer than five metres to the wire. Anyone who did so was shot by the SS guards without warning, since this transgression was already considered attempted escape. For shooting a prisoner who "attempted escape," an SS man received three days' special leave.

It is not hard to imagine, therefore, how keen the SS were to organize "escapes" of this kind, for the sake of their extra leave. In the relatively short time that I worked in the quarry, I myself witnessed at least ten occasions when SS men seized a prisoner's cap and threw it against the wire. They would then demand that the prisoner fetch his cap back. Naturally enough, the prisoner tried to refuse, as everyone knew this meant certain death. The SS men then started beating the poor devil with sticks, so that he could only choose the way in which he was to die. Either beaten to death by the SS beasts, or be shot by the guards for "attempted escape."

It happened several times, too, that a prisoner would himself run up against the wire in despair, to get shot and to be freed from pain and hunger and the unbearable toil...

One way of tormenting Jews and homosexuals that the SS in the quarry were very fond of was to drive crazy prisoners who were already physically at the end of their tether. A man who had not done anything in particular, but was simply picked upon by the SS officer in charge, would have a metal bucket placed over his head. Two men held him down, while the SS men and the capos banged on the bucket with their sticks. The terrible noise amplified through the bucket soon brought the victim to such a pitch of terror that he completely lost his mind and his sense of balance was destroyed. Then the bucket was suddenly removed from his head and he was pushed towards the wire fence. He could seldom right himself in time. And if he staggered inside the 5-metre zone, he was fired on in the usual way. "Games" such as these were a favorite pastime for some of the SS guards, who had no need to fear any disciplinary measures, their victims just being homosexuals and Jews whose extermination was planned for in any case...

[Through a combination of good luck, hard work, and ingratiating himself with camp officers, Heger survived for two years working at Flossenbürg, when a new program to deal with gay prisoners was announced in 1943.]

On the express order of *SS-Reichsfuhrer* Heinrich Himmler, "Reichsheini" as he was known to both friend and foe, a prison brothel was established in Flossenbürg in summer 1943, known by the euphemism of the "special block"...

Himmler's idea, however, was that those of us in the pink-triangle category should be "cured" of our homosexual disposition by compulsory regular visits to the brothel. We were obliged to show up there once a week, in order to learn the "joys" of the other sex. Of course, this instruction only showed how little the SS leadership and their scientific advisors understood homosexuality, seeing a human emotional orientation as simply a disability and prescribing brothel visits as "treatment"...

One day the lorry [truck] with the "girls" arrived at the camp gate and rolled up at the special block, impatiently anticipated by many people. Ten young women got out, and were taken into their quarters. They came from the women's camp at Ravensbrück, and were almost all Jews and gypsies. The SS had brought them to Flossenbürg on the pretext that after six months "service to clients" they would be released from concentration camp. The tortures and sufferings in the women's camps must have been just as bad as those inflicted on the male prisoners at Flossenbürg, otherwise it would be incomprehensible that girls such as these would have volunteered for brothel service. The promise of freedom was a gleaming one, an end to torture and brutality, as well as the pangs of hunger.

Believing in the promises of their concentration camp jailers, they offered themselves up as victims for six months, whereupon they would allegedly be relieved by a further batch of "volunteers" from Ravensbrück. But rather than freedom, they were taken to the extermination camp at Auschwitz, completely exhausted by the almost 2000 "acts of love" that they had to submit to in these six months...

Towards the end of 1943 a new instruction on "the eradication of sexual degenerates," i.e., homosexuals, came down from Himmler. He now stipulated that any homosexual who consented to castration, and whose conduct was good, would shortly be released from concentration camp. Many of the pink-triangle prisoners actually believed Himmler's promises, and consented to castration with a view of escaping their murderous persecutions. But in spite of good conduct — and this was assessed by the SS block leader and camp commander — when they were released from concentration camp this was only to be sent to the SS Dirlewanger penal division on the Russian front, to be butchered in the partisan war and die a hero's death for Hitler and Himmler...

[Heger continued to work in the camp for two years, until the end of the war approached in 1945. He was then transferred to another camp, Dachau, as Russian troops overran his old camp. Dachau was liberated in April 1945 by the American Army, and Heger was able to return home to his mother in Vienna.]

My mother and I wept tears of joy when we met again after years of separation, with her ignorant of whether I was alive or dead, tears of joy mixed with bitter tears over the fate of my father ... I was back in my room once more, surrounded by all the books of my student days, a comforting and confident vision. Everything in the same place, quite unchanged from the day six years ago when I was called in by the Gestapo and never returned. Only we were changed, my mother and I. Myself, by violence and oppression, my mother by worry and grief.

I wanted to resume and complete the studies I had begun so many years before, but I lacked the strength or the will for systematic learning. I could not banish from my mind the terrible tortures of the concentration camp, the dreadful and beastly brutalities of the SS monsters. I would be listening to a professor, but soon my attention would wander, I would think of the camp, see the tortures again in my mind, and forget the lecture. In hours of quiet, too, pictures of the camp would rise up before my eyes, pictures that I shall never forget as long as I live. Today, people have stopped talking about the sufferings and the killings of the Nazi concentration camps, and no longer want to be reminded of them, but we, the ex-prisoners, will always remember what we suffered.

My request for compensation for the years of concentration camp was rejected by our democratic authorities, for as a pink-triangle prisoner, I had been condemned for a criminal offense, even if I had not harmed anyone. No restitution is granted to "criminal" concentration camp victims...

Scarcely a word has been written on the fact that along with the millions whom Hitler butchered on the grounds of "race," hundreds of thousands of people were sadistically tortured to death simply for having homosexual feelings. Scarcely anyone has publicized the fact that the madness of Hitler and his gang was not directed just against Jews, but also against us homosexuals, in both cases leading to the "final solution" of seeking the total annihilation of these human beings.

May they never be forgotten
these multitudes of dead,
our anonymous, immortal martyrs.

IMPORTANT TERMS

Magnus Hirschfeld
Paragraph 175
Weimar Republic (1919–1933)
Nazi Party
Adolf Hitler
Heinrich Himmler
concentration camp
extermination camp
pink triangle

QUESTIONS/ACTIVITIES

1. Keep an imaginary diary, or write "internal monologues," which could be read aloud in class, of what is going on in Heger's mind, at these moments in the account:

- when he is standing in the SS official's office waiting to hear why he has been called to Gestapo headquarters
- when the officer reveals the photograph of him with his friend Fred
- when he finds out he is to be transported to a concentration camp
- on his first night in a concentration camp
- after the war, when he attempts to return to his studies but cannot
- when the editor of this book approaches him to ask him to share his story.

2. More difficult than understanding Heger is understanding the Nazis who persecuted him. Try to understand Nazi thinking under the rationale that "We cannot defeat our enemies unless we understand them." It is important to remember that, in these exercises, you are adopting a character, and that you are not representing your own views in writing or speaking as these characters.

a. Write an "internal monologue" of what the following individuals were thinking at the time, with the goal of having them explain how they could see their actions as justified:

- the SS officer who interviews Heger at Gestapo headquarters
- the SS guard who greets the prisoners at Heger's first camp
- the SS guards who played the "fence game"

b. Choose a partner who has written one of the accounts in question 1. Have a conversation, after the war, as if you were still these characters. These can be done simultaneously, with volunteers afterwards offering to perform before the whole class.

c. Imagine you are Nazi officials in charge of the details of implementing the Holocaust. Write memos explaining:

- why you've chosen to imprison members of those groups on the "triangle list," offering a rationale for why each is a threat to society. [This can also be done in small groups, with each group given a specific population to justify.]
- why concentration camp work should involve tasks such as the snow shoveling
- why you would attempt the prostitute and castration "cures" for homosexuals.

What would it take to write such memos and then return home each night feeling good about your work? How could you do this?

3. Debate, either orally or in writing, whether or not to submit to the castration "cure" as if you were a gay prisoner.

4. Address this question: How was it that Heger survived? What qualities does he have that enabled him to "make it" under conditions that would destroy most of us?

5. The film *Europa, Europa* depicts the dramatic true story of a Jewish teenager who "passed" for Christian to survive the Holocaust. Watch the film. What parallels are there between "passing" for straight and the kind of "passing" the character must do to survive in this film?

6. In the postwar era, particularly in the United States, the pink triangle became the symbol of the gay liberation movement. This may seem ironic after reading this account. Debate the use of this symbol, what it means, what kind of message it sends, and whether or not you feel it is appropriate.

CHAPTER 9

World War II and a "New Minority" in the United States

INTRODUCTION

As seen in Chapter 6, gays have been a presence in the American military since before the nation itself won its independence. This does not mean that this presence was welcomed. "Sodomy," or same-sex sexual activities, was grounds for being discharged from the military, and the first individual to be so punished was Lt. Gotthold Enslin, expelled from the army in February 1778 at Valley Forge.[1] Gays may have fought for America, but America was strangely ungrateful for this sacrifice. However, only a small number of gay Americans actually suffered from these discriminatory regulations. The difficulty of "catching someone in the act" of sodomy meant that few were actually prosecuted: only a few hundred soldiers were discharged on this basis until World War II.[2]

World War II was a turning point in American history, for the nation as a whole and gays and lesbians in particular. The United States traditionally had maintained a very small military, relying on volunteers when war broke out. World War II called upon the country to mobilize as never before. Eventually, sixteen million Americans (including over a quarter of a million women) served in the war.[3] With so many male workers gone, just as industrial production had to reach new heights in order to defeat the enemy, the domestic labor force changed dramatically. Millions of women worked outside the home for the first time, in jobs that had always been reserved for men, such as welding. African-Americans were drawn to northern cities to fill jobs made available by the labor shortage and Latinos immigrated to the United States in record numbers to take advantage of these opportunities. Cities grew as many left small-town and rural areas for the first time to live in urban areas. Postwar America was a drastically different society from what it had been in 1941.

For gay Americans, the war ended the sense of isolation that had dominated gay life in the years before the war. With the exception of one group, the Chicago-based Society for Human Rights (see Chapter 14), no gay-rights organizations had been founded before World War II, and the entire topic of homosexuality was generally not discussed in "polite society" or the media. However, as historian Allan Bérubé points out, the war brought together previously isolated gays, profoundly changing their sense of self:

> During the 1930s and 1940s, young men and women who grew up feeling homosexual desires had little help coming out. They were likely to lead isolated lives, not knowing anyone else like themselves, with no one to talk to about their feelings and often unsure of who or what they were...
>
> The massive mobilization for World War II relaxed the social constraints of peacetime that had kept gay men and women unaware of themselves and each other, "bringing out" many in the process. Gathered together in military camps, they often came to terms with their sexual desires, fell in love, made friends with other gay people, and began to name and talk about who they were.[4]

Through these experiences, gays and lesbians began to develop a greater "group consciousness," and the silence that had characterized gay life before the war was forever shattered.

However, all was not well for gays in the military. Military policies were revised during the war to make life much harder for gay soldiers. In seeking to develop the best possible fighting force, military officials turned to the medical establishment for help in screening out "unfit" soldiers. Under the influence of psychiatry, medical procedures included mental health in their evaluations to determine fitness. One of the disqualifying "illnesses" was homosexuality. Psychiatrists convinced the military to take a new view of gays. Instead of lawbreakers, homosexuals became a group of "sick" people who needed treatment. All gays, whether or not they had actually had sex with someone of the same sex, needed to be either "cured" or kept out of the military altogether. As Bérubé explains, this change was dramatic:

> [The new policy resulted in] the widening of the net in which gay men and lesbians could be caught, vastly expanding the military's

> antihomosexual apparatus and creating new forms of surveillance and punishment. When previously only those who had been caught in the sexual act and convicted in court were punished, now merely being homosexual or having such "tendencies" could entrap both men and women, label them as sick, and remove them from the service with an undesirable discharge. Because the discharge system punished both gay men and women even if they remained celibate, it demanded that they police their social behavior and appearance as well, so that no one would suspect them of being homosexual.[5]

In order to enforce the new, broader policies, a whole system of repression had to be developed. It became standard to ask all recruits about their sexual orientation (a practice not to be discontinued until 1993), with a "yes" answer leading to rejection from the military; new agencies were set up to investigate suspected gays; special facilities for "treatment" were established; and a new form of discharge was developed to expel those who had "undesirable habits or traits of character," such as homosexuals. These were called the "blue discharges," because of the color of the paper on which they were printed.[6] The numbers of those victimized soared: Over 9000 individuals were discharged during the war on gay-related charges.[7] Ironically, the military itself deserves much of the credit for breaking the silence around homosexuality; its new regulations brought the issue into the consciousness of military members as never before, with the insistent questioning, investigating, and prosecution the new approach required.

This repression helped gays develop a sense of themselves as a "minority" group deserving of equal rights. Having fought for their country and feeling entitled to full citizenship in it, some gays began to speak out publicly against anti-gay discrimination. As Bérubé explains in Reading 9-A, one of the legacies of the Second World War was that, for the first time, a sense of solidarity arose among previously isolated gay Americans. The political effects would be felt until this day. This solidarity grew from the personal tragedies gay soldiers suffered. As Pat Bond explains in Reading 9-B, there were very real human casualties from this second war the military waged, against not a foreign enemy but an "enemy" within, gay men and lesbians. Bond's first-person account helps us see how this affected one person, but her experience is typical of hundreds of thousands of others. Together, these readings help us understand the vital role the war played in the emergence of an organized gay community and political movement.

READING 9-A

After the War

from *Coming Out under Fire: The History of Gay Men and Women in World War Two,* by Allan Bérubé

The minor sexual revolution regarding homosexuality that gay veterans had experienced during the war brought about more changes than the efforts of blue dischargees to fight discrimination. The vast majority of gay male and lesbian veterans who received honorable discharges returned home with a sense of pride and accomplishment for having done their part in winning the war and a sense of entitlement to the GI benefits that awaited them. With heightened awareness of themselves as homosexual persons, familiarity with gay social life, and stronger bonds with each other, they adjusted to postwar civilian society with raised expectations of how they should be treated as homosexuals and as veterans...

Veterans who had formed their first gay relationships or discovered gay social life while in the military had an even stronger need to resolve questions regarding their own homosexuality. They had to make important life decisions about marriage and partners, education, where to live and work, how much to reveal about their sexuality to their families, and how deeply to become involved in a gay social life. They often had to choose between their families' expectations and their own needs. Some based their civilian life decisions on their loyalty to their families and home communities, while others embarked on lives organized around their homosexuality. After brief visits home, many lesbian and gay male veterans left their parents, abandoned small towns, and joined the majority of other veterans who headed toward the more expansive and tolerant conditions in American cities after the war.

The choice between staying in their hometowns or moving to the big city was for many veterans the choice between heterosexual marriage and the gay life. Some eagerly chose the gay life. "I can't change," wrote a gay GI in a letter shortly before his discharge in 1946, "have no desire to do so, because it took me a long, long time to figure out how to enjoy life ... I'm not going back to what I left."

Others who did go back faced deep conflicts between their love for their hometown and their attraction to the urban gay life they had discovered during the war. "Naturally I was afraid to return to Maysville," wrote one gay veteran to another about his trip home to Kentucky, "a town of ten thousand that I had left as a fair youngster ... Yet I have found the same things which always gave Maysville its charm are still here. I have my little circle of admirers — the river still flows — and drives on country roads are still as restful ... As far as really gay life," he continued, "there will be none here. At least not for a long while. I have spotted a few sisters — but in a town of this size — and being as well known as I am..."

A great many gay male, lesbian, and bisexual veterans got married, settled down, and raised families after the war, putting their homosexuality on hold or finding ways to have homosexual relationships within the context of their marriages. Robert Gervais got married, raised three children, and was "happy I didn't make it a completely gay life," yet for decades after the war remained the occasional lover of the communications officer he met aboard his destroyer. "My wife knows," he explained, and "understands when he comes to visit with us." Other bisexual veterans had clandestine sex with men in bathhouses, public toilets, and parks, while hiding their homosexuality from their wives. Some lesbian veterans who got married after the war waited until their children were grown or their husbands died to resume a lesbian life; others remained part of a lesbian circle of friends or had a female lover throughout their married life. With so little support for maintaining gay relationships, the temptation to lead a more respectable married life was always present, as was the fear that one's lover would abandon one to get married, leaving the gay life behind.

Gay male and lesbian veterans who moved to the cities found an anonymity, independence, and safety in numbers allowing them to lead gay lives without the scrutiny of unsympathetic family members and small-town neighbors who could condemn them or threaten their livelihood. They created their own circles of friends and risked going to the growing number of postwar lesbian and gay bars. Some used the GI Bill to go to school. "If it hadn't been for the Army, I probably wouldn't have been educated," explained Robert Fleischer, who used the GI Bill to go to fashion design school in New York City. Many used GI loans to open their own small businesses as florists, antique dealers, hairdressers, and shop owners, protected from the antigay prejudices of employers. Others worked for the government, universities, industry, private corporations, and other employers, where they could be fired if their homosexuality was discovered. Those who had found lovers during or after the war often settled down to quiet private lives, even joining the postwar migration to the mostly white suburbs. Sometimes reuniting with wartime buddies, they socialized with friends, neighbors, and other couples in their homes and avoided gay bars where they would risk public exposure and arrest.

Many poor and working-class veterans who had been raised in minority neighborhoods or on Indian reservations had to choose between trying to fit their homosexuality into the extended family of their home cultures or trying to fit as minorities into the gay culture of white society, where people had more economic resources and privacy to live independently gay lives. When Todd Grison, who had had his first gay experience in the Army, returned home to his mother in Alabama, he at first married a young woman he got pregnant, although he really wanted to go to Detroit to live with his aunt, which he eventually did after divorcing his wife. In the racially segregated city of Detroit, he discovered other gay black men and female prostitutes who hung out with the gay crowd in their own bars. One night he ventured into a white gay bar to see what it was like, but he "really got the cold shoulder, no one would even talk to me." When his black friends found out, they accused him of "goin' hiking on us," of thinking he was better than they were. Todd Grison, living with his aunt, faced much social pressure to keep his gay life within the black community.

The camaraderie in combat that both heterosexual and homosexual veterans missed after the war had been especially important to those gay men who had not previously felt themselves part of an all-male community. The gay life in the civilian world offered them a camaraderie that approximated what they had known in the military. Maxwell Gordon was such a veteran. In the spring of 1946 Gordon felt a restlessness and a nostalgia after being discharged from the Navy in San Francisco. "I hated it when the war ended," he recalled. "Everything stopped too quick. I felt very uncomfortable." Gordon hitchhiked across the country, "sort of looking for something," and ended his journey in New York City. "When I got there," Gordon recalled, "I found out that there were literally hundreds and thousands of people just like me, who'd been in either Europe or the Pacific," veterans who had gone back home but had discovered that they didn't fit in. "So they all ended up in New York for one more party. They didn't want it to end." Gordon began working as an office clerk and lived at the Sloane House YMCA, which was notorious for harboring clandestine homosexual activity. All of his friends were honorably discharged veterans his own age who also were trying to come to terms with their homosexuality. They ate meals together, went out to the gay bars together, and slept on each other's sofas when it was too late or too expensive to take the subway home.

Gordon described the difficult process he and his friends went through to decide who they were sexually and where they belonged. They would "express it in different ways," he explained, "but they would go home, [after having] had an experience or a friendship in the service with a man. They'd say, 'Well, the war's over and I'll put that behind me. Now I'm going home and I'm going to marry and we're going to settle down.' They'd go home and they could not fit in. Everything was too odd. They had responsibilities and there was a lot of peer pressure: get married, have kids, start a home. They just weren't ready. Then they'd come back to New York. We would say, 'Well, you can go back all you want, but it won't work. Because you're gay.'" Gordon recalled getting calls in the middle of the night from friends who had returned home to get married. They would say, "'Hey, you remember me? Can I come over and stay?' So we'd take them in. A lot of them knew they would never fit in again. So they'd stay in New York."...

Gay men and lesbians relied on each other to smooth their transitions from soldiers to civilians. They wrote letters and visited each other in their hometowns, hung out with each other in the cities or became roommates or lovers. "I want to hold the best of the friends I've met in the army," wrote one gay veteran in late 1945, "to ease my way into what will be a new era in my life." Burt Gerrits, who served as a Navy hospital corpsman at Treasure Island, moved to Oakland to live with the lesbian head nurse of the ward and her lover. Pat Bond [see Reading 9-B] moved in with lesbian roommates and immersed herself in the gay night life that flourished in San Francisco's North Beach after the war. Betty Somers and Phillis Abry each set up households with the women who had been their lovers in the service. When Bob Ruffing returned from the Pacific, he reunited with the gay GI he had met at the baths in San Francisco during the war, and they set up house together as life partners. Others drifted apart from their wartime buddies as they let go of the past and made new friends rooted in their lives as civilians...

As they tried to adjust to their new live as civilians, some gay veterans realized that their identity as homosexuals was integral to the way they lived. The military, ironically, encouraged gay veterans to assume a stronger gay identity when it began to identify and manage so many people as homosexual persons rather than focus narrowly on the act of sodomy. Their shared memories of the war helped them to identify more closely with each other's struggles as veterans and as members of a homosexual minority. Having served their country well in a time of national emergency, gay veterans, especially those who had fought in combat, felt a heightened sense of legitimacy as citizens, entitlement as veterans, and betrayal when denied benefits. The rhetoric used and the actions taken to appeal blue discharges and bring about reform in the military's antigay policies reinforced their sense of legitimacy. A few began to speak of rights, injustice, discrimination, and persecution as a minority, expressing a hope that the war had led to social changes that would improve their status in American society.

A handful of gay veterans tried on their own after the war to bring about improvements in their social status as homosexuals. In New York City, four dishonorably discharged veterans reached beyond their immediate circle of friends to form an organization of and for gay veterans, called the Veterans' Benevolent Association. Like many other veterans' groups that proliferated across the nation in 1945, the VBA attempted to meet the needs of veterans who felt out of place in established organizations. Its seventy-five to one hundred members met regularly for social gatherings, attended by as many as four or five hundred additional guests. Through informal networks, its members assisted gay veterans in matters concerning the military, the law and employment. Edward Sagarin, a sociologist who in the early 1960s interviewed former members of the VBA, explained that its leaders came to the organization unapologetic about their homosexuality because "the hardships they had endured" as soldiers during the war had made them believe they were entitled to some respect. They expected that their status as veterans would help protect them from persecution as homosexuals. The Veterans' Benevolent Association existed until 1954, and was the first major gay membership organization in the United States.

Some gay veterans, who had met in the military so many others like themselves, began to feel more normal than "queer" and to sense that there might be power in their numbers. "The real revelation was when I went to London," recalled Bill Wynkoop, who served in the medical corps and was stationed in England during the war, "and saw the large number of servicemen of all nations and ranks cruising each other in Picadilly and Leicester Square. Here were thousands of female prostitutes wandering around, but these men were choosing each other. This was far beyond anything I had known before, and I began to think there would have to be some kind of social revolution because too many good people were homosexual ... for there to be anything wrong with their relationships or for them to remain perpetually suppressed and oppressed." The publication of the Kinsey Report in 1948, which the press interpreted to mean that 10 percent of the United States male population was homosexual, only added to this sense of being normal, one of many, and potentially powerful...

Having survived fear and death on the battlefield, some gay combat veterans began to cast off the veil of secrecy that so seriously constrained their lives. For them, "coming out" to family and friends was not nearly as terrifying as facing an armed enemy in battle. Frank Jacober explained that, having survived combat, his fears about coming out were nothing like "the time we went in the first wave. Nothing like that, boy." Robert Fleischer believed that it was his combat experience that enabled him to come out to his family after he returned home to Manhattan. "The first six months," he recalled, "my family was trying to get me dates. They were getting me the most eligible Jewish girls in New York. Finally one day at my sister's home, the entire family practically was there for a summer weekend having a barbecue in the back yard. I lined everybody up and I said, 'Listen. Enough!' And I stood up and made my speech. I said, 'I prefer men and I'm not going to accept any more blind dates with women. Leave me alone! Let me live my life.' And all it did was make my life much easier and much happier."...

Articles in the popular press gave the minority issue even wider exposure. From June 4 through October 8, 1949, a heated debate surfaced in the letter column of the *Saturday Review of Literature* with the heading "Homosexual Minority." The opening letter referred to homosexuals as "another minority which suffers from its position in somewhat the same way as the Jews and Negroes."

The previous month, *Cosmopolitan* magazine had run a feature article about homosexuals entitled "The Unmentionable Minority." In June 1947 *Newsweek* magazine, in a remarkable article entitled "Homosexuals in Uniform," broke the press's silence about gay veterans. It reviewed the history of the Army's wartime policies against homosexuals and revealed that many blue discharge veterans had been homosexual. The growing public perception that homosexuals might be members of a persecuted minority contributed to a climate increasingly favorable to the emergence of a gay political movement.

The war experiences of black and gay veterans ran parallel in more ways than suggested by the rhetorical comparisons in postwar literature. Both groups had received a disproportionate number of blue discharges, and both had experienced overseas an unexpected acceptance, respect, and relaxation of prejudices. This, together with the rhetoric of war propaganda that condemned fascism and promoted freedom, democracy and equality for all, raised their expectations for a better life as civilians. When they returned home to find discrimination, violence, and arrests based on their color or sexuality, many felt a heightened sense of injustice and betrayal. As a result some black veterans, both heterosexual and homosexual, became a force for social change within their already-existing movement for civil rights. A few white gay veterans, beginning to imagine the possibility of a similar movement for themselves, wrote about their own sense of injustice and hope for change, even arguing passionately that tolerance and equal rights were the things they had fought for in the war.

Gay men and women often tried out these new ideas in letters, sometimes stating their case with a righteousness not usually associated with homosexuals before the beginning of the gay-rights movement in the 1950s. In July 1946 Henry Gerber, who served in the Army during the war, wrote to the director of the Mental Hygiene Bureau in Washington, D.C., to protest proposals to increase the prison sentences for "sex perverts." "Shall these thousands of homosexuals," he asked, "who fought in this war have come back to this country to find that they fought in vain and that persecution of them is still going on as before in this land of ours, disgraced by the presence of stupid and hypocritical fanatics?" Jerry Watson, who also served in the Army, envisioned a future when the nation's homosexuals would fight back against bar raids, arrests, discharges, and prison sentences with anger and even revenge. "Our perversion is our destiny," he wrote to a friend, "our right. And we'll fight for what we know to be our right." Someday, he imagined, homosexuals would take their fight to "the newspapers, magazines and radio programs from coast to coast ... The fear that the world has given *us* will soon be *their* fear, for the fight will be one of monstrous proportions."

The WAC officer from Ohio who in November 1945 wrote to *Yank* ended her letter with her own vision of a better future for gay people, one she based on the ideals for which the war had been fought. "I use the word us," she admitted, "for I have voluntarily drunk from the Lesbian cup and have tasted much of the bitterness contained therein as far as the attitude of society is concerned. I believe there is much that can and should be done in the near future to aid in the solution of this problem, thus enabling these people to take their rightful places as fellow human beings, your sister and brother in the brotherhood of mankind." The idea these veterans all agreed on was that homosexuals were human beings who belonged side by side with others in society and had a right to be left alone.

Such visions for the future and anger at injustice indicated that the changes brought about by the war were leading to a redefinition of homosexuality as a political issue. Those veterans who appealed their discharges were engaging in an early form of protest, as individuals and in small groups, against the government's discrimination against them as homosexuals. The fact that the military now had procedures for guiding their protests through new administrative channels only affirmed and strengthened their cause. The GI Bill of Rights, which was meant to protect veterans from the inequities of the discharge system, together with the campaign against blue discharges, introduced the concepts of "rights," "injustice," and "discrimination" to public discussions of homosexuality. Popular magazines and novels began to publicize the notion that homosexuals constituted a persecuted "minority." This was the language of politics, not the language of therapy or military efficiency that had dominated the discussion of homosexuality in the military during the war. Such changes in political awareness and action began to anticipate the emergence of a movement for homosexual civil rights...

Until he died in 1985, Robert Fleischer saved a personal letter that President Harry Truman had sent him and other veterans upon their return from the war. "To you who answered the call of your country," the president wrote, "and served in its Armed Forces to bring about the total defeat of the enemy, I extend the heartfelt thanks of a grateful Nation. As one of the Nation's finest, you undertook the most severe task one can be called upon to perform. Because you demonstrated the fortitude, resourcefulness and calm judgment necessary to carry out that task, we now look to you for leadership and example in further exalting our country in peace." Such words of thanks were difficult for Robert Fleischer and his generation to forget.

READING 9-B

"Tapioca Tapestry"
by Pat Bond

from *Long Time Passing: The Lives of Older Lesbians,*
edited by Marcy Adelman

I went to high school out in the middle of Iowa, and somehow I got a copy of *The Well of Loneliness* and read it. And then a German film was being shown in my town. I just had a gut feeling it was about lesbians so I went to see it; sure enough it was about lesbians. Of course it was disastrous — the lesbian kid kills herself. I had crushes on women so I decided, "Aha! That's what I am. I'm a lesbian." It was those crushes on teachers that convinced me. Not gym teachers; nothing so shabby as a gym teacher. I had to have a *French* teacher to have a crush on. Then I went to a Catholic college and fell in love with a nun ... so I knew.

I wanted to be an intellectual; therefore all lesbians were intellectuals. Dreadful mistake. All lesbians played softball and football — in my generation — and they hadn't read a book in their lives. Until feminism, dykes weren't intellectuals at all, because they were imitating men — the worst side of men — the truck driver man. Nobody ever thought of imitating a college professor.

I just knew the army had to be full of lesbians, so I ran off and joined the army. And, to my horror, the army was filled with lesbians who hated the fact that I read a book once in a while. Terrible, anti-intellectual — like the rest of this country. It was awful. Not only was I rejected by the women I had fallen in love with and by my mother, but now all these ... lesbians in the army were rejecting me.

I had hoped the army would provide me with a community of women, but it didn't. I felt like an outsider. I tried like crazy to be a good butch, a real dyke, but it wasn't my nature. I'd sneak and put Chanel behind my ears. I tried to do the walk but I couldn't carry it off. I tried to put on men's clothes and I looked like Laurel and Hardy. My figure is just not cut out for men's clothes. I'm too round.

So, mostly I hung out with a lot of faggots I met in Davenport. I remember sitting in this park right by the Mississippi; while they cruised the park I would sit there and memorize Shakespeare's sonnets. They had me over for dinner. They liked opera and they liked the theater and it was my milieu. These were people I could talk to about my interests...

While I was stationed in San Francisco, they sent me to Japan for a little over a year. I got there just in time for the witch-hunt. I didn't know what was going on — none of us did. Well, there we were in Japan, all these kids. We were twenty, twenty-one, and MacArthur had said he wanted American women in Japan so that Japanese women could see what free American women looked like. I'm sure that what he meant was not the five hundred dykes that got off that boat. And I mean, *dykes*. We had an all-woman band and they were all in men's band uniforms. We had girl's night home, one night a week when we were all dancing and drinking, falling in and out of love.

It was like there wasn't any risk at first because everybody was gay. The officers, all of us. Our favorite song was "Prisoner of Love": "Alone from night to night you'll find me, to break the chains that bind me. I need no shackles to remind me, I'm just a prisoner of love." And we drank like fish. It was nothing to polish off five or six quarts of beer a night. We were young. Hangover victims. We started in again the next night. Just lucky I didn't get to be an alcoholic. And the woman I was in love with ran off with a man. She fell in love with a man. God, I was miserable. I was going to kill myself.

Then they decided to crack down. After the war, when we were no longer needed, they decided to get rid of the dykes. So they had court martials. Every day you came up for a court martial against one of your friends. They turned us against each other. When I was living it, I didn't have any idea why they were doing this to us. I only knew they were throwing us out of the army with dishonorable discharges. One woman killed herself, for God's sake. She was twenty-one years old. Helen. Her family will never know why she died. And then they gave her a military funeral. It was just insane. And it was *our* officers who were conducting these summary court martials. Lesbian officers.

But I had married Paul Bond; in those days gays got married to protect themselves and their families. Paul was gay and wanted to marry to make his family happy — so that they would think he was straight. I did it for a lark. It was a marriage in name only; we divorced in 1955. But if you were married, you could get out of the military. I wanted to protect the woman I was involved with, so I went to my CO and I said, "I want to get out because I'm married." She said, "You're *what?"* And I produced my wedding license and got out. The only way I could figure out to save my lover was to get out. If I had been there, they could have gotten us both because other women would have testified against us...

So I went home. Which made me feel kind of guilty, like people who survived Buchenwald. So I waited and everybody came home. They sent the five hundred women home for dishonorable, but a lot of them got off because the Attorney General's Office looked at it and said, "Come *on,* five hundred??" What they didn't know was that all five hundred were dykes.

We were angry. Especially when Helen killed herself and they did that military funeral for her. We sat around, wouldn't go to our jobs, just sat and drank for days and days, crying and drinking, drinking and crying. And you suspected everybody. You thought your best friend was going to turn you in. The military does turn you against each other...

I hope those officers are miserable now. I hope they live with guilt all their lives. I did a show called "Murder in the Women's Army Corps" because I consider that they murdered Helen, literally...

We wound up being afraid of each other. One woman went out and got pregnant, she was so terrified...

When I was flown back, I was miserable. I was leaving my true love behind. I was coming back to San Francisco, what was I going to do then? Again I was isolated and alone. I felt the witch-hunt was dastardly, unforgivable. It was totally unjust. We all thought so and we couldn't think of any way we could combat it ... Even the civil liberties union I don't think would — *then* — have been willing to take the case.

When I got back to the Presidio in San Francisco, I was too busy running around to the gay bars to do any of my allotted chores. It was wonderful. You got out of uniform and you went to the gay bars ... You got to know everybody in the bar, so it was a kind of community...

We certainly knew everyone. If you went to the gay bars in San Francisco, you knew everybody who was gay in San Francisco. We were open in the bars, but when you walked outside ... We used to say, "Don't ever leave North Beach. Don't cross the color line." ... I knew people who were harassed on the streets by the cops. When civilians stopped us — "Oh, look at that big dyke" — we'd just stick out our tongues. We *liked* that. It was like a confrontation. It was neat. And I think gays still like that — they're always trying to shock straights. Most of the time anymore it doesn't work, so it's kind of boring. You used to be able to shock them. It was fun.

The bars were really family; there was no community at all outside of the bars. If you were a closet dyke then — there were lots of them, I'm sure — you stayed home. You had your own little circle of friends that you saw. That was about it. My family never knew and I was terrified that they'd find out. Very often if you broke up with a lover, the lover would call your parents and tell them you were gay. Or they would call up your job and tell them you were gay and you would get fired. There were lots of stories about gays abusing gays. It went on all the time. I knew a lot of people who that happened to. I wasn't threatened by that because they always broke up with *me*. I was always the rejectee. People weren't just afraid of the straight community; they were afraid of each other...

All the bar owners then were straight ... they had a sort of disdain for us really. We were just their moneymakers. And they had rules that were unbelievably rigid. Like if you put your arm around another woman or held her hand you were thrown out. And if you were thrown out, you were out of touch with your world. I had a friend whose sister came in one night; they hadn't seen each other in a couple of years and they embraced each other. They both got thrown out. And Roberta was saying, "But she's my *sister.*" Didn't make any difference. There was no dancing. No touching. In the male bars *and* the female bars.

IMPORTANT TERMS

sodomy
blue discharges
GI Bill
Veterans' Benevolent Association

QUESTIONS/ACTIVITIES

1. Bérubé covers an enormous amount of material. Answer the following questions based on Reading 9-A, writing your answers in one-sentence thesis statements and then offering specific, underlined examples from the text as evidence:

- How did the war affect gay peoples' self-image?
- How did it affect their view of their role and rights in society?
- What problems did they face in the postwar era?
- How did they cope with these problems?
- How did society's image of gays begin to change after the war?
- How did the way gays represented themselves to society change after the war?

2. A key skill in history is being able to generalize from specific examples. Where does Bond's account, as a primary source, reflect Bérubé's account, as a secondary one? Does Bond's experience seem typical or atypical of the gay or lesbian World War II veteran? Does Bérubé seem to have done a good job in making accurate generalizations?

3. Using Bond's account, how did people seem to cope with the pressures placed on them by the military's anti-gay policy? Underline specific examples.

4. Why did Robert Fleischer forever treasure his letter from President Truman? Might he have had mixed feelings toward the letter? Write an answering letter from Fleischer to President Truman about the government's policies on gay soldiers.

5. After reading Chapter 10, write a letter to the Senate authors of the "Employment of Perverts" report as if you were Pat Bond or one of the veterans in Bérubé's account. How would you answer these kinds of charges against gay Americans?

6. Interview an older friend who was alive during World War II. If possible, interview both someone who remained in the United States and someone who served overseas in the armed forces. How did the experience of the war seem to change their lives?

CHAPTER 10

McCarthyism and the Witch-Hunt Mentality

INTRODUCTION

If the anti-gay regulations of World War II made life more difficult for gay soldiers, things only worsened for the general gay population in the late 1940s and early 1950s. This was the "McCarthy Era," so-called because of the influence of Senator Joseph McCarthy (R-WI) in American life. The hoped-for peace after the war turned instead into a "Cold War" as the United States and the Soviet Union became locked in a worldwide competition for supremacy. To meet the ever-present "Communist threat," the United States needed for the first time to maintain a "standing" or permanent army, instead of relying on volunteers and draftees to fills its ranks when a crisis arose. In 1949 two events, the Soviet explosion of their first atomic bomb, and the victory of the Chinese Communists over American ally Chiang Kai-Shek, drove fear to new heights, and people were eager to find scapegoats for this startling rise of communist power.

Senator McCarthy had the answer. "Subversives" working within the United States government were giving away our secrets and undermining our nation. They had to be found out and eliminated from the government. McCarthy would often wave lists of "subversives" at press conferences, lists that were entirely imaginary, and claim that Democratic president Harry Truman's administration was sheltering these traitors instead of investigating and purging them. McCarthy's answer seemed convincing enough to many frightened Americans, and he became wildly popular. Desperate to prove their loyalty, government bureaucrats did indeed search for "subversives" and discharge them in large numbers during these years.

Who were these "subversives"? Members or former members of the Communist Party were chief suspects. The Party had been popular among union organizers and intellectuals during the Depression, and hundreds of thousands of Americans had at that time been members. They were obvious suspects for participation in the "Communist conspiracy." Although not directly named as such, Jews also came under suspicion. The trial and execution of Julius and Ethel Rosenberg for supposedly giving away our atomic bomb secrets to the Soviets fueled these suspicions. Perhaps on an unconscious level, many found it easier to believe Jews would betray the United States than to believe good "Christian Americans" would.

Beginning in 1950, gays were added to this list. During a February 1950 Senate investigation hearing into "subversives," Undersecretary of State John Puerifoy spoke of a shadowy "homosexual underground" in Washington that was participating in the "Communist conspiracy" against America.[1] Senator McCarthy and others quickly seized upon this. They whipped up a controversy about the new "pervert peril." In April 1950 Republican National Committee Chairman Guy Gabrielson charged that a "conspiracy" was under way:

> As Americans, it is difficult for us to believe that a National Administration would go to such lengths to cover up and protect subversives, traitors, working against their country in high Government places ... Perhaps as dangerous as the actual Communists are the sexual perverts who have infiltrated our Government in recent years ... The country would be more aroused over this tragic angle of the situation if it were not for the difficulties of the newspapers and radio commentators in adequately presenting the facts, while respecting the decency of the American people.[2]

These "difficulties" in talking about the "facts" did not stop the media from filing numerous reports of the "pervert peril" throughout the spring of 1950[3]; The *New York Times* alone ran at least seven stories on the subject in May and June of 1950. The charge was led by Senator Kenneth Wherry (R-NB) and Senator McCarthy. Ironically, Senator McCarthy's anti-homosexual campaign was planned by his top aide, Roy Cohn, a closeted gay man who would eventually die of AIDS in the mid-1980s.[4] Because of these efforts, the Senate ordered a full-scale investigation into "perverts" in June 1950.[5] In the meantime, terrified government bureaucrats, fearful of being charged with protecting "subversives," dramatically increased their efforts to rid their departments of gays. In the period before the controversy arose (1947 through April 1950), dismissals of gays averaged about five a month in civilian government jobs; in the April–December 1950 period, more than sixty a month were fired.[6]

As seen in Chapter 9, new anti-gay regulations had led to the discharge of over 9,000 service members during World War II, and the intensity of these witch-hunts only increased in the McCarthy era. Approximately 100,000 gay and lesbian Americans have been discharged from the military over the past fifty years.[7]

In December 1950, the Senate investigators released the report included in this chapter. Its argument that homosexuals were, by their very nature, traitorous became the basis for strict new anti-gay government regulations in the early 1950s. The Democratic Truman administration tried to prove it was not sympathetic to gays by increasing dismissals after the Senate report was released: firings in the State Department alone rose from 54 in 1950, to 119 in 1951, and to 134 in 1952.[8]

These anti-gay efforts were just the beginning, however; the Republicans regained the White House with Dwight D. Eisenhower winning the 1952 election largely because of the suspicions raised about the Democrats by Senator McCarthy's charges. Once in office, Eisenhower moved swiftly against gays: in April 1953, after holding office for barely a month, Eisenhower signed Executive Order 10450, which made "sexual perversion" grounds for firing any person working for the government and for barring federal hiring of any gay man or woman. This dramatically extended existing regulations, which had applied only to those working in "national security" areas such as the military and the State Department.[9] Soon, state and local governments were also requiring workers to sign "loyalty oaths" swearing their "moral purity" before they would be given jobs. These federal, state, and local rules governed over 12 million government employees by the mid-1950s, over 20 percent of the entire American workforce.[10] These regulations ended up affecting even more workers, as private businesses and organizations such as the American Red Cross adopted similar techniques to screen their employees.[11] For a tremendous number of gays, simply being gay now meant automatic dismissal from your job, if you were found out.

Even some of America's allies adopted anti-gay practices. One casualty was British mathematician Alan Turing, whose breaking of the Nazi secret code was a major reason for Allied victory in World War II. Turing was entrapped for being gay in the early fifties, and he was thereafter watched by the British government as a potential "subversive." He eventually killed himself in 1954.[12]

As for Senator McCarthy, he was discredited in 1954 when it was discovered that his "lists" were all false and that many of his charges were simply lies made up to win political support. He died soon thereafter of complications from his alcoholism. His legacy, however, far outlived him: Regulations banning gays from federal civil jobs were not repealed until 1975.[13] For nearly a quarter century, gay and lesbian Americans lived in fear of being caught in one of the periodic "witch-hunts" to round up and eliminate "subversives" from government service.

Readers of this report should keep in mind the mentality of the fifties, with its hysteria over the "Communist threat" and fear of sudden atomic attack. With this as a backdrop, the arguments of the Senate subcommittee carried unusual weight, especially in an era when there had been little public discussion of homosexuality at all.

READING 10-A

"Employment of Homosexuals and Other Sex Perverts in Government"

(Report made to the Committee on Expenditures in the Executive Departments by its Subcommittee in Investigations, United States Senate, 81st Congress, 2nd Session, Dec. 15, 1950)

...The primary objective of the subcommittee in this inquiry was to determine the extent of the employment of homosexuals and other sex perverts in the Government; to consider reasons why their employment by the Government is undesirable; and to examine into the efficacy of the methods used in dealing with the problem. Because of the complex nature of the subject under investigation it was apparent that this investigation could be not be confined to a mere personnel inquiry. Therefore, the subcommittee considered not only the security risk and other aspects of the employment of homosexuals, including the rules and procedures followed by Government agencies in handling these cases, but inquiries were also made into the basic medical, psychiatric, sociological and legal phases of the problem. A number of eminent physicians and psychiatrists, who are recognized authorities on this subject, were consulted and some of these authorities testified before the subcommittee in executive session. In addition, numerous medical and sociological studies were reviewed. Information was also sought and obtained from law-enforcement officers, prosecutors, and other persons dealing with the legal and sociological aspects of the problem in 10 of the larger cities in the country...

The subcommittee found that most authorities agree on certain basic facts concerning sex perversion and it is felt that these facts should be considered in any discussion of the problem. Most authorities believe that sex deviation results from psychological rather than physical causes, and in many cases there are no outward characteristics or physical traits that are positive as identifying marks of sex perversion. Contrary to a common belief, all homosexual males do not have feminine mannerisms, nor do all female homosexuals display masculine characteristics in their dress or actions. The fact is that many male homosexuals are very masculine in their physical appearance and general demeanor, and many female homosexuals have every appearance of femininity in their outward behavior...

Psychiatric physicians generally agree that indulgence in sexually perverted practices indicates a personality which has failed to reach sexual maturity. The authorities agree that most sex deviates respond to psychiatric treatment and can be cured if they have a genuine desire to be cured. However, many overt homosexuals have no real desire to abandon their way of life and in such cases cures are difficult, if not impossible. The subcommittee sincerely believes that persons afflicted with sexual desires which result in their engaging in overt acts of perversion should be considered as proper cases for medical and psychiatric treatment. However, sex perverts, like all other persons who by their overt acts violate moral codes and laws and the accepted standards of conduct, must be treated as transgressors and dealt with accordingly.

Sex perverts as government employees

Those charged with the responsibility of operating the agencies of Government must insist that Government employees meet acceptable standards of personal conduct. In the opinion of this subcommittee homosexuals and other sex perverts are not proper persons to be employed in Government for two reasons; first, they are generally unsuitable, and second, they constitute security risks.

General unsuitability of sex perverts

Overt acts of sex perversion, including acts of homosexuality, constitute a crime under our Federal, State, and municipal statutes and persons who commit such acts are law violators. Aside from the criminality and immorality involved in sex perversion such behavior is so contrary to the normal accepted standards of social behavior, that persons who engage in such activity are looked upon as outcasts by society generally. The social stigma attached to sex perversion is so great that many perverts go to great lengths to conceal their perverted tendencies. This situation is evidenced by the fact that perverts are frequently victimized by blackmailers who threaten to expose their sexual deviations...

In further considering the general suitability of perverts as Government employees, it is generally believed that those who engage in overt acts of perversion lack the emotional stability of normal persons. In addition there is an abundance of evidence to sustain the conclusion that indulgence in acts of sex perversion weakens the moral fiber of an individual to a degree that he is not suitable for a position of responsibility.

Most of the authorities agree and our investigation has shown that the presence of a sex pervert in a Government agency tends to have a corrosive influence upon his fellow employees. These perverts will frequently attempt to entice normal individuals to engage in perverted practices. This is particularly true in the case of young and impressionable people who might come under the influence of a pervert...

Another point to be considered in determining whether a sex pervert is suitable for Government employment is his tendency to gather other perverts about him. Eminent psychiatrists have informed the subcommittee that the homosexual is likely to seek his own kind because the pressures of society are such that he feels uncomfortable unless he is with his own kind. Due to this situation the homosexual tends to surround himself with other homosexuals, not only in his social, but in his business life. Under these circumstances if a homosexual obtains a position in Government where he can influence the hiring of personnel, it is almost inevitable that he will attempt to place other homosexuals in Government jobs.

Sex perverts as security risks

The conclusion of the subcommittee that a homosexual or other sex pervert is a security risk is not based upon mere conjecture. That conclusion is predicated upon a careful review of the opinions of those best qualified to consider matters of security in Government, namely, the intelligence agencies of the Government. Testimony on this phase of the inquiry was taken from representatives of the Federal Bureau of Investigation, the Central Intelligence Agency, and the intelligence services of the Army, Navy and Air Force. All of these agencies are in complete agreement that sex perverts in Government constitute security risks.

The lack of emotional stability which is found in most sex perverts and the weakness of their moral fiber, makes them susceptible to the blandishments of the foreign espionage agent. It is the experience of intelligence experts that perverts are vulnerable to interrogation by a skilled questioner and they seldom refuse to talk about themselves. Furthermore, most perverts tend to congregate at the same restaurants, night clubs, and bars, which places can be identified with comparative ease in any community, making it possible for a recruiting agent to develop clandestine relationships which can be used for espionage purposes.

As has been previously discussed in this report, the pervert is easy prey to the blackmailer. It follows that if blackmailers can extort money from a homosexual under the threat of disclosure, espionage agents can use the same type of pressure to extort confidential information or other material the might be seeking...

...The present danger of this security problem is well illustrated by the following excerpt from the testimony of D. Milton Ladd, Assistant to the Director of the Federal Bureau of Investigation, who appeared before this subcommittee in executive session:

> The Communists, without principles or scruples, have a program of seeking out weaknesses of leaders in Government and industry. In fact, the FBI has in its possession information of unquestionable reliability that orders have been issued by high Russian intelligence officials to their agents to secure details of the private lives of Government officials, their weaknesses, their associates, and in fact every bit of information regarding them, hoping to find a chink in their armor and a weakness upon which they might capitalize at the appropriate time.

The subcommittee in pointing out the unsuitability of perverts for Government employment is not unaware of the fact that there are other patterns of human behavior which also should be considered in passing upon the general suitability or security-risk status of

Government employees. There is little doubt that habitual drunkards, persons who have engaged in criminal activities, and those who indulge in other types of infamous or scandalous personal conduct are also unsuitable for Government employment and constitute security risks. However, the subcommittee, in the present investigation, has properly confined itself to the problem of sex perverts...

Conclusion

There is no place in the United States Government for persons who violate the laws or the accepted standards of morality, or who otherwise bring disrepute to the Federal service by infamous or scandalous personal conduct. Such persons are not suitable for Government positions and in the case of doubt the American people are entitled to have errors of judgment on the part of their officials, if there must be errors, resolved on the side of caution. It is the opinion of this subcommittee that those who engage in acts of homosexuality and other perverted sex activities are unsuitable for employment in the Federal Government. This conclusion is based upon the fact that persons who indulge in such degraded activity are committing not only illegal and immoral acts, but they also constitute security risks in positions of public trust.

The subcommittee found that in the past many Government officials failed to take a realistic view of the problem of sex perversion in Government with the result that a number of sex perverts were not discovered or removed from Government jobs, and in still other instances they were quietly eased out of one department and promptly found employment in another agency. This situation undoubtedly stemmed from the fact that there was a general disinclination on the part of many Government officials to face squarely the problem of sex perversion among Federal employees and as a result they did not take the proper steps to solve the problem. The rules of the Civil Service Commission and the regulations of the agencies themselves prohibit the employment of sex perverts and these rules have been in effect for many years. Had the existing rules and regulations been enforced many of the perverts who were forced out of Government in recent months would have been long since removed from the Federal service...

While this subcommittee is convinced that it is in the public interest to get sex perverts out of Government and keep them out, this program should be carried out in a manner consistent with the traditional American concepts of justice and fair play. In order to accomplish this end every reasonable complaint of perverted sex activities on the part of Government employees should be thoroughly investigated and dismissals should be ordered only after a complete review of the facts and in accordance with the present civil-service procedures. These procedures provide that the employee be informed of the charges against him and be given a reasonable time to answer. Furthermore, in view of the very serious consequence of dismissal from the Government on charges of sex perversion, it is believed that consideration should be given to establishing a board of review or similar appeal machinery whereby all persons who are dismissed from the Government on these charges may, if they so desire, have their cases reviewed by higher authority outside of the employing agency...

Since the initiation of this investigation considerable progress has been made in removing homosexuals and similar undesirable employees from the positions in the Government. However, it should be borne in mind that the public interest cannot be adequately protected unless responsible officials adopt and maintain a realistic and vigilant attitude toward the problem of sex perverts in the Government. To pussyfoot or to take half measures will allow some known perverts to remain in Government and can result in the dismissal of innocent persons.

In view of the importance of preventing the employment of sex perverts in Government the subcommittee plans to reexamine the situation from time to time to determine if its present recommendations are being followed and to ascertain whether it may be necessary to take other steps to protect the public interest.

IMPORTANT TERMS

Cold War
Joseph McCarthy
McCarthyism
"Communist conspiracy"
"subversives"
Julius and Ethel Rosenberg
Roy Cohn
witch-hunts
"loyalty oaths"
Alan Turing

QUESTIONS/ACTIVITIES

1. The following questions outline the central points of the document:
   - What are the objectives of the report?
   - Where did the committee get its evidence? From whom?
   - What are the "facts" about "sex perversion" they uncover?
   - Why are gays considered "unsuitable for employment"?
   - Why are gays deemed "security risks"?

2. Many issues are raised by the report, some of which are addressed in these questions:
   - What are the biases of the sources of evidence the committee relies on? How might this shape their report?
   - How many of the "facts" the committee presents about "sexual perversion" are actually "facts"? What evidence to support these "facts" is offered?
   - How many of the conditions that make gays "unsuitable" and "security risks" seem valid? How many are the fault of gays and how many of society's attitudes?

3. In the report's conclusion, the committee recommends procedures for removing gays and claims these procedures are "consistent with traditional American concepts of justice and fair play." Does the report seems consistent with those concepts to you? Keeping in mind that the body which investigated such claims was called the "House Committee on Un-American Activities," divide your class into two groups and, either orally or in writing, represent whether the committee was "Un-American" or that the gays were.

4. Write letters to your senators from that time (whose names you will have to research), either attacking or supporting the committee's report. Find out what position your senators back then took on McCarthyism.

5. Interview an older friend or relative who was an adult in the early fifties and ask about the attitudes of the time and about what they remember of McCarthyism. How would the conditions this person describes have affected the public's reaction to the committee's findings?

6. Investigate the lives of famous individuals who were victims of McCarthyism (such as Lillian Hellman) and report on them.

7. The character of Roy Cohn is fascinating and mysterious. How and why could Cohn have participated in such anti-gay activities, given his own sexuality? "Internal monologues" or diary entries might help us "get inside his head"; for the morbid, a deathbed reflection might prove dramatic.

8. McCarthyism has generated numerous artistic responses. Two plays include *The Crucible* by Arthur Miller, about the Salem "witches" that is an allegory concerning McCarthyism, and Hugh Whitmore's *Breaking the Code,* an account of Alan Turing's life. McCarthy hearings are widely available on videotape and make interesting viewing. Numerous Hollywood films, such as *The Way We Were,* deal in part with the era. Excerpts from any of these might be helpful in understanding the tenor of the times, which may be hard to grasp in the aftermath of the collapse of the USSR.

9. Could this happen again? Think of a group in today's society and write a brief "report" explaining why its members should be excluded from government employment. Share these in class (either in pairs, small groups, or with the whole class), and ask others to evaluate whether or not their scenarios are believable.

CHAPTER 11

Harry Hay and the Beginnings of the Homophile Movement

INTRODUCTION

Growing oppression often creates growing resistance. When people feel they are being unjustly persecuted, they often organize to demand fairer treatment. Thus, while the late forties and early fifties were an understandably discouraging time for gays and lesbians (see Chapters 9 and 10), it also saw the first emergence of widespread, organized political groups fighting to win gay rights. Although the Society for Human Rights in Chicago had been founded in 1924 (see Chapter 14), it was short-lived, and the first successful gay-rights group was not founded in the United States until 1950. Then, a teacher and artist named Harry Hay met up with a few other gay men in Los Angeles and persuaded them to join him in a dream he had had for many years — an organization for gay liberation.

Harry Hay was born in 1914 and had worked for many years in the entertainment industry in Hollywood. He had numerous gay relationships during his early adulthood, including one with Will Geer, the actor who would later play Grandpa on the classic seventies "family values" television series, *The Waltons*. However, driven by a desire to better things for disadvantaged Americans, Hay, like many other young idealists during the thirties, joined the Communist Party in 1938. At that time, the Communist Party was no more sympathetic to gays than conservative political groups were: Homosexuality was seen as an unhealthy lifestyle produced by an unhealthy capitalist society that would cease to exist once pure communism had been achieved, and Party membership was open only to heterosexuals. In 1938, Hay married a fellow Party activist named Anita Platsky, in an effort to "go straight" and be a good Party member. He spent the next thirteen years as both Anita's husband and a Party member, teaching classes in political theory, organizing unions, and performing folk music designed to inspire workers to demand their rights.

Hay's involvement with the Communist Party and Anita, however, did not wipe away his homosexuality. He found himself still drawn to men, and he maintained contact with the homosexual community in Los Angeles. In the late forties, he came up with the idea of organizing gays as a political force. This was a new and revolutionary concept; until that time, homosexuality had largely been thought of as a "private matter," an "illness" with which an individual was afflicted. Hay's argument was that homosexuals were not sick individuals but an oppressed minority, and they should organize to demand fairer treatment just as groups such as African-Americans and Jews had. Hay eventually founded the Mattachine Society in 1950, the first-ever ongoing gay-rights group in the nation.[1] But the beginning was not an easy one, as this excerpt from Stuart Timmons's biography of Hay shows.

READING 11-A

Mattachine

from *The Trouble with Harry Hay,*
by Stuart Timmons

On August 10, 1948, Harry Hay first formulated what later became the Mattachine Society ... What Harry later described as a "beer bust" was actually a sedate gathering of seminarians and music students in a Victorian-style apartment. He found to his delight that all the two dozen guests chatting and sipping beer on plush sofas were male and seemed to be "of the persuasion." The first he spoke to, a seminary student from France, asked if Harry had heard of the recently published Kinsey report. Its first volume, *Sexual Behavior in the Human Male,* was the season's most talked-about book, especially among homosexuals, with its claim that thirty-seven percent of adult men had experienced homosexual relations. To Harry, this newly revealed number suggested the dimensions of an organizable minority. He voiced the idea. When his friend protested that organizing homosexuals was impossible, Harry rebutted him. There could be millions of people who might fall into a group that would find great benefit to organizing. Certainly it would be difficult, but it was not impossible.

Others were listening and added their objections. There was too much hatred of homosexuals. Any individual who went public could be entrapped and discredited. There were too many different kinds of homosexuals; they'd never get along. And anyway, people belonging to such an organization would lose their jobs. Hay countered each objection enthusiastically, further convincing himself of the viability of organizing homosexuals...

He spun forth ideas anyway. One was to pool funds to provide fast bail money and legal help for victims of police entrapment. This he referred to as "a fraternal Civil Insurance and Mutual Protection League." Since lewd conduct arrests — or fear of them — threatened most homosexuals with severe debts to corrupt lawyers and officials, this insurance fund was a high priority. Another was education; hygiene classes in high schools could discuss homosexuality as a way of life.

...Both skepticism and seriousness faded with the beer, but Harry forged ahead. On a large sheet of butcher paper, he wrote out a homosexual agenda. One inebriated partygoer started to run out the door with the list, waving it like a banner to show the world. Harry stayed with the idea for five hours that night, buttonholing every party guest to extol its merits.

...Once home, in his study, he wrote two papers. "One was the plank for the Progressive Party, and the other was the structure for an organization to go on after the convention was over."

This second, much more elaborate paper, based in a Marxist perspective, forged a principle that Hay had struggled years to formulate: that homosexuals were a minority, which he temporarily dubbed the "Androgynous Minority." Since 1941, Harry had taught Stalin's four principles of a minority; these were a common language, a common territory, a common economy, and a common psychology and culture. "I felt we had two of the four, the language and the culture, so clearly we were a social minority." This concept of homosexuals as a minority was the contribution of which Hay was proudest — and one of his greatest struggles was to convince others of its validity...

The writing of "the Call," as Hay referred to the organization prospectus ever afterwards, marked the dedication of his life to gay activism. The original was lost during the 1950s, but a revised version he wrote two years later survives. By its next draft the organization was called "Bachelors Anonymous," in reference to

Alcoholics Anonymous, the new organization that relied on a grass-roots, self-help model. But the structure and most of the text remained essentially the same. At the end of the first page, he proclaimed a formal incorporation:

> WE, THE ANDROGYNES OF THE WORLD, HAVE FORMED THIS RESPONSIBLE CORPORATE BODY TO DEMONSTRATE BY OUR EFFORTS THAT OUR PHYSIOLOGICAL AND PSYCHOLOGICAL HANDICAPS NEED BE NO DETERRENT IN INTEGRATING 10% OF THE WORLD'S POPULATION TOWARDS THE CONSTRUCTIVE SOCIAL PROGRESS OF MANKIND.

Some of this would change radically; the term "handicap" soon vanished from his language. Still, the keystones of the Mattachine Society and of Hay's lifework were laid down that night; to bring homosexuals together for the purpose of self-understanding and, even more unheard-of, to recognize their contribution to humanity.

"The bubble soared to burst promptly in the dawn's early light," he wrote. The next morning at Leahy's he got the phone numbers of everyone who had shown enthusiasm the night before. But they had all lost interest in the light of a sober day. "Many gasped in fear, as if I were trying to tear away their Divinity degrees. Others simply sneered, 'Honey! That was the *beer!'* I heard that over and over again." ... No one gave him a shred of encouragement. He turned for support to several progressives who were well established as social workers, teachers, and ministers, but their response was politely evasive. "Several said, 'Tell you what you do. You get a discussion group on your ideas going, and we'll come. If we think this is promising, we'll loan our names as sponsors.' And the progressive-minded gays I spoke to said, 'Now, tell you what you do. You get a couple of prominent people who'd be willing to lend their support to such an endeavor, and we'll look over their names. If it looks like we've got good allies and good protection, maybe we'll come and bring friends.' So — there it was! I couldn't get a list of sponsors until I got a discussion group going, and I couldn't get a discussion group going until I had a committee of sponsors."

He looked for both constantly, and without success. It took Harry Hay two years to find even one person who was interested in his unlikely dream.

After two years of dead-end pleading Harry found support from an unexpected turn of events — he fell in love. His relationship with the young Rudi Gernreich changed everything. It brought to an end Harry's marriage, terminated his membership in the Party, and, most important, lifted his deep psychic distress. The day he met Gernreich, he often said, they created a "society of two" that became the Mattachine...

[Two days after meeting Gernreich] he took Rudi to the Chuckwagon, a new restaurant just west of the Sunset Strip. He passed the prospectus over the table. Rudi was intrigued. "It's the most dangerous thing I've ever seen, and I'm with you one hundred percent," Hay recalled him responding. While he encouraged Hay's undertaking, Gernreich counseled extreme caution and discretion, both for the sake of individuals and for the stability and potential of such an American movement. He explained that before leaving Europe, he had been aware of the homosexual movement led by Magnus Hirschfeld, whose publicly known Institute for Sexual Research had been easily smashed by the Nazis; its records sent homosexuals to death camps. [See Chapter 8] They talked about many aspects of "our kind of love." The vastness of the subject and the prospect of an organization excited both men. "We sat there, by law unable even to hold hands, but looking warmly at one another, a sort of glowing through the tears across the table."...

Harry explained to Rudi the frustrations he had experienced since writing the first prospectus the night of the beer bust. After the rejection of the initial plan for meetings, he had devised a facade: He would announce a public meeting to "objectively" discuss the Kinsey report, a cautious and security-minded approach to organizing. But even with such a buffer, he found himself caught in the maddening impasse of paralyzed homosexuals and noncommittal sponsors. "I had talked to hundreds of people between Bachelors for Wallace and Mattachine, and people on both sides were afraid to take the first step. It was like being told you had to have a harp to get into heaven and that you had to go to heaven to get a harp." So the organization remained unborn...

Within a month of their meeting, the two set out on a field trip to drum up a discussion group on homosexuality. As an icebreaker they armed themselves with copies of the Stockholm Peace Petition, a Leftist initiative to recall the early troops that had been sent to Korea. With his gay agenda in mind, Harry took the petitions to a strategic spot. "We set about discovering new adherents on the two slices of beach Gays had quietly made their own," he wrote later.

"The section of the beach below the Palisades just west of Marion Davies's huge waterfront estate, and that slice of Malibu between the pier and the spit — which would be taken over by the surfers in the 1960s."

Nearly five hundred sunbathers signed the petition, and while chatting, Hay and Gernreich asked each if he or she would be interested in attending a discussion on new findings about social deviancy. Not one was: "They were willing enough to designate themselves Peaceniks by signing our petitions in the teeth of the Korean War and its accompanying patriot-mongering ... but were *not* willing to commit themselves to participating in easily disguised public forums, oh-so-diffidently fingering the newly published Kinsey report." Altogether, the canvasing only repeated the disappointment Harry had gone through during the previous two years. All he managed to glean was a mailing list of extremely tentative supporters.

Even if the beachgoers had eagerly joined up, however, the roster would have fallen far short of the solid organization and "movement" Harry envisioned. Rudi counseled perseverance. By November, after more unproductive weeks of outreach, Rudi proposed that Harry take a chance on Bob Hull, a man who had come to his music classes. Very blond, small, and boyishly handsome, he was one of those who had repeated the course often. Harry thought Hull was homosexual, but he was not sure he would join a homosexual organization. He nervously gave Hull a copy of the prospectus at the next Thursday evening class. Chuck Rowland, who lived with Hull, recalled how that night, "Bob came home and told me about this delightful and brilliant teacher who had approached him about this."

On November 11, 1950, late autumn's strong winds blew up Cove Avenue. Around noon, Bob Hull called Harry and asked if he and a couple of friends could come over to discuss the paper he had received two days earlier. He gave no indication of his reaction, but indicated that he would be over at about three o'clock. Anita and the girls were away that day, so Harry called Rudi over and together they waited pensively outside to steer the visitors to a quiet spot on the oak-studded hillside overlooking Silver Lake. A thrill broke over Harry when he saw Rowland "running up the hill, waving the thing like a flag, saying, 'We could have written this ourselves! When do we get started?'" Rowland's later recollection was similar. "We were enchanted with it. I did say, 'My God, I could have written this myself.' I don't remember actually waving the thing in the air and running up that steep hill with it, but I might have." The five sat on the hill overlooking the restless water that windy Armistice Day, talking and basking in each other's excitement. "We sat there," Harry wrote, "with fire in our eyes and far-away dreams, *being* Gays."

As a result of that fateful meeting, Robert Hull and Charles Dennison Rowland became two founding members of the Mattachine Society [along with Dale Jennings, a friend whom they had brought to the meeting]...

The five met weekly over the next season, trying out formats for a discussion group on homosexuality. They told their life stories and pooled scraps of gay knowledge to, as Jennings later wrote, "make a little sense out of much nonsense." They were frequently amazed by how much they had in common but had never before expressed, and a heady intimacy bonded them. On Hay's cue, the founders sometimes referred to the group as "Parsifal," after his beloved operatic knights in search of the Holy Grail, but officially they were known as the Steering Committee, or, more commonly, as the Fifth Order. Harry continued to live as a married man, keeping his straight world and his new gay world carefully separated. His success at this prompted Rowland to remark in 1987, "By the time Mattachine got started, Harry was already divorced and the wife was out of the picture," though this was not the actual circumstance until the following autumn.

The very real possibility of a police raid and legal persecution required that their meetings always be held in secret. When the occasional guest was invited, it was a standard security process for him to meet a Mattachine member at some public landmark, then to be driven around for a few blocks before being taken to the meeting place. "We did not want to lead the police to our meetings, so we did not give guests the address," said Rowland, and they tried not to use the same location too many times. Blinds were always drawn. ("All those *men*— people would be very curious!") Because they had read that telephones could be used to bug a room, Rowland always put the phone in a dresser drawer and put a pillow over it. When people left the meetings, they kept their voices down...

The laws and customs of the era were stringently anti-homosexual; in California, as in most states, any sexual act except the missionary position between a heterosexual couple was a crime punishable by up to twenty years in prison. Anyone caught doing anything else could be made to register as a sex offender. Repeat offenders and those whose partners were minors were often sent to Atascadero State Prison and given electroshock "therapy," or even subjected to castration. Since any public mention of homosexuality was equated with scandal, few workplaces would retain an employee whose involvement with such an organization became public. Harry knew his own job at Leahy's was on the line, but by this time he had completely reset his priorities. By the fall of 1951, as he later told historian Jonathan Katz, he decided that organizing the Mattachine was "a call to me deeper than the innermost reaches of the spirit, a vision-quest more important than life."

It is hard to imagine today what a new and exciting prospect this was in 1950. For homosexuals to meet and share with each other in a nonsexual environment was rare, and for most, being identified as homosexual bore a distinctly negative connotation. Jim Gruber, who joined the Fifth Order that winter, emphasized that "the population in general tended to be sedate in sexual matters, not only in behavior but even what they said, how they phrased things. Talking about gay sex was something you just didn't do." Those early meetings, which continued through the winter and into the spring of 1951, probed topics such as the homosexual personality and society as well as sex. Chief among their challenges was overcoming the negative, cynical mentality of gay life — epitomized by the cuttingly bitchy language of bar talk — so prevalent in homosexual gathering places. Hay and Rowland thus stressed the development of an "ethical homosexual culture" as a steady theme of their work. This sort of social context, where homosexuals were supportive of one another instead of being sexually competitive and acid-tongued, was rare. Harry described it as a "glorious shock" simply to sit in a room with other gay men "and suddenly find one another good, and find ourselves so at home and 'in family,' perhaps for the first time in our lives."...

The new group's endless talk sessions often sought to give an articulate voice to "the love that dared not speak its name." Common parlance was deliberately evasive to protect homosexuals from persecution — terms like "nervous," "sensitive," "musical," and Harry's favored "temperamental" were politically useless, and other terms — like "deviant" and "invert" — were defensive at best. This problem was shared by other organizers of that time. Del Martin and Phyllis Lyon, pioneers of the Daughters of Bilitis, the first American lesbian organization, recalled how during the early days they used the subtly homophobic phrase "the problems of children with mothers who were lesbians" before the term "lesbian mothers" evolved. "If you weren't living in that era," Jim Gruber stressed, "you would have a hard time understanding this. There was a prevalent attitude that there wasn't a middle ground. You were either straight or a screaming faggot and mentally unstable. A healthy acceptance of oneself as a gay man was just an unheard-of idea."...

What were later called, with great sensationalism, the "Communist origins" of the Mattachine became its most explosive issue. But in reality, only one central concept was heavily influenced by Marxism: Harry's application of the term "cultural minority" to homosexuals. "That was a new idea, " Chuck Rowland said. "Harry was the first person I know who said that gays are a minority — an oppressed minority. This was a profound contribution, and really the heart and core of the Mattachine movement and all subsequent gay movements." This started, Rowland recalled, "once we decided we were going to organize. With my Communist background, I knew I could not work in a group without a theory. I said, 'All right, Harry, what's our theory?' And he said, 'We are an oppressed minority culture.' I agreed instantly."

Harry extrapolated that as such a minority, homosexuals had to rely on a change of consciousness, an active evaluation of their identity and relationship to society, to obtain further power. Harry's inspiration had been Marxist discussions of minorities and what constitutes them. As the Mattachine grew to include more people, many resisted the minority model. "They thought I was making 'niggers' out of them," Harry recounted. "They thought this identity was mere 'predilections.'" Konrad Stevens remembered another argument — that identifying as a minority diminished individuality. "They steadfastly said, 'We are *not* a minority.' I think they didn't want to be. To admit that meant you were in an inferior position."...

[In 1951, new member Howard] Senn suggested that the ideals of the new organization be set in writing. Begun in late March and ratified in July, the Mattachine "Missions and Purposes" was arrived at after countless hours of discussion. The document identified homosexuals as "one of the largest minorities in America today." Using Harry's emphatic capital letters, it stated the group's threefold purposes: "TO UNIFY" homosexuals "isolated from their own kind and unable to adjust to the dominant culture ... [to] a consensus of principle around which all of our people can rally and from which they can derive a feeling of 'belonging'"; "TO EDUCATE" and improve the "woefully meager and inconclusive" information about homosexuality, and to further research in various academic disciplines "for the purpose of informing all interested homosexuals, and for the purpose for informing and enlightening the public at large"; and "TO LEAD ... the whole mass of social deviates" to achieve the missions of unification and education.

The document called political action on a legislative basis "imperative." The founders also insisted on the emergence of "a highly ethical homosexual culture" as a result of their work. Citing Negroes, Jews, and Mexicans as "our fellow minorities," they proclaimed that "homosexuals can lead well-adjusted, wholesome and socially productive lives once ignorance and prejudice against them are successfully combatted, and once homosexuals themselves feel they have a dignified and useful role to play in society." In an era where the outer world threatened anti-gay imprisonment, electroshock, and castration, and guilt, alcoholism, and suicide plagued gays internally, these ideals were astounding...

Entry into the society was by attendance at a discussion group. Ideally these held about twenty, though as the groups sprang up with increasing frequency, numbers could rise toward one hundred or more. Jim Kepner, who first went to one toward the end of 1952, remembered nearly 150 people there. "It was a large home belonging to a doctor and his wife; they were one of the couples that seemed to be sympathetic straights, though a lot of those types eventually came out. Their large living room was full; and a circular staircase coming down into it was also packed. More people listened from the balcony and the foyer."

An air of polite formality ruled most of these groups. The Fifth Order produced a simple guide called "How to Lead a Discussion Group." Suggested topics ranged from "Camping, Pro and Con" to

"The Case for Homosexual Marriage," which produced earnest conversations. Often personal emergencies would overtake the agenda, and these were the liveliest, most meaningful sessions. Men wore a suit and tie or at least a sports coat and often brought a woman they claimed was a wife ... The formality could be stiff, depending on who was running the discussion. Kepner saw "two guys sitting in each other's laps, being somewhat lovey-dovey, which upset a number of people." "Nevertheless," he said, "there was really the feeling that for thousands of years we'd been secret and hiding and alone. Now we were on the march and convinced of the idea, 'We'll solve this problem — within a few years!'"...

The Mattachines themselves soon provided their own "prestigious person" by creating a hero of Dale Jennings, the salty writer whose entrapment case for "lewd and dissolute conduct" was a turning point for the Mattachine and is a little-remembered milestone in gay history. In Rudi Gernreich's blocky printing in the Mattachine minutes notebook for 1952 are the bare details of its beginning:

> March 28. Attendance 12.
> Swearing in 2 new guild members, Cliff, Tommy.
> Second Order report: Entrapment case. Decision to fight on basis of 5th Amendment — politically, not morally. Test case — willing to fight from lowest courts to highest. Try to get support from ACLU and other civic groups. Wire sent to [Donald Webster] Cory. Every minority in danger on entrapment basis. George Shibley being approached to defend. Suggestion by Second Order to cancel Saturday night party. Motion unanimously accepted.

What started as a commonplace arrest diverted to its unusual course when Dale Jennings, in jail and needing fifty dollars bail money, called Harry at two a.m. Harry had just enough cash on hand, and by six-thirty Dale was released. Over a cheer-up breakfast at the Brown Derby, Harry learned what had happened. He recalled, "Dale had just broken off with Bob Hull and was not, I know, feeling great. He told me that he had met someone in the can at Westlake Park. The man had his hand on his crotch, but Dale wasn't interested. He said the man insisted on following him home, and almost pushed his way through the door. He asked for coffee, and when Dale went to get it, he saw the man moving to the window blind, as if signaling to someone else. He got scared and started to say something, when there was a sudden pounding on the door, and Dale was arrested."

The practice of entrapment, which still lingers today, was a grim standard in the fifties. It amounted to a financial and emotional lynching, in which an officer accused a gay man of making a sexual advance. Often the officer had engaged in no more than a glance; sometimes he encouraged advances to the point of full participation. (A joke from the time went, "It's been wonderful but you're under arrest.") These arrests created a victim in a victimless situation and served as a controlling threat to all male homosexuals. Harry knew dozens of men whose lives had been marred by this, and some went into a permanent decline following an entrapment arrest. Most respectable lawyers would not touch such cases.

Two lawyers in Los Angeles did defend these cases, a middle-aged woman named Gladys Towle Root and a man still practicing today. Many gay men considered these two more an injury than a remedy, as they invariably instructed those accused to plead guilty and then charged a fee ranging from $300 to $3,000, depending on the person's ability to pay. Often, men convicted of "vag-lewd" (vagrancy and lewdness) charges paid large fines rather than spend time in jail, where they would be singled out for beatings and rape. The dilemma, Harry recalled, made "everyone plead guilty, and plea bargaining was a tactic not yet in practice. So to the average ribbon clerk this could mean years of debt."

That morning while Harry listened to Dale, a light came on. "I said, 'Look, we're going to make an issue of this thing. We'll say you are homosexual but neither lewd nor dissolute. And that cop is lying.' "

An emergency meeting was called for eight o'clock that night. Aware that this untried strategy might sound foolhardy, Harry prepared "a firebrand harangue on how this is the perfect opportunity to press the issue of oppression," which he delivered at Jennings's apartment on Lemoyne Avenue in Echo Park. There was surprisingly little opposition to the proposal, but the air was still thick with tension. Next, Rowland stood up in support. As Harry recalled, "His eyes dark and blazing, Chuck said passionately, *'The Hinger of Fistory points!'* There was a pause while everyone stared at each other. Rudi gasped and dissolved into uncontrollable laughter, and the rest of the group followed." That mirthful moment sealed the decision to take on the Jennings case. "We seized on it as a rallying point," Gruber recalled. "There wasn't much arm-twisting at all. Inasmuch as I was often a dissenter, I was aware that any of the dissenters would have spoken up at that point."...

The Citizen's Committee to Outlaw Entrapment was set up by the Mattachine Foundation to defend Jennings ... The Foundation ... could raise funds and command public awareness through a series of fliers addressed to "the community of Los Angeles" and spread through gay beach areas, bus stops, and selected men's rooms. One, discreetly titled "Are You Left-Handed?," compared homosexuality to any other inborn trait. Another, with cautious militancy, was entitled "An Anonymous Call to Arms."

This second leaflet hammered home the "guilt by association" idea in Harry's original prospectus. It began with the declaration, "We, the CITIZEN'S COMMITTEE AGAINST ENTRAPMENT, an anonymous body of angry voters in full sympathy with the spirit of rebellion in our community concerning police brutality against Minorities in general, ARE CONVINCED THAT NOW, ALSO, IS THE TIME TO REVEAL IN THE CLEAREST POSSIBLE MANNER THE FULL THREAT TO THE ENTIRE COMMUNITY OF THE SPECIAL POLICE BRUTALITY AGAINST THE HOMOSEXUAL MINORITY." The "Call to Arms" leaflet detailed the bitter harvest of entrapment. It recounted "the man who parted with his valuable art collection ... piece by piece ... his savings account ... and when he was wrung dry was turned in anyway; the professional man who paid $3,000 to get a trumped-up charge reduced to 'disturbance of the peace'; the West Los Angeles businessmen who pay for protection against false witnessing every week; the dozens of youngsters who are offered rides by 'lonely or maudlin' decoys in wolf's clothing and stampeded into milking the family's savings or turning over the names and addresses of acquaintances who might make likely entrapment candidates." To break this cycle, the Committee promised to fight to the Supreme Court if necessary. Members hit up everyone they could think of for donations, including the owners of decorator shops on Robertson Boulevard. Some of these slipped the fliers into the shopping bags of clients and associates they thought might be sympathetic...

The trial began on June 23, 1952, and after [attorney] Shibley caught the arresting officer in a lie on the witness stand, the jury deadlocked and the judge dismissed the charges. Jennings later described it in *One* magazine:

> The trial was a surprise. The attorney, engaged by the Mattachine Foundation, made a brilliant opening statement to the jury when he pointed out that homosexuality and lasciviousness are not identical after stating that his client was admittedly homosexual, that no fine line separates the variations of sexual inclinations and the only true pervert in the courtroom was the arresting officer. He asked, however, that the jury feel no prejudice merely because I'd been arrested: these two officers weren't necessarily guilty of the charges of beating another prisoner merely because they were so accused ... the jury deliberated for forty hours and asked to be dismissed when one of their members said he'd hold out for guilty till hell froze over. The rest voted straight acquittal.

The Mattachine Society called the result a victory and cited it as the first time in California history that an admitted homosexual was freed on a "vag-lewd" charge. But the story went unreported in the newspapers. "We informed every paper in Southern California, every journal, radio, and television station, on every hearing date and on the date of the judge's decision not to renew — *to no avail!*" Hay recalled bitterly. "This was a deliberate conspiracy of silence." The triumph could only be celebrated as it was rallied — by leaflet...

The greatest product of the Jennings case was an explosion of interest in Mattachine, marked by the steady growth of its discussion groups and guilds. During the waning summer of 1952, word of the victory spread like wildfire. In circles of friends, among "ribbon clerk" professionals like costumers and clerks, in the gay crowds at bars like the Golden Carp on Melrose Avenue and the Pink Poodle on Pico Boulevard, people talked of little else. Dorr Legg heard it in the office where he worked as a city planner. "A guy asked me, 'Have you heard about the guy here who has fought the police and won?' I said no. 'Well, he has, and there's an organization about it.'"

The impression that Mattachine was a savior from police entrapment caused a sudden flood of requests from areas wanting to be instantly organized. Chuck Rowland recalled that the crowds at these meetings were enormous. "In Long Beach I had maybe a hundred kids at one meeting. Bob Hull told us about a meeting in the Valley with nearly two hundred people." This began to throw off the original plan of a tight-knit, secret organization. By the time Jim Kepner heard about Mattachine, the fervent secrecy had largely evaporated. With almost two dozen guilds and what Hay termed a "sphere of influence" of thousands, mostly in California, the frustrations of former years, when no on would dare attend a meeting, was completely reversed. Groups sprang up in Whittier, Laguna, Capistrano, San Diego, Bakersfield, Fresno, Monterey, and the San Francisco Bay Area. The dream of organizing homosexuals had succeeded beyond their wildest hopes.

AFTERWORD

The good times for Hay and the Mattachine Society were soon clouded by difficulties. His involvement with gay politics convinced Hay he had to "come clean" about who he really was with family and friends. As a result, he endured a bitter divorce from his wife Anita and was expelled from the Communist Party, both in 1951. Immediately afterwards, a harsh leadership struggle broke out within the rapidly growing Mattachine Society. New members were suspicious of the secrecy of the organization's leadership. In addition, the general anti-communist atmosphere of the time led to deep mistrust of anyone seen as being sympathetic to "reds." Bitterly attacked at a Mattachine Convention in 1953, Hay and other early leaders resigned from their positions, and were soon forced out of the organization altogether. Within a few years, Harry had lost both of his communities, the one he had lived in as a heterosexual, and the new circle of gay friends he had met through organizing Mattachine. He was eventually called before the notorious House Un-American Activities Committee in its 1954 hearings on "subversives," where he managed to escape without criminal punishment. Because of his earlier expulsion from the Communist Party (because of his homosexuality), Hay was technically innocent of any crime. The secrecy of Mattachine's organizing meant he was not even suspected by the committee of being homosexual.

Hay largely dropped from sight in the years that followed. He turned much of his attention to researching gay history, becoming one of the first to do so. It was his way of contributing to the movement he so loved. In fact, his early discoveries on the Native American institution of the "berdache" (see Chapter 4) paved the way for today's scholarship. By the late seventies, the growth of academic interest in gay history restored Hay to his place as one of the founders of the movement. He was regularly interviewed by scholars as well as filmmakers working on historical documentaries such as *Before Stonewall.* His main involvement in the eighties and nineties has been with Radical Faeries, a countercultural group that blends elements of Native American, New Age, and other philosophies with gay rights. He is still living in the Los Angeles area as of this writing in late 1993.[2]

Mattachine also went through its troubles in the mid-to-late fifties. The new leadership adopted very different strategies from Hay's. Instead of trying to make society more accepting of gays, the new Mattachine leadership argued that homosexuals should try to "fit in" more. Mattachine argued that "the sex variant is no different from anyone else except in the object of his sexual expression" and that homosexuals should "adopt a pattern of behavior that is acceptable to society in general; and compatible with [the] recognized institutions of home, church, and state."[3] The "homophile" movement, as it was called, did experience some successes: Mattachine chapters were established in a number of cities, including Los Angeles, San Francisco, Boston, Denver, Philadelphia, Detroit, Chicago, and Washington. Its affiliated publication, *One* magazine, won a crucial Supreme Court decision in January 1958, overturning a ban that considered all literature relating to homosexuality to be "obscene."[4] The first lesbian rights organization, the Daughter of Bilitis, was founded in 1955 in San Francisco by Del Martin and Phyllis Lyon. In addition to holding social activities, it published a magazine called *The Ladder,* which broke the silence on the existence of lesbians.[5]

Nevertheless, by 1960 Mattachine had only 230 members nationwide and DOB enrolled a mere 110.[6] Membership figures are a bit deceptive, however: The organization's influence spread to thousands who may not have been official members but who read the organization's publications, participated in discussion groups they organized, or merely read or heard about their efforts. Mattachine and DOB had much more impact than their small membership totals would suggest. Two factors conspired to keep those totals so low. First, gay people were aware of the risk of job loss that accompanied joining such an organization in the McCarthy era (see Chapter 10). The FBI, in fact, did infiltrate Mattachine meetings and maintained files on its members.[7] Hostility to gays was simply too strong in the fifties for all but the bravest of individuals to "come out" by joining a political organization such as Mattachine.

A second factor was the philosophy of Mattachine's leadership. Gays had been energized by Mattachine's willingness to fight oppression in its early years through actions like the Jennings trial. When the focus shifted to trying to "fix" homosexuals so that they "adjusted" to society better, many gays simply lost interest. After all, some must have reasoned, why join an organization that says *we're* the problem? As Historian John D'Emilio put it:

> ...DOB and Mattachine often reflected back to their potential constituency some of society's most condemnatory attitudes. Their criticisms of the bars and the gay subculture undoubtedly alienated some of the men and women with the strongest commitment to gay life. If fear kept most homosexuals and lesbians away from the movement, contempt for its seeming acceptance of a negative view of the gay world may have turned off the rest.[8]

Members of the young gay movement ran into the dilemma that many oppressed people have faced in American society: should they "go along to get along," trying to "fit in" to win acceptance or should they "fight back," announcing an unapologetic pride in their difference and disregarding the opinions of the majority while demanding (not asking for) equality? In the 1960s a new generation would scorn the former approach, favored by the Mattachine leaders of the fifties, and found a liberation movement based on the notion that "Gay is Good."

IMPORTANT TERMS

Harry Hay
Kinsey report
police entrapment
Mattachine Society
Jennings case
Daughters of Bilitis
One
The Ladder
homophile movement

QUESTIONS/ACTIVITIES

1. Recreate the scene in the apartment the night Harry Hay first gets the idea for a gay-rights organization. This can be done by: writing a "sales pitch" that Hay delivers to prospective members; role-playing the parts of Hay and the partygoers; or writing diary entries, from the point of view of Hay or others, as if you have just gotten home from the party.

2. Either role-play or write a dialogue depicting a phone conversation the next day between Hay and a partygoer, who suddenly has lost interest in the idea.

3. What obstacles does Hay encounter throughout his efforts to organize Mattachine? Cite specific examples. Why? What do you think of his strategies to overcome them?

4. When Hay finally meets some others interested in his idea and discusses it with them, he describes it as finally *"being* Gays." Since these men already knew they were homosexuals, what does Hay mean when he says they were finally "being Gays"? What does "being gay" involve for him that being homosexual does not?

5. Hay's "most important" contribution, in the eyes of many, was his notion that gays were a "cultural minority." What does this mean? Why would it be important? (You may want to look at the life of Ulrichs in Chapter 7 for a comparison.)

6. Make a "pro and con" list on the advantages and disadvantages to joining Mattachine. Write a brief statement afterwards about what you think you would have done. Keep in mind the conditions described in Chapter 10. It is easy for us to be "presentist," judging decisions of the past from the perspective of today. Be sure to try to think as if you are a person from the fifties, not today!

7. Write a diary entry as if you have just been to your first Mattachine meeting. Be sure to describe the conditions you found on your way to and at the meeting in addition to your emotional and mental reactions.

8. Gernreich said Hay's ideas were "the most dangerous thing I've ever heard of." Taking into account the content of Mattachine's 1951 "Missions and Purposes" Statement, what was revolutionary about the group's beliefs about being gay and its ideas about how to deal with social attitudes toward gays?

9. The key argument Hay came up with in the groundbreaking Jennings case was that Jennings had been homosexual but not "lewd or dissolute." What made this a dramatic new argument at the time?

10. You've just gotten home from grocery shopping and, in emptying your bags, find one of the "Citizen's Committee to Outlaw Entrapment" flyers. How would you react? Why?

11. You learn from a friend about Jennings's victory. Write another friend to tell them about it, explaining how you feel about its impact on your life.

12. Every minority group has debated the "assimilation or resistance" question. Put yourself in the late 1950s and imagine you are a member of Mattachine or DOB. Justify your group's political strategies. Others can represent a more "resistance" point of view. After a debate, vote on which argument would be more convincing, given the conditions in the United States for gays of that period.

CHAPTER 12

Before Stonewall: Portraits of Lesbian and Gay Lives before Gay Liberation

INTRODUCTION

While the history of political organizing is important, the fact remains that in the gay community, as in every community, the number who choose to become political activists is always a small minority. Focusing our account of gay history on events in the "public sphere" of politics, such as McCarthyism and the founding of Mattachine, not only leaves out the majority of gay people but also gives us a distorted sense of what individual gay lives are all about. Most of life is not taken up in meetings or protests but in just *living:* finding a job, making a home, spending time with loved ones, and the everyday acts that make up a life.

For lesbian and gay people before the emergence of gay liberation, making a life as a gay person took considerable courage, ingenuity, and creativity. Chapters 9, 10, and 11 gave us a sense of the political conditions under which pre-Stonewall gay life was lived. Facing discrimination and social ostracism, members of earlier gay communities committed an astoundingly brave act by simply choosing to live as gay people. Such a choice could involve the loss of freedom, family, friends, career, and community. Nevertheless, countless numbers did so, creating the basis for the modern gay community and movement.

The readings in Chapter 12, all taken from Marcy Adelman's *Long Time Passing: The Lives of Older Lesbians,* are what we call "oral history." They are called "oral history" because they are literally stories told by the subject to an interviewer and then written down. They offer us vivid, personal portraits of how lesbians made their lives in an era when there was relatively little support for living a gay life. In the process, the stories remind us that, like all people, gay people are *people* first, people who love, hope, dream, cry, and suffer, feeling the same emotions that all other humans share.

READING 12-A

"If You Live, You're Going to Get Old"
by Alma Adams

I was born in 1910 in Elgin, Illinois, where they used to make watches. My cousin tells me they've torn the watch factory down and there's some senior citizen housing there now. My mother worked at the factory. My dad worked at the factory. If you weren't at the watch factory you were at Moody's Publishing. Or you worked at the Elgin State Hospital. Elgin was one of the Underground Railroad stations. It has quite a history to it. We celebrated Emancipation Day. It was a good place to grow up.

Until I was about six years old I thought I was Jewish. The Fishers lived down the street. I played with their kids — Sylvia, Ann, and Irving. I ate at their house all the time. Mrs. Fisher made good stuff and she was always inviting me. At Easter it was Seder. Fridays, Mr. Fisher would have his cap on for the Sabbath. I spoke a lot of Hebrew. And I thought I was Jewish. Nobody said anything about me being anything else. Nobody said anything about being black or white; they talked about being Jewish, Italian, Irish.

So, even though I was black, since I associated more with Jewish children I became Jewish. I went to synagogue. My mother never said anything about religion although she was an ordained Methodist Evangelist minister. We had to go to Sunday school, but she didn't mind me going to synagogue. She and Mrs. Fisher hung over the back fence and talked about their children. Mr. Fisher pushed a vegetable cart. My dad drove a coal wagon. Everyone was friendly. There was never any animosity. There was never any bickering. But that came all too soon.

When I was eleven we moved from Elgin in northern Illinois to Columbus in southern Illinois and it was full of rednecks. You had to go to the back door of restaurants to get your sandwich or your coffee. We weren't called "black," we were called "colored folks." We were driving one time and this little kid said, "Hi, colored folks." I didn't know what they meant. My sister said, "I wasn't dipped in a pot of dye."

One day after we had moved, we went to the movies and we couldn't watch the show for seeing all these colored people. Well, come to find out, it was a colored theater. It was in the black section of Columbus. I couldn't watch the show for seeing all these colored people — I'd never seen so many colored people in my life. I didn't know there was that many in the world. I was simply amazed. When we saw all these colored people in the streets, my sister and I didn't say anything; we just had our mouths hanging open. And we talked to each other at home. My sister said, "Where did they all come from?" I said, "I don't know. I wonder, do they all live here or did they just come here like we did from some other place where there's just a few?"

It made me laugh, it was such a good feeling to see all these black people. At school, all black kids. In Elgin, there weren't half a dozen black kids. It blew my silly little mind. I walked backwards, looking at all these people. My uncle had this Flint — it was a great, big, beautiful, ugly car. Now I know it was ugly, but then I thought, "Gee, my uncle is rich with this car." There were black people with cars! At home *no one* had cars, only a few rich people. There were no streetcars, either; you walked in Elgin.

Later my mother worked in a frat house and we moved down near the university. There weren't so many black people out there in the north end. East Columbus was where the blacks were...

My mother knew about me and girls because I told her when I was in high school. I asked her, "Mama did you ever like to kiss girls?" And she said, "You mean kissing? We always kiss." I said, "I don't mean like at church. Did you ever feel like you like to kiss a girl?" She said, "I never thought about it, honey. Why do you ask?" I said, "I feel like I like to kiss girls..."

She didn't get angry. She just kept saying, "Oh my Lord." I think she said it a dozen times. She kept looking at me. I said, "Well, what?" But she accepted it, just like she accepted me not going to church. My sister was baptized, taught Sunday school, sang in the choir, prayed and all that stuff. Married and children. And there was just the two of us. We were all very tight. But Mama never got through saying, "Oh my Lord."...

I didn't go to gay bars until I got to San Francisco. There were a couple of places in Chicago — sort of secretive places where you run the risk of getting beat up. Not very healthy places to go, but when I came to San Francisco, Jesus God! That was in '54. There were about twenty bars here. It was almost a year before I got into the swing of things.

If it wasn't for my mother, I wouldn't have learned all these things. I brought her out here. My mother came out to cook at the convent. Sister Mary Ann, our superior in Elgin, had come to California and asked Mama to come out here. The Father asked me if I'd cook for the priests; I stayed three years cooking for the priests. And in staying I discovered San Francisco and the girls. You know how I discovered it? Through the Red Cross!

I volunteered to drive for the Red Cross and one of the drivers asked me what else I did on my days off and I said, "Nothing. That's the reason I'm driving for the Red Cross. There isn't anything else to do." She said, "Do you go to San Francisco — to the bars?" I said, "No, I can't go to the bars by myself." She said, "Why don't you go with me sometime?" I said, "Okay." I always bless the Red Cross. That's where I got started...

I got involved with the gay movement because it was the thing to do. Oh my God, I was so happy to find all this stuff here. I was down at the nude beach at Half-Moon Bay. It was Moonlight Night and I was laying on the beach. I met this guy and we started talking. He asked me if I'd heard of SIR [the Society for Individual Rights, an early homophile organization]. I made some smart-ass remark, "Sissies in Retirement?" He said, "Why don't you come to a meeting sometime?"

Anything I'm invited to, I go. I went to DOB [Daughters of Bilitis] and to their parties and to their open meetings...

You didn't see too many black lesbians in the bars. A few black gay men. There was a leather bar the boys used to invite us to after bowling. There were no blacks. Gerry and I were the only blacks in the bar the several times that we were there. There was no friction. No feeling of not belonging. The feeling was that you were with your own people. More than if you *were* with your own people. I never went to black women's bars...

It's hard to find women my own age. It seems like I'm the only one who's old ... I haven't made any friends in the last ten years that are my own age. There's no one as old as I am. I was talking to my sister. I said, "Do you suppose that I'm the oldest living lesbian in the world?"

READING 12-B

"A Charmed and Lucky Life"
by Dr. Eileen

My first gay encounter was in medical school in 1941. After that I never really questioned that I was gay. I had never felt attracted to men nor they to me. Being "unpopular" with men was not something to which I gave much thought. The reality was that being gay created for me, for the first time, a community — a place where I could actually belong.

For the rest of the world it might have been a subculture, but my experience was that it gave me an identity, a self-identity, and for the first time a community identity ... with my first gay encounter I met people who were like me. It was something I had never felt.

And then I met Ann. I had actually met her many years before in Korea when I was twelve years old and she was sixteen. When I "found" her in New York it completed my sense of having found a home community. In those days the gay community was very much different than it is today. It was a large community that was almost entirely closeted to the outside world. We were not openly gay — it didn't seem like an option to us. I think we all felt it would be a mistake to "broadcast" that we were gay. I don't remember ever talking to anyone in those years about being gay — not to gay friends and certainly not to straight acquaintances. But we did have a gay identity.

In those days, during the fifties and sixties, there were large parties. Because I was a doctor I met many interesting and different gay people in my practice. Ann and I would get invited to dinner parties and Halloween parties. There would be fifty gay men and women. It seemed fantastic to us. Everyone would dance and drink — we drank a great deal. They were wonderful parties where we could be ourselves. People were vital; you could see they were involved with the world. We were informed and concerned about the world as a group, though we weren't too involved with politics.

Even though we were closeted, I felt support from my community. Gay men and women came to see me as a doctor, and I got many referrals from the people I met at parties. I felt like I was serving "my community."

Ann and I also had an identity together, a world we created for ourselves. Because Ann was a nurse, we had a great deal to share.

After medical school Ann and I decided to open a practice. We worked side by side after it opened in 1955 on. In our practice we were never openly a couple — not many non-gays knew that Ann lived with me. But even though no one talked about being gay, I know they knew, because they sent me gay patients. I never felt comfortable talking about being gay, yet I was comfortable with being gay.

I was proud of Ann. She was the kind of person everyone liked, warm and outgoing. She was generous to everyone she met. She truly loved people and was always trying to find ways to help people who needed help. She shared many things with me: her love of art, music, and literature. We loved to go skiing together. We met most of our friends in a lesbian investment club. (That club is not operating anymore but it was an example of how gay people used such organizations for social and personal support.) With Ann I had a family.

Our community was very present when Ann got sick. She smoked, and in 1976 she lost a lung to cancer. Eight months later she had a convulsion and became paralyzed. Toward the end, it became worse and she could only speak every once in a while. I knew she understood me, and was aware of me but she was not able to talk much in those last few weeks. It was then that our gay friends stood by us; they came right to the end and took care of Ann and me. They gave us 24-hour care.

Ann died in 1977; we had shared thirty years together. I spent most of the next two years crying. It seemed like I could not stop. I was shattered. Everything I counted on was Ann. My grief was total. I had a hard time continuing my life, and even my work became a burden. I almost couldn't work, I often cried between patients. My work has always been important to me, so it helped pull me through this period of grieving. It gave me a way to keep going.

I was sixty when Ann died. I didn't feel my own aging until I was sixty-five. I began to feel, "God, I *am* old. I'm a senior citizen."...

I probably have some regrets about my life ... but I'd do it all over again. I'd go into medicine, I'd certainly pick Ann. I don't know if I'd stay as a GP [general practitioner] — maybe I should have gone into one of the specialties. I probably regret being harsh with people sometimes — patients and friends.

Now when I walk down the street, I usually smile at people because I figure it's nicer than not saying or doing anything and they just go right by you and never see you. You're just not there when you're older. Your own age group almost always smiles at you.

I realize there's a new community of gays and lesbians out there, but I don't think about it much or what they do. Maybe I should look into it, but it's just not my style to join things. I've never been involved with the gay movement or the women's movement...

...I think, though, that as you grow older, you don't feel any different than when you first started, except that you mellow, you learn more about coping and how to get along with people whether they're gay or not. I feel I've had a charmed and lucky life.

READING 12-C

"A Free Spirit"
by Barbara Tymbios

I was born after the close of the nineteenth century in Sumter, South Carolina.

We lived in a bungalow on Liberty Street. I was the seventh of eleven children. In the back of the bungalow was a forest. When I wanted to get away from my family I roamed the forest and communicated with the trees.

We had two huge iron pots where we bathed and servants washed our clothes and starched our petticoats and dresses, which were as stiff as cardboard. We had a privy, or outhouse as it is called today. We used newspapers to wipe our behinds.

My parents had a store on Main Street called "The New York Racket Store." It had a swinging shingle. Father employed two clerks; one black, Pinckney, and the other, Mr. Burgess, who was white. I believe Father was the first white to employ a Negro clerk. Mind you, this was ninety years ago. We sold Hoyt's cologne at a nickel a vial, ginghams, clothing for men and women, spools of thread, needles — a general store. But thank heavens, no groceries.

Papa was an Orthodox Jew — actually a rabbi — who did not believe in making money at the pulpit. He was strict, all right — kosher food, and don't mix milk products with meat products. A separate set of dishes for milk products and for meat. At Passover, Mama had to sterilize her cutlery. How did she do this? By digging a hole in the earth and pouring boiling water over knives, forks, spoons, etc....

In 1917, I left home to live in New York with my sister Sarah ... Through my sister Sarah, I met Herman Defremery, who was a psychologist at Columbia University. We became friends. I confided in him how very perturbed I was at liking women. I thought I was insane. He assured me that I was not crazy, saying there were homos, bi's, and heteros, and that I was bisexual. You can imagine how grateful I was to him for straightening out my thinking about being gay. It was a time in my life when I was truly confused and in need of guidance...

I started going to bars and parties. I met lesbians and had numerous affairs, primarily with married women. During the Depression, I took any job that was available. For a while I worked as a water inspector in buildings. I got this job through the WPA. I would check toilets and waterlines.

After a while I met lesbian friends who introduced me to women with whom I was compatible. I met Joy Perry in the thirties. She was an administrator who sold to wholesalers. I fell in love the first time I saw her...

A friend of Joy's who worked for the *Times,* Maria Saurez, introduced me to Lorena Hickok at a party. [See Chapter 6 for details on Hickok's life.] I had an affair with her. I met a lot of newspaper people. She would take me to restaurants that literary people frequented. This was in the thirties. I had a job with AMTOG — the American Trading Organization — working on *The Economic Review of the Soviet Union.* We tried to explain what the Soviet Union was trying to do and to contribute to world industry. Hickok would come to the office for information. I was a clerk/secretary there. She would speak with one of the head people.

I never loved her but I found her extremely interesting. She knew a lot. I enjoyed conversations with her. She wanted me as a lover, not as a friend. When I ended the relationship, I never saw her again. I'm sorry for that as I admired her greatly...

...I hope I proved that an old dame like me can be gay. Just because I'm old and sick and eighty-five doesn't mean I didn't have quite a gay life. You see I've loved a lot of women and a lot of women have loved me. In fact, if I weren't sick that would still be the case...

I have friends who come by and cook me dinner now and then and I have friends who take me to my doctors' appointments. These are new and younger gay friends.

At one point, I thought gay people were no good. But now all these gay people are helping me. It's not my family that is taking care of me; it's my gay friends. They have been wonderful to me...

You know, young gay people are a revelation to me. They participate in gay parades. One gal I know, she is a young person of thirty-five, is going to study politics. I told her, "For God's sake, don't vote for a person just because they are gay. Be more objective in your outlook on life."

These young people flaunt themselves. They march in parades. They represent gay people on TV. I admire that but I don't do it myself. I've always been conservative about being gay. I can't imagine I could be any different. I have to be guarded but I think it's good that others reveal themselves.

READING 12-D

"Not Always a Bed of Roses"
by Wilma and Roberta

ROBERTA: I remember how I first met Wilma. It was in 1949; we were stationed in Germany. She walked into the mess hall with this other girl. I thought, "Boy, I bet she's a bitch to work with."

WILMA: I was in my room later on that same day and Roberta came in. I hadn't gotten my trunk so I didn't have any dresser scarves and she said, "I have some extra ones, I'll bring them down." I thought that was pretty nice, that someone would offer me dresser scarves. So she got two and gave them to me. That's how we started running around together. We became lovers — I'd go up to her room or she'd come down to my room at night. We'd take our leaves together.

ROBERTA: It was very risky, two women in the service being lovers. I'm the more cautious type. She liked any kind of risk...

I came home because of alcoholism in '51 ... I was offered the alternative of resigning so I took it ... I didn't think I was an alcoholic — I thought I got stuck in a bad situation. I knew I was going to do something about my drinking but it was always tomorrow — never today.

I continued to drinking until 1954. I was living with my brother and his wife and children. My brother called our family physician about my drinking; the doctor said, "I can't do a thing for her but I have a friend who's running an outfit called AA." So a woman from AA came out to see me — which is unusual, because we don't normally make third-party calls in AA; the alcoholic has to take the initiative. I knew I had to get these people off my back so I went to the meetings.

I was impressed with the meetings and I felt comfortable in them. But I didn't do the first step; we have a first step in AA where we admit that we are powerless over alcohol and that our lives have become unmanageable. I could see I was powerless over alcohol but I would have never conceived of my life as unmanageable. I thought I could manage my life just fine.

I was dry for ten months. At the end of ten months I decided I would go back to social drinking. That was a mistake because I never drank socially in my life. On my job, I was working for a fellow that was in AA and when he saw that I was drinking again, he saw to it that I got to a drying-out place. And it was there that I saw a psychiatrist who asked if I wanted to talk to him about my sexuality. I did and his comment was, "It's neither wrong nor right. There's no wrong or right to it. It's whatever you're comfortable with."

That was the first time I had spoken to a professional person about my sexual orientation. It had a real impact. I didn't feel guilty, but I did feel it wasn't normal. I said to him, "I understand that I probably have two choices — to continue to do as I am or sublimate." He said, "Yes, that's true. Whatever you're more comfortable with. Do you feel that you're doing wrong?" I said no. He said, "Well, it's your feeling about it that's important." It really made me feel better to hear that. I thought, "I'm not doing anything wrong in my life; if society doesn't accept me then I have to live with that aspect of it. I might be in the closet but I don't have to feel guilty about it." Up until that time I'd never heard anybody say anything about it.

WILMA: I'd never heard anything about it either. I'd read *The Well of Loneliness*. You just didn't hear anything...

ROBERTA: But we both felt, when we realized that we were gay, that we were abnormal. It wasn't the socially accepted thing to be.

WILMA: You just knew that there was something wrong with you ... I drank, too. But I never knew I was an alcoholic until the day I called AA. I was in all kinds of trouble, too. But I always blamed it on the other person. I never accepted that I had a problem with alcoholism. So I never saw her problem either. We drank together in the service. We had a good time together. My advice to her was, "Just don't drink where they can see you. Get away." And that's exactly what I did. I came back to Los Angeles; I had a sister living there. And I'd drink at my sister's or in the city of Los Angeles, but not where they could catch you.

I was sent home in '52 also. It was alcoholism, but they called it "dementia melancholia." I was no psychiatric nurse — I had to look that up. Then I got so mad I could have killed them because I was thirty-eight and dementia melancholia is a disease of senility. I thought, "Well, you damn idiots." I had the D.T.'s; it was pure and simple alcoholism. But they tried to be nice to me because an alcoholic diagnosis would have gotten me kicked out of the service.

I was lonely when I came up here to the military hospital. I was missing Roberta a lot ... I only knew one person that I'd take a chance on and that was Roberta. So I flew back to Atlanta in March. I wanted to see if I could get her to come out here. We talked about our drinking — I was still drinking and Roberta had stopped. She said, "This isn't going to be very mature of me if I go out there." And I said, "Let's take a chance on your maturity."

ROBERTA: The story of my life!

WILMA: So then she agreed to come to California. But before she got out here in June, I got into a driving accident. I came around a corner and hit a car. I was stoned, absolutely out of my mind. The police came and I blamed my little dog, said she jumped on me as I made the turn. But I was cited; I had to appear before a judge in August, soon after Roberta was out here.

That's when I called AA. It was going out to get Roberta and seeing her sober. That was a great influence on me ... I couldn't understand why she was so damn happy and she wasn't making any money and living in a boardinghouse. And here I was — I had a car, my career, and the bank and I owned this house ... And I was miserable. I was contemplating suicide very seriously. It was partially my drinking, and partially what I had been through with this woman [I'd been involved with] and the military. The day of the hit-and-run, I went to the cupboard and got out this full bottle of Scotch. I was a Scotch drinker. Every time something happened to me that I didn't like, I just said, "Well, I'll show them. I'll get drunk." And I always got drunk, too. When I got the bottle down, I opened it up and smelled it. I just smelled it and thought, "Well, you damn fool, you can't drink." I called Roberta first. In Atlanta. I asked her if anybody out here would help me the way they helped her or would they think I was crazy. And she said, "Well, they'll know you're crazy and they'll help."

That was the end of May and she came out on the sixteenth of June. So I only had a couple of weeks in between to get on a program.

So our commitment didn't start in the military; it started in 1956 when she came out here and we were both sober. It was wonderful being sober together. In the service we had gotten into some physical fights with each other when we'd been drunk. I don't know what Roberta thought, but I knew that somewhere I was thinking that those fights were all drink oriented.

It's only been in the last few years that I've reflected way back on my own life and realized that I've always been gay. In eighth grade I fell in love with a teacher. I knew at the time that I thought a lot of her and I saved up money to give her a Christmas gift. I knew that I was probably in love with a girl in training and another one in the military. But you didn't hear about it, you didn't know about it. I don't know if my drinking had anything to do with how I felt about being gay. Maybe yes. Maybe no...

We wouldn't have each other without AA.

ROBERTA: AA made all the difference in the world. Sobriety gave me my life back.

WILMA: We have friends over here that are gay that we have known since 1964 — twenty-one years. It was only about seven years ago that it came out that any one of us was gay. Yet all of us felt that the others were.

ROBERTA: But we never said anything, we never talked about it. When we first started going to AA here, we never wore slacks there or anything like that. There were no other gay women in AA. We were very careful not to let anyone know that we were sexual, but we always went together. We let it be known that we lived together. But women have historically lived together.

WILMA: Women can get away with a lot more than men can.

ROBERTA: But it was fifteen years before any of us said anything to the others.

WILMA: It came up in a very strange way. Marge gave a birthday party for Elly. She took us all to dinner at a gay bar, Tuxedo Junction. And Elly said, "I hope we're not shocking you." And I said, "No, not exactly." It was the first we knew. It never came up that they were gay. We've never discussed it since. We didn't have any gay friends before them. They did. They were our first gay friends, but we didn't know it. We never talked about it. There was no community the way there is now...

ROBERTA: It is a support. There's no doubt about that. The community has become more important to us as we have gotten older ... I think we have been too conditioned to being closeted to be totally out. We are out with a number of people, but I'm not totally out. I'm not out with what family I have left. But I think we were conditioned for too long to be comfortable with that. I don't think it's necessary. I'd like to see a time when it's an accepted form — when your sexual orientation is your own business and you move on from there.

QUESTIONS/ACTIVITIES

1. Some useful documentary films are now available to supplement these readings, among which are: *Before Stonewall,* a history of gay and lesbian life from the early twentieth century to the sixties; *Last Call at Maud's,* which provides a vibrant sense of lesbian life in this period through the lens of a well-known San Francisco lesbian bar; and *Forbidden Love,* which brings to life lesbian experiences through the fifties "pulp" novels that were many women's first contact with lesbian culture.

2. One of the important skills for students of history to learn is how to make generalizations from specific cases. Try to make generalizations about lesbian and gay life based on these accounts. List them on the board. Analyze what we can accurately say, using these oral histories.

3. Similarly, look for important differences in the experiences of these women. What are these differences, and what are the factors (race, class, personality) responsible for them?

4. In this highly discriminatory time period, enormous stresses existed for gay people. Find examples of what these stresses were, and how these women coped with them, in these readings.

5. A danger in studying gay history is that we can see everything as a function of an individual's sexual orientation. Choose a specific account and look for those experiences that are universal to all people as well as those that might be particular to gay people.

6. Imagine you had the chance to meet one of these women. If you could ask one question, what would it be? Put the questions into a hat, and have everyone draw a question out. Reread the account of the person to which your question is addressed and write a first-person answer as if you were the individual to whom the question was addressed. You may need to do other research to answer the question. Answers can be read aloud, followed by discussion over whether or not they are realistic.

7. Make two lists of different facts from the readings: things you might have expected would be the case, and things you found surprising. These can be used as sources for reflection about the biases of the reader, our misconceptions about that period, or revelations about previously unknown facts.

8. Eileen says, "I never felt comfortable talking about being gay, yet I was comfortable with being gay." What does she mean? What does this reflect about her generation's attitude toward gayness?

9. Barbara says, "Young gay people are a revelation to me." Reading the accounts, have students look for statements about how these older women feel about today's gay community. Is there a generation gap? What does it consist of?

10. It may be useful to read Chapter 17 or portions of it in conjunction with these readings. What has stayed the same for gay people? What has changed? Were they to meet, what would these two generations have to say to one another? Imagine or write a dialogue between two individuals, one from Chapter 12 and one from Chapter 17.

CHAPTER 13

Stonewall and the Dawning of a New Day

INTRODUCTION

Stonewall — the very word is synonymous with gay and lesbian history. Commemorated annually each June in "gay pride" parades in many of the world's major cities, the Stonewall Riots (which took place in New York City in June 1969) are considered by many to be the beginning of the gay movement. Though the factual details of Stonewall are unknown to most people, these riots have become legendary.

As historians have turned their professional attention to gay history, though, we have begun to see these riots in a different light. As seen in Chapters 7–12, Stonewall was hardly the "beginning" of the gay movement, not even in the United States. It would probably come as a shock to the millions who march each June that Karl Heinrich Ulrichs, for example, was delivering public speeches in Germany about gay rights over a century before Stonewall, in 1867. (See Chapter 7). And certainly organized gay political groups in the United States had been around for decades in the United States before the riots broke out. Few readers of this book could still see Stonewall as the "beginning" of the gay movement.

So is Stonewall overrated as a historical event? Hardly. Those nights of violence in Greenwich Village in late June, begun in response to a routine police raid on a gay bar called the Stonewall Inn, marked a crucial turning point in gay history. As seen in Chapter 11, the "homophile" movement of the 1950s and 1960s was a generally cautious, small one, which preached "fitting in" as the way to win acceptance. Its strategies did not appeal to the average gay American, and its visibility and effectiveness were limited. Events of the sixties, such as the civil rights movement, the Vietnam War, and the assassinations of the Kennedys and Martin Luther King, Jr., had caused many Americans to question the traditional attitudes of society. Nonconforming individuals began wondering if it was perhaps society's attitudes (and not themselves) that were the problem to begin with. Gays, like others such as African-Americans and women, were ready for a more direct challenge to the system that oppressed them. Many gays wanted to fight back, and Stonewall was their opportunity to do so. After the riots, a more militant attitude and new leadership emerged. The new strategy called for confrontation instead of compromise. "Gay is Good," "Gay Power," and "Gay Liberation" became the order of the day.

Historian Martin Duberman has given us the first full account of the Stonewall Riots in his landmark work *Stonewall*. In this book, Duberman traces the stories of three gay men and two lesbians to explain the conditions that produced the riots. In Reading 13-A, Duberman sets the stage for the actual event itself, explaining the Stonewall Inn as an institution, the circumstances of the riots themselves, and the results of their immediate aftermath. In this section, he tells his story through the eyes of three men actually present that night: Craig Rodwell, a 28-year-old "radical activist in the Mattachine Society [who] opened the Oscar Wilde Memorial Bookstore" (a gay bookstore still operating in New York); Sylvia (Ray) Rivera, an 18-year-old "street transvestite ... fixture in the Times Square area, [and] fearless defender of her sisters"; and Jim Fouratt, a 25-year-old "actor, hipster, antiwar protestor, and a major spokesperson for the countercultural Yippie movement."[1] Based on extensive archival research and interviews with living participants, *Stonewall* is an invaluable study of how and why turning points of history happen when and where they do.

Reading 13-A

The Stonewall Riots

from *Stonewall*, by Martin Duberman

Craig [Rodwell] was ... fed up with the gay bar scene in New York — with Mafia control over the only public space most gays could claim, with the contempt shown the gay clientele, with the speak-easy, clandestine atmosphere, the watered, overpriced drinks, the police payoffs and raids. His anger was compounded by tales he heard from his friend Dawn Hampton, a torch singer who, between engagements, worked the hatcheck at a Greenwich Village gay bar called the Stonewall Inn. Because Dawn was straight, the Mafia men who ran Stonewall talked freely in front of her — talked about their hatred for the "faggot scumbags" who made their fortunes.

Indeed, the Stonewall Inn, at 53 Christopher Street, epitomized for Craig everything that was wrong with the bar scene. When a hepatitis epidemic broke out among gay men early in 1969, Craig printed an angry article in his newsletter, *New York Hymnal,* blaming the epidemic on the unsterile drinking glasses at the Stonewall Inn. And he was probably right. Stonewall had no running water behind the bar; a returned glass was simply run through one of two stagnant vats of water kept underneath the bar, refilled, and then served to the next customer. By the end of an evening the water was murky and multicolored...

...[A]s for the Stonewall Inn, it had, in the course of its two-and-a-half-year existence, become the most popular bar in Greenwich Village. Many saw it as an oasis, a safe retreat from the harassment of everyday life, a place less susceptible to police raids than other gay bars and one that drew a magical mix of patrons ranging from tweedy East Siders to street queens. It was also the only gay male bar in New York where dancing was permitted...

The Stonewall Inn had, in its varied incarnations during the fifties, been a straight restaurant and a straight nightclub. In 1966 it was taken over by three Mafia figures who had grown up together on Mulberry Street in Little Italy: "Mario" (the best-liked of the three), Zucchi, who also dealt in firecrackers, and "Fat Tony" Laura, who weighed in at 420 pounds. Together they put up $3,500 to reopen the Stonewall as a gay club; Fat Tony put up $2000, which made him the controlling partner, but Mario served as the Stonewall's manager and ran it on a day-to-day basis...

Tony and his partners, Mario and Zucchi, had opened Stonewall as a private "bottle club." That was a common ruse for getting around the lack of a liquor license; bottles would be labeled with fictitious names and the bar would then — contrary to a law forbidding bottle clubs from selling drinks — proceed to do a cash business like any other bar...

...The Stonewall partners also had to pay off the notoriously corrupt Sixth Precinct. A patrolman would stop by Stonewall once a week to pick up the envelopes filled with cash — including those for the captains and desk sergeants, who never collected their payoffs in person. The total cash dispensed to the police each week came to about two thousand dollars.

Despite the assorted payoffs, Stonewall turned a huge weekly profit for its owners. With rent at only three hundred dollars a month, and with the take (all in cash) typically running to five thousand dollars on a Friday night and sixty-five hundred on a Saturday, Stonewall quickly became a money machine...

Once inside Stonewall, you took a step down and straight in front of you was the main bar ... Behind the bar some pulsating gel lights went on and off — later exaggeratedly claimed by some to be the precursor of the innovative light shows at the Sanctuary and other gay discos that followed. On weekends, a scantily clad go-go boy with a pin spot on him danced in a gilded cage on top of the bar. Straight ahead, beyond the bar, was a spacious dance area, at one point in the bar's history lit only with black lights. That in itself became a subject for camp, because the queens, with Murine in their eyes, all looked as if they had white streaks running down their faces. Should the police (known as Lily Law, Alice Blue Gown — Alice for short — or Betty Badge) or a suspected plainclothesman unexpectedly arrive, white bulbs instantly came on in the dance area, signaling everyone to stop dancing or touching...

The jukebox on the dance floor played a variety of songs, even an occasional "Smoke Gets in Your Eyes" to appease the romantics. The Motown label was still top of the heap in the summer of 1969; three of the five hit singles for the week of June 28 — by Marvin Gaye, Junior Walker, and the Temptations — carried its imprint. On the pop side, the Stonewall jukebox played the love theme from the movie version of *Romeo and Juliet* over and over, the record's saccharine occasionally cut by the Beatles' "Get Back" or Elvis Presley's "In the Ghetto." And all the new dances — the Boston Jerk, the Monkey, the Spider — were tried out with relish. If the crowd was in a particularly campy mood (and the management was feeling loose enough), ten or fifteen dancers would line up to learn the latest ritual steps, beginning with a shouted "Hit it, girls!"...

Very few women ever appeared in Stonewall. [Stonewall employee] Sascha L. flatly declares that he can't remember *any,* except for the occasional "fag hag" ... or "one or two dykes who looked almost like boys." But Chuck Shaheen, who spent much more time at Stonewall, remembers — while acknowledging that the bar was "98 percent male" — a few more lesbian customers than Sascha does, and, of those, a number who were decidedly femme. One of the lesbians who did go to Stonewall "a few times," tagging along with some of her gay male friends, recalls that she "felt like a visitor." It wasn't as if the male patrons went out of the way to make her feel uncomfortable, but rather that the territory was theirs, not hers: "There didn't seem to be any hostility, but there didn't seem to be any camaraderie."

Sylvia Rivera had been invited to Marsha P. Johnson's birthday party on the night of June 27, but she decided not to go. It wasn't that she was mad at Marsha; she simply felt strung out. She had been working as an accounting clerk in a Jersey City chain-store warehouse, keeping tally sheets of what the truckers took out — a good job with a good boss who let her wear makeup whenever she felt like it. But it was an eleven-to-seven shift, Sundays through Thursdays, all-night stints that kept her away from her friends on the street and decidedly short of the cash she had made from hustling...

No, she was not going to Marsha's party. She would stay home, light her consoling religious candles (Viejieta [her grandmother] had taught her *that* much), and say a few payers for Judy [Garland, the entertainer who was extremely popular with gay men, whose funeral had been earlier that day]. But then the phone rang and her buddy Tammy Novak — who sounded more stoned than usual — *insisted* that Sylvia and Gary join her later that night at Stonewall. Sylvia hesitated. If she was going out at all — "Was it all right to dance with the martyred Judy not cold in her grave?" — she would go to Washington Square. She had never been crazy about Stonewall, she reminded Tammy: Men in makeup were tolerated there, but not exactly cherished. And if she was going to go out, she wanted to *vent* — to be just as outrageous, as grief-stricken, as makeup would allow. But Tammy absolutely *refused* to take no for an answer and so Sylvia, moaning theatrically, gave in. She popped a black beauty and she and Gary headed downtown.

Jim [Fouratt]'s job at CBS required long hours, and he often got back to his apartment (after a stopover at Max's Kansas City) in the early morning. On the night of June 27 he had worked in the office until midnight, had gone for a nightcap at Max's, and about one a.m. had headed back to his apartment in the Village. Passing by the Stonewall Inn — a bar he despised, insistent it was a haven for marauding chicken hawks [men who seek underage partners] — Jim noticed a cluster of cops in front of the bar, looking as if they were about to enter. He shrugged it off as just another routine raid, and even found himself hoping that *this* time (Stonewall had been raided just two weeks before) the police would succeed in closing the joint.

But as Jim got closer, he could see that a small group of onlookers had gathered. That was somewhat surprising, since the first sign of a raid usually led to an immediate scattering; typically, gays fled rather than loitered, and fled as quietly and quickly as possible, grateful not to be implicated at the scene of the "crime." Jim spotted Craig Rodwell at the top of the row of steps leading up to a brownstone adjacent to the Stonewall Inn. Craig looked agitated, expectant. Something was decidedly in the air.

Craig had taken up his position only moments before. Like Jim, he had been on his way home — from playing cards at a friend's — and had stumbled on the gathering crowd in front of the Stonewall. He was with Fred Sargeant, his current lover, and the two of them had scrambled up the brownstone steps to get a better view. The crowd was decidedly small, but what was riveting was its strangely quiet, expectant air, as if awaiting the next development. Just then, the police pushed open the front door of the Stonewall and marched in. Craig looked at his watch: It was one-twenty a.m.

Sylvia was feeling *very* little pain. The black beauty had hopped her up and the scotch had smoothed her out. Her lover, Gary, had come along; Tammy, Bambi, and Ivan were there; and rumor had it that Marsha Johnson, disgusted at all the no-shows for her birthday, was also headed downtown to Stonewall, determined to party *somewhere*. It looked like a good night. Sylvia expansively decided that she did like Stonewall after all, and was just saying that to Tammy, who looked as if she was about to keel over — "that chile [Tammy was seventeen, Sylvia eighteen] could not control her intake" — when the cops came barreling through the front door. (The white warning lights had earlier started flashing on the dance floor, but Sylvia and her friends had been oblivious.)

The next thing she knew, the cops, with their usual arrogance, were stomping through, ordering patrons to line up and get their IDs ready for examination. "Oh my God!" Sylvia shouted at Gary, "I didn't bring my ID!" Before she could panic, Gary reached in his pocket and produced her card; he had brought it along. "Praise be to Saint Barbara!" Sylvia shrieked, snatching the precious ID. If the raid went according to the usual pattern, the only people who would be arrested were those without IDs, those dressed in the clothes of the opposite gender, and some or all of the employees. Everyone else would be let go with a few shoves and a few contemptuous words. The bar would soon reopen and they would all be back dancing. It was annoying to have one's Friday night screwed up, but hardly unprecedented.

Sylvia tried to take it in stride; she'd been through lots worse, and with her ID in hand and nothing more than face makeup on, she knew the hassling would be minimal. But she was pissed; the good high she had was gone, and her nerve ends felt as raw as when she had been crying over Judy earlier in the evening. She wished she'd gone to Washington Square, a place she preferred anyway. She was sick of being treated like scum; "I was just not in the mood" was how she later put it. "It had got to the point where I didn't want to be bothered anymore." When one of the cops grabbed the ID out of her hand and asked her with a smirk if she were a boy or a girl, she almost swung at him, but Gary grabbed her hand in time. The cop gave her a shove toward the door, and told her to get the hell out...

The Stonewall management had always been tipped off by the police before a raid took place — this happened, on average, once a month — and the raid itself was usually staged early enough in the evening to produce minimal commotion and allow for a quick reopening. Indeed, sometimes the "raid" consisted of little more than the police striding arrogantly though the bar and then leaving, with no arrests made. Given the size of the weekly payoff, the police had an understandable stake in keeping the golden calf alive...

When the raid, contrary to expectations, did get going, the previous systems put in place by the Mafia owners stood them in good stead. The strong front door bought needed time until the white lights had a chance to do their warning work: Patrons instantly stopped dancing and touching; and the bartenders quickly took the money from the cigar boxes that served as cash registers, jumped from behind the bar, and mingled inconspicuously with the customers...

Some of the campier patrons, emerging one by one from the Stonewall to find an unexpected crowd, took the opportunity to strike instant poses, starlet style, while the onlookers whistled and shouted their applause-meter ratings. But when a paddy wagon pulled up, the mood turned more somber. And it turned sullen when the police officers started to emerge from Stonewall with prisoners in tow and moved with them toward the waiting van. Jim Fouratt at the back of the crowd, Sylvia standing with Gary near the small park across the street from Stonewall, and Craig perched on top of the brownstone stairs near the front of the crowd — all sensed something unusual in the air, all felt a kind of tensed expectancy.

The police (two of whom were women) were oblivious to it initially. Everything up to that point had gone so routinely that they expected to see the crowd quickly disperse. Instead, a few people started to boo; others pressed against the waiting van, while the cops standing near it yelled angrily for the crowd to move back. According to Sylvia, "You could feel the electricity going through people. You could actually feel it. People were getting really, really pissed and uptight." A guy in a dark red T-shirt danced in and out of the crowd, shouting "Nobody's gonna f*** with me!" and "Ain't gonna take this sh**!"

As the cops started leading their prisoners into the van — among them, Blond Frankie, the doorman — more people joined in the shouting. Sylvia spotted Tammy Novak among the three queens lined up for the paddy wagon, and along with others in the crowd started yelling "Tammy! Tammy!," Sylvia's shriek rising above the rest. But Tammy apparently didn't hear, and Sylvia guessed that she was too stoned to know what was going on. Yet when a cop shoved Tammy and told her to "keep moving! keep moving!," poking her with his club, Tammy told him to stop pushing and when he didn't, she started swinging. From that point on, so much happened so quickly as to seem simultaneous.

Jim Fouratt insists that *the* explosive moment came when "a dyke dressed in men's clothing," who had been visiting a male employee inside the bar, started to act up as the cops moved her toward the paddy wagon. According to Jim, "the queens were acting like queens, throwing their change and giving lots of attitude and lip. But the dyke had to be more butch than the queens. So when the police moved her into the wagon, she got out the other side and started to rock it."

Harry Beard, the Stonewall waiter who had been inside the bar, partly corroborates Jim's account, though differing on the moment of explosion. According to Beard, the cops had arrested the cross-dressed lesbian inside the bar for not wearing the requisite (as mandated by a New York statute) three pieces of clothing "appropriate to one's gender." As they led her out of the bar, so Beard's version goes, she complained that the handcuffs they had put on her were too tight; in response, one of the cops slapped her in the head with his nightstick. Seeing the cops hit her, people standing immediately outside the door started throwing coins at the police.

But Craig Rodwell and a number of other eyewitnesses sharply contest the view that the arrest of a lesbian was *the* precipitating incident, or even that a lesbian had been present in the bar. And they skeptically ask why, if she did exist, she has never stepped forward to claim the credit; to the answer that she may long since have died, they sardonically reply, "And she never told another soul? And if she did, why haven't *they* stepped forward to claim credit for her?" As if all that isn't muddled enough, those eyewitnesses who deny the lesbian claimant, themselves divide over whether to give the palm to a queen — Tammy Novak being the leading candidate — or to one of the many ordinary gay male patrons of the bar. Craig Rodwell's view probably comes as close as we are likely to get to the truth: "A number of incidents were happening simultaneously. There was not one thing that happened or one person, there was just ... a flash of group — of mass — anger."...

From this point on, the mêlée broke out in several directions and swiftly mounted in intensity. The crowd, now in full cry, started screaming epithets at the police — "Pigs!" "Faggot cops!" Sylvia and Craig enthusiastically joined in, Sylvia shouting her lungs out, Craig letting go with a full-throated "Gay power!" One young gay Puerto Rican went fearlessly up to a policeman and yelled in his face, "What you got against faggots? We don't do you nuthin'!" Another teenager started kicking at a cop, frequently missing as the cop held him at arm's length. One queen smashed an officer with her heel, knocked him down, grabbed his handcuff keys, freed herself, and passed the keys to another queen behind her.

By now, the crowd had swelled to a mob, and people were picking up and throwing whatever loose objects came to hand — coins, bottles, cans, bricks from a nearby construction site. Someone even picked up dog shit from the street and threw it in the cops' direction. As the fever mounted, [Stonewall co-owner] Zucchi was overheard nervously asking [fellow co-owner] Mario what the hell the crowd was upset about: the Mafia or the police? The *police,* Mario reassured him. Zucchi gave a big grin of relief and decided to vent some stored-up anger of his own: He egged on bystanders in their effort to rip up a damaged fire hydrant and he persuaded a young kid named Timmy to throw the wire-mesh garbage can nearby. Timmy was not much bigger than the can (and had just come out the week before), but he gave it his all — the can went sailing into the plate-glass window (painted black and reinforced from behind by plywood) that stretched across the front of the Stonewall.

Stunned and frightened by the crowd's unexpected fury, the police, at the order of Deputy Inspector Pine, retreated inside the bar. Pine had been accustomed to two or three cops being able to handle with ease any number of cowering gays, but here the crowd wasn't cowering; it had routed eight cops and made them run for cover. As Pine later said, "I had been in combat situations, [but] there was never any time that I felt more scared than then." With the cops holed up inside Stonewall, the crowd was now in control of the street, and it bellowed in triumph and pent-up rage...

...[Stonewall bouncer] Blond Frankie, meanwhile — perhaps taking his cue from Zucchi — uprooted a loose parking meter and offered it for use as a battering ram against the Stonewall's door. At nearly the same moment somebody started squirting lighter fluid through the shattered glass window on the bar's façade, tossing in matches after it. Inspector Pine later referred to this as "throwing Molotov cocktails into the place," but the only reality *that* described was the inflamed state of Pine's nerves.

Still, the danger was very real, and the police were badly frightened. The shock to self-esteem had been stunning enough; now came an actual threat to physical safety. Dodging flying glass and missiles, Patrolman Gil Weisman, the one cop in uniform, was hit near the eye with a shard, and blood spurted out. With that, the fear turned abruptly to fury. Three of the cops, led by Pine, ran out the front door, which had crashed in from the battering, and started screaming threats at the crowd, thinking to cow it. But instead a rain of coins and bottles came down, and a beer can glanced off Deputy Inspector Charles Smyth's head. Pine lunged into the crowd, grabbed somebody around the waist, pulled him back into the doorway, and then dragged him by the hair, inside. [This individual turned out to be a well-known, heterosexual folk singer, Dave Van Ronk.]...

...The cops then found a fire hose, wedged it into a crack in the door, and directed the spray out at the crowd, thinking that would certainly scatter it. But the stream was weak and the crowd howled derisively, while inside the cops started slipping on the wet floor. A reporter from *The Village Voice,* Howard Smith, had retreated inside the bar when the police did; he later wrote that by that point in the evening "the sound filtering in [didn't] suggest dancing faggots anymore; it sound[ed] like a powerful rage bent on vendetta." By now the Stonewall's front door was hanging wide open, the plywood brace behind the windows was splintered, and it seemed only a matter of minutes before the howling mob would break in and wreak its vengeance. One cop armed himself with [employee] Tony the Stiff's baseball bat; the others drew their guns, and Pine stationed several officers on either side of the corridor leading to the front door. One of them growled, "We'll shoot the first m*****f***** that comes through the door."

At that moment, an arm reached in through the shattered window, squirted more lighter fluid into the room, and then threw in another lit match. This time the match caught, and there was a whoosh of flame. Standing only ten feet away, Pine aimed his gun at the receding arm and (he later said) was preparing to shoot when he heard the sound of sirens coming down Christopher Street. At two fifty-five a.m. Pine had sent out an emergency signal 10-41 — a call for help from the fearsome Tactical Police Force — and relief was now rounding the corner.

The TPF was a highly trained, crack riot-control unit that had been set up to respond to the proliferation of protests against the Vietnam War. Wearing helmets with visors, carrying assorted weapons, including billy clubs and tear gas, its two dozen members all seemed massively proportioned. They were a formidable sight as, linked arm in arm, they came up Christopher Street in a wedge formation that resembled (by design) a Roman legion. In their path, the rioters slowly retreated, but — contrary to police expectations — did not break and run. Craig, for one, knelt down in the middle of the street with the camera he'd retrieved from his apartment and, determined to capture the moment, snapped photo after photo of the oncoming TPF minions.

As the troopers bore down on him, he scampered up and joined the hundreds of others who scattered to avoid the billy clubs but then raced around the block, doubled back behind the troopers, and pelted them with debris. When the cops realized that a considerable crowd had simply re-formed to their rear, they flailed out angrily at anyone who came within striking distance. But the protesters would not be cowed. The pattern repeated itself several times: The TPF would disperse the jeering mob only to have it re-form behind them, yelling taunts, tossing bottles and bricks, setting fires in trash cans. When the police whirled around to reverse direction at one point, they found themselves face to face with their worst nightmare: a chorus line of mocking queens, their arms clasped around each other, kicking their heels in the air Rockettes-style and singing at the tops of their sardonic voices:

We are the Stonewall girls
We wear our hair in curls
We wear no underwear
We show our pubic hair...
We wear our dungarees
Above our nelly knees!

It was a deliciously witty, contemptuous counterpoint to the TPF's brute force, a tactic that transformed an otherwise traditionally macho eye-for-an-eye combat and that provided at least the glimpse of a different and revelatory kind of consciousness. Perhaps that was exactly the moment Sylvia had in mind when she later said, "Something lifted off my shoulders."...

The cops themselves hardly escaped scot-free. Somebody managed to drop a concrete block on one parked police car; nobody was injured, but the cops inside were shaken up. At another point, a gold-braided police officer being driven around to survey the action got a sack of wet garbage thrown at him through the open window of his car; a direct hit was scored, and soggy coffee grounds dripped down the officer's face as he tried to maintain a stoic expression. Still later, as some hundred people were being chased down Waverly Place by two cops, someone in the crowd suddenly realized the unequal odds and started yelling, "There are only two of 'em! Catch 'em! Rip their clothes off! F*** 'em!" As the crowd took up the cry, the two officers fled.

Before the police finally succeeded in clearing the streets — for that evening only, it would turn out — a considerable amount of blood had been shed. Among the undetermined number of people injured was Sylvia's friend Ivan Valentin; hit in the knee by a policeman's billy club, he had ten stitches taken at St. Vincent's Hospital. A teenager named Lenny had his hand slammed in a car door and lost two fingers. Four big cops beat up a young queen so badly — there is evidence that the cops singled out "feminine boys"— that she bled simultaneously from her mouth, nose, and ears. Craig and Sylvia both escaped injury (as did Jim, who had hung back on the fringe of the crowd), but so much blood splattered over Sylvia's blouse that at one point she had to go down to the piers and change into the clean clothes Gary had brought back for her.

Four police offers were also hurt. Most of them suffered minor abrasions from kicks and bites, but Officer Scheu, after being hit with a rolled-up newspaper, had fallen to the cement sidewalk and broken his wrist. When Craig heard the news, he couldn't resist chuckling over what he called the "symbolic justice" of the injury. Thirteen people (including Dave Van Ronk) were booked at the Sixth Precinct, seven of them Stonewall employees, on charges ranging from harassment to resisting arrest to disorderly conduct. At three thirty-five a.m., signal 10-41 was canceled and an uneasy calm settled over the area. It was not to last.

Word of the confrontation spread throughout the gay grapevine all day Saturday. Moreover, all three of the dailies wrote about the riot (the *News* put the story on page one), and local television and radio reported it as well. The extensive coverage brought out the crowds, just as Craig had predicted (and had worked to achieve). All day Saturday, curious knots of people gathered outside the bar to gape at the damage and warily celebrate the implausible fact that, for once, cops, not gays, had been routed.

The police had left Stonewall a shambles. Jukeboxes, mirrors, and cigarette machines lay smashed; phones were ripped out; toilets were plugged up and overflowing; and shards of glass and debris littered the floors. (According to at least one account, moreover, the police had simply pocketed all the money from the jukeboxes, cigarette machines, cash register, and safe.) On the boarded-up front window that faced the street, anonymous protesters had scrawled signs and slogans — THEY INVADED OUR RIGHTS, THERE IS ALL COLLEGE BOYS AND GIRLS IN HERE, LEGALIZE GAY BARS, SUPPORT GAY POWER—and newly emboldened same-gender couples were seen holding hands as they anxiously conferred about the meaning of these uncommon new assertions...

Something like a carnival, an outsized block party, had gotten going by early evening in front of the Stonewall. While older, conservative chinos-and-sweater gays watched warily, and some disapprovingly, from the sidelines, "stars" from the previous night's confrontation reappeared to pose campily for photographs; hand-holding and kissing became endemic; cheerleaders led the crowd in shouts of "Gay power!"; and chorus lines repeatedly belted out refrains of "We are the girls from Stonewall."

But the cops, including Tactical Police Force units, were out in force, were not amused at the antics, and seemed grim-facedly determined not to have a repeat of Friday night's humiliation. The TPF lined up across the street from the Stonewall, visors in place, batons and shields at the ready. When the fearless chorus line of queens insisted on yet another refrain, kicking their heels high in the air, as if in direct defiance, the TPF moved forward, ferociously pushing their nightsticks into the ribs of anyone who didn't jump immediately out of their path.

But the crowd had grown too large to be easily cowed or controlled. Thousands of people were by now spilling over the sidewalks, including an indeterminate but sizable number of curious straights and a sprinkling of street people gleefully poised to join any kind of developing rampage. When the TPF tried to sweep people away from the front of the Stonewall, the crowd simply repeated the previous night's strategy of temporarily retreating down a side street and then doubling back on the police. In Craig's part of the crowd, the idea took hold of blocking off Christopher Street, preventing any vehicular traffic from coming through. When an occasional car did try to bulldoze its way in, the crowd quickly surrounded it, rocking it back and forth so vigorously that the occupants soon proved more than happy to be allowed to retreat...

But the cops needed no additional provocation; they had been determined from the beginning to quell the demonstration, and at whatever cost in bashed heads and shattered bones. Twice the police broke ranks and charged into the crowd, flailing wildly with their nightsticks; at least two men were clubbed to the ground. The sporadic skirmishing went on until four a.m., when the police finally withdrew their units from the area. The next day, *The New York Times* insisted that Saturday night was "less violent" than Friday (even while describing the crowd as "angrier"). Sylvia, too, considered the first night "the worst." But a number of others, including Craig, thought the second night was the more violent one; that it marked "a public assertion of real anger by gay people that was just electric."

When he got back to his apartment early Sunday morning, his anger and excitement still bubbling, Craig sat down and composed a one-page flyer. Speaking in the name of the Homophile Youth Movement (HYMN) that he had founded, Craig headlined the flyer GET THE MAFIA AND THE COPS OUT OF GAY BARS — a rallying cry that would have chilled Zucchi (who had earlier been reassured by co-owner Mario that the gays *only* had it in for the cops). Craig went on in the flyer to predict that the events of the previous two nights "will go down in history"; to accuse the police of colluding with the Mafia to prevent gay businesspeople from opening "decent gay bars with a healthy social atmosphere (as opposed to the hell-hole atmosphere of places typified by the Stonewall)"; to call on gay people to boycott places like the Stonewall ("The only way ... we can get criminal elements out of the gay bars is simply to make it unprofitable for them"); and to urge them to "write to Mayor Lindsay demanding a thorough investigation and effective action to end this intolerable situation."

Using his own money, Craig printed up thousands of the flyers and then set about organizing his two-person teams. He had them out on the streets leafleting passersby by midday on Sunday. They weren't alone. After the second night of rioting, it had become clear to many that a major upheaval, a kind of seismic shift, was at hand, and brisk activity was developing in several quarters.

But not all gays were pleased about the eruption at Stonewall. Those satisfied by, or at least habituated to, the status quo preferred to minimize or dismiss what was happening. Many wealthier gays, sunning at Fire Island or in the Hamptons for the weekend, either heard about the rioting and ignored it (as one of the later put it: "No one [at Fire Island Pines] mentioned Stonewall"), or caught up with the news belatedly. When they did, they tended to characterize the events at Stonewall as "regrettable," as the demented carryings-on of "stoned, tacky queens" — precisely those elements in the gay world from whom they had long since dissociated themselves. Coming back into the city on Sunday night, the beach set might have hastened off to see the nude stage show *Oh, Calcutta!* or the film *Midnight Cowboy* (in which Jon Voight played a Forty-second Street hustler) — titillated by such mainstream daring, while oblivious or scornful of the real-life counterparts being acted out before their averted eyes.

Indeed some older gays, and not just the wealthy ones, even sided with the police, praising them for the "restraint" they had shown in not employing more violence against the protesters. As one of the leaders of the West Side Discussion Group reportedly said, "How can we expect the police to allow us to congregate? Let's face it, we're criminals. You can't allow criminals to congregate." Others applauded what they called the "long-overdue" closing of what for years had been an unsightly "sleaze joint." There have even been tales that some of the customers at Julius', the bar down the street from Stonewall that had long been favored by older gays ("the good girls from the fifties," as one queen put it), actually held three of the rioters for the police...

The Mattachine Society had still another view. With its headquarters right down the street from the Stonewall Inn, Mattachine was in 1969 pretty much the creature of Dick Leitsch, who had considerable sympathy for New Left causes but none for challenges to his leadership. Randy Wicker, himself a pioneer activist and lately a critic of Leitsch, now joined forces with him to pronounce the events at Stonewall "horrible." Wicker's earlier activism had been fueled by the idea that gays were "jes' folks" — just like straights except for their sexual orientation — and the sight (in his words) "of screaming queens forming chorus lines and kicking went against everything that I wanted people to think about homosexuals ... that we were a bunch of drag queens in the Village acting disorderly and tacky and cheap." On Sunday those wandering by the Stonewall saw a new sign on its boarded-up façade, this one printed in neat block letters:

WE HOMOSEXUALS PLEAD WITH
OUR PEOPLE TO PLEASE HELP
MAINTAIN PEACEFUL AND QUIET
CONDUCT ON THE STREETS OF
THE VILLAGE — MATTACHINE

The streets that Sunday evening stayed comparatively quiet, dominated by what one observer called a "tense watchfulness"...

The police on Sunday night seemed spoiling for trouble. "Start something, faggot, just start something," one cop repeated over and over. "I'd like to break your ass wide open." (A brave young man purportedly yelled, "What a Freudian comment, officer!" — and then scampered to safety.) Two other cops, cruising in a police car, kept yelling obscenities at passersby, trying to start a fight, and a third, standing on the corner of Christopher Street and Waverly Place, kept swinging his nightstick and making nasty remarks about "faggots."

At one a.m. the TPF made a largely uncontested sweep of the area and the crowds melted away. [Poet] Allen Ginsberg strolled by, flashed the peace sign, and, after seeing "Gay Power!" scratched on the front of the Stonewall, expressed satisfaction to a *Village Voice* reporter: "We're one of the largest minorities in the country — 10 percent, you know. It's about time we did something to assert ourselves."

By Sunday some of the wreckage inside the bar had been cleaned up, and employees had been stationed out on the street to coax patrons back in: "We're honest businessmen here. We're American-born boys. We run a legitimate joint here. There ain't nuttin' bein' done wrong in dis place. Everybody come and see." Never having been inside the Stonewall, Ginsberg went in and briefly joined the handful of dancers. After emerging, he described the patrons as "beautiful — they've lost that wounded look that fags all had 10 years ago." Deputy Inspector Pine later echoed Ginsberg: "For those of us in public morals, things were completely changed ... suddenly they were not submissive anymore."...

[Another disturbance took place on Wednesday.] That proved the last of the Stonewall riots, but when it came time only two days later for the fifth annual picket of Independence Hall [in Philadelphia], the repercussions could be clearly measured...

The demonstration in front of Independence Hall began in much the same way it had in previous years: the group of some seventy-five people — men in suits and ties, women in dresses, despite the ninety-five-degree heat — walked silently in a circle, radiating respectability, eschewing any outward sign of anger. (Craig even kept his temper when a mean-looking man on the sidelines hissed "Suck!" in his face every time he passed by.) But the events at Stonewall had had their effect. After a half hour of marching quietly in single file, two of the women suddenly broke ranks and started to walk together, holding hands. Seeing them, Craig thought elatedly, "O-oh — that's *wonderful!*"

But Frank Kameny, the Washington, D.C., leader who had long considered himself to be in charge of the demonstration, had a quite different reaction. Back in 1966 Kameny hadn't hesitated in pulling a man from the line who had dared to appear without a jacket and wearing sneakers, and Kameny was not about to tolerate this latest infraction of his rule that the demonstration be "lawful, orderly, dignified." His face puffy with indignation and yelling, "None of that!

None of that!" Kameny came up behind the two women and angrily broke their hands apart.

Craig instantly hit the ceiling. When Kameny went over to talk to the two reporters who had turned up for the event (one from a Philadelphia paper and one from Reuters), Craig barged up to them and blurted out, "I've got a few things to say!" And what he said — in his own description, "ranting and raving" — was that the events in New York the previous week had shown that the current gay leadership was bankrupt, that gays were entitled to do whatever straights did in public — yes, wearing cool clothes in the heat, and, if they felt like it, holding hands too.

Kameny was furious at this unprecedented challenge to his authority; and, on different grounds, the veteran activists Barbara Gittings and Kay Tobin chided Craig for calling so much "personal attention" to himself. But, as had not been the case in previous years, many of those who had come down on the bus from New York were young people personally recruited by Craig at his bookstore. Some of them were students at NYU and, being much younger than Kameny or Gittings, had no prior movement affiliation (and no respect for what the homophile movement had accomplished). They had been energized by Stonewall, were impatient for further direct confrontation with oppressive traditions and habits — and vigorously applauded Craig's initiative.

All the way back on the bus, they argued with their recalcitrant elders for a new impetus, a new departure that would embody the defiant spirit of Stonewall. As the contention continued, it became clear to Craig that this would be the final Reminder [the name of the Philadelphia protest] — that a new day had dawned, which required different tactics, a different format. Yet it saddened him to think that a common enterprise of five years' standing would pass from the scene without any immediate replacement in sight. And then it came to him. Why shouldn't there be an immediate replacement? Didn't the events at Stonewall themselves require commemoration? Maybe the Annual Reminder simply ought to be moved to New York — but, unlike the Reminder, be designed not as a silent plea for rights but as an overt demand for them. Craig thought of a name right then and there: Christopher Street Liberation Day.

AFTERWORD

Craig Rodwell's dream of the Christopher Street Liberation Day was realized on Sunday, June 28, 1970. In what would become known as "Gay Pride Day," this first parade in New York drew 2,000 people, while simultaneous parades in Los Angeles, Chicago, and Boston drew smaller crowds. London and Paris joined the list the next year. Today, dozens of cities hold annual parades, ranging from smaller events attended by a few hundred to the half million each that attend the annual events in New York, Los Angeles, and San Francisco. Rodwell, unfortunately, died of stomach cancer in 1993, not living to see the Stonewall 25 Commemorative March that is expected to draw a million people to New York in 1994.[2]

QUESTIONS/ACTIVITIES

1. Numerous straightforward questions arise from the reading, including:
   - Why did the Stonewall exist? What was it like as a place to go?
   - Why would people go to a place like the Stonewall? What does this show us about the social conditions for gays at that time?
   - What conditions, both specific and general, existed the night of June 27 that made such a conflict more likely to happen?
   - What specific events seem to have caused the riot to break out?
   - What kind of reactions did gays have to the police violence, that night and afterwards?
   - Why did the police act the way they did, that night and subsequently?
   - Why did the conflict continue?
   - How did gays seem to view their oppression differently after Stonewall?

2. There is a tendency to view historical events as if fated to happen. This way of thinking is called "historical inevitability." Focusing on Jim, Craig, and Sylvia, examine the factors that caused them to be involved in the Stonewall Riots. How much of history is an accident? How much of what happened at Stonewall could have been expected, both for those three individuals and for the group as a whole? Were the events of late June 1969, "historically inevitable"?

3. Building on Question 2, rewrite accounts of the night of June 27, changing some of the circumstances or actions so that the outcome might have been different. Read these aloud in class. Are they

believable? Could Stonewall not have turned out the way it did, or not even have happened at all?

4. Imagine you are a historian. What problems did Duberman run into trying to reconstruct those nights? In particular, why is it so hard to pinpoint the exact event that caused the full-fledged violence to break out? How and why does he come to these conclusions? Do you agree with them? Are certain types or pieces of evidence better than others?

5. Write diary entries from the day after the first riot from the point of view of one of these people: a police officer; a gay person who fought the police; a Mattachine leader; and a gay person vacationing at Fire Island. How do you feel about these events and why?

6. What does Allen Ginsberg mean when he says, "They've lost that wounded look that fags all had 10 years ago?"

7. Imagine you are on the bus returning from the Independence Hall demonstration. Break into groups, having one represent the traditional Mattachine point of view (like Kameny and Gittings) and another the new attitude (represented by Rodwell), debating how gays should proceed in terms of tactics and strategy. How have things changed as a result of Stonewall?

PART 3

The Ongoing Struggle

Gays and Lesbians in the Eighties and Nineties

INTRODUCTION

Since the Stonewall Riots, the gay and lesbian movement has achieved a level of success that would astound its early leaders. Seemingly invisible in 1969, gays and lesbians were seemingly everywhere by 1993. Indeed, the gay community will commemorate the twenty-fifth anniversary of Stonewall with a march expected to draw up to one million people to New York City in June 1994. This event will coincide with the Gay Games, an international athletic competition with competition in dozens of events that will draw over 15,000 athletes — making it comparable in size to the Olympics. Much has changed in the quarter century since Stonewall.

The list of changes can go on and on. In 1973 the American Psychiatric Association declared that homosexuality was indeed not an "illness," removing a label that had haunted gays for a century. In 1974 a lesbian, Elaine Noble, became the first openly gay person elected to public office when she became a Massachusetts state representative. In 1983 Wisconsin became the first state to pass a law forbidding discrimination on the basis of sexual orientation. In the same year, Representative Gerry Studds became America's first openly gay congressman. And in 1993 hundreds of thousands of gay people marched on Washington for gay and lesbian rights in one of the largest demonstrations in American history. As of this writing in 1994, eight states (in alphabetical order, California, Connecticut, Hawaii, Maine, Massachusetts, Minnesota, New Jersey, and Vermont) and numerous municipalities have laws protecting gays from discrimination; many cities and corporations are beginning to grant "domestic partnership" status to gay couples, entitling them to the same benefits married heterosexual couples receive; over one hundred openly gay and lesbian people hold elective office in the United States; and openly gay artists have won such awards as the National Book Award, the Academy Award for Motion Pictures, and the Grammy Award, for their work. Abroad, gays can legally marry in Denmark and Norway, seek political asylum from homophobia in Canada, and are generals in the Dutch army. Gay rights have become a global phenomenon.

At the same time, the recent years have been times of struggle for gays as well. The AIDS crisis, while not unique to the gay community, has killed tens of thousands of gay men since the appearance of the disease in 1981, and will kill hundreds of thousands more thanks to the slowness of the United States government's response in the 1980s; anti-gay violence is so prevalent that the United States Department of Justice says that homosexuals are "probably the most frequent victims of hate crimes" in America; gay youth suicide has reached epidemic proportions, with a gay adolescent attempting suicide every thirty-five minutes, according to the United States Department of Health and Human Services; and the state of Colorado became the first state in the nation to ban laws protecting gays from discrimination after a 1992 ballot question passed, with numerous other states planning to take up this question in coming years. Gays can hardly feel safe in America today, and the day when safety will be assured is not in the near future.

The readings in this section introduce readers to some of the key issues of recent years. They provide a window into important battles, in the United States and abroad, that are yet to be resolved. As the adage goes, "History is not *was*— History *is*"— as this part of the book shows. Readers should look for echoes of old fights and see how, despite change, the times still resonate with the dilemmas faced by pioneers such as Ulrichs, Hirschfeld, and Hay decades and even a century ago.

CHAPTER 14

Changing Times, Changing Demands: A Collection of Manifestoes and Platforms, 1865–1993

INTRODUCTION

Organized efforts to win rights for gay and lesbian people have been going on for well over a century in the Western world. Thousands of groups have been founded and innumerable protests have been launched, all with specific aims in mind, stated in written form. These documents are invaluable to historians, for they provide insight into the motivations, concerns, and needs of the people involved in social change.

In this chapter, documents spanning the gay movement from 1865 to 1993 are included. Through these proclamations, we gain a better sense of how gay people were oppressed, what their goals were, and how they planned to achieve those goals. They offer us a window through which we can see the evolution of a people and their movement.

READING 14-A

Germany, 1865 — The Founding of an "Urning" Union

Editor's note: *In Germany in 1865, Karl Heinrich Ulrichs, an attorney, began one of the first documented efforts to better the status of gay people. An account of his early efforts, which included inventing a word — urning — to describe those who loved members of their own sex* (homosexual *wasn't coined until 1869), is offered in Chapter 7. Once he had defined the topic, Ulrichs began drawing up a structure for an organization to advance the rights of "Urnings" by writing the bylaws below:*

Bylaws for the Urning Union

2. Its goals are:

a. to bring Urnings out of their previous isolation and unite them into a compact mass bound together in solidarity.

b. to champion the inborn human rights of Urnings in opposition to public opinion and the agencies of the State, namely to vindicate their equality with Dionings [heterosexuals] before the law and in human society in general.

c. to found an Urning literature.

d. to further the publication of appropriate Urning writings...

e. to work for the goals of Urnings in the daily press.

f. to assist individual Urnings, who suffer because of their Urning nature, in every need and danger and, when possible, to also help them find a suitable livelihood.

[Ulrichs then wrote a series of demands to present to the Congress of German Jurists, a body charged with legal reforms. He put forth the following resolution for their consideration in a speech whose full story is told in Chapter 6:]

The Congress, as a pressing requirement of legal justice, resolves that the present German penal legislation concerning the so-called carnal violations is to be submitted immediately to a revision, and that in two directions:

I. that inborn love for persons of the male sex is to be punished under the same conditions, under which love for persons of the female sex are punished; that it is, therefore, to remain free of punishment, so long as:

neither rights are violated (through application or threat of force, misuse of prepubescent persons, the unconscious, etc.)

nor public offense is given;

II. that, however, the present, often thoroughly unclear requirements for "giving public offense by sexual acts" be replaced by such as preserve legal guarantees.[1]

READING 14-B

The Chicago Society for Human Rights, 1924

Editor's note: *Founded in 1924, the Society for Human Rights was the first organization devoted to gay rights in America. Media and* *legal harassment forced the Society to dissolve in 1925, however, so its impact was limited. Nevertheless, its records are historically valuable, as they show the beginnings of gay organizing in America.*

The society's charter of incorporation with the state of Illinois defined the following mission:

[The Society's goal is] to promote and to protect the interests of people who by reasons of mental and physical abnormalities are abused and hindered in the legal pursuit of happiness which is guaranteed them by the Declaration of Independence, and to combat the public prejudices against them by dissemination of facts according to modern science among intellectuals of mature age. The Society stands only for law and order; it is in harmony with any and all general laws insofar as they protect the rights of others, and does in no manner recommend any acts in violation of present laws nor advocate any matter inimical to the public welfare.[2]

[In 1962, the Society's founder, Henry Gerber, described its program thusly:]

1. We would cause the homosexuals to join our Society and gradually reach as large a number as possible.

2. We would engage in a series of lectures pointing out the attitude of society in relation to their own behavior and especially urging against the seduction of adolescents.

3. Through a publication named *Friendship and Freedom* we would keep the homophile world in touch with the progress of our efforts. The publication was to refrain from advocating sexual acts and would serve merely as a forum for discussion.

4. Through self-discipline, homophiles would win the confidence and assistance of legal authorities and legislators in understanding the problem; that these authorities should be educated on the futility and folly of long prison terms for those committing homosexual acts, etc.[3]

READING 14-C

The Daughters of Bilitis, 1956

Editor's note: *Founded in 1955, the Daughters of Bilitis was the first lesbian organization in the United States. A year later it began* *publishing* The Ladder, *the nation's first lesbian magazine, in October 1956. In stating its purpose in the first issue of* The Ladder, *DOB identified itself as*

a Women's Organization for the Purpose of Promoting the Integration of the Homosexual into Society [by:]

1. Education of the variant with particular emphasis on the psychological and sociological aspects, to enable her to understand herself and make her adjustment to society in all its social, civic, and economic implications by establishing and maintaining a library of both fiction and non-fiction on the sex deviant theme; by sponsoring public discussions on pertinent subjects to be conducted by leading members of the legal, psychiatric, religious and other professions; by advocating a mode of behavior and dress acceptable to society.

2. Education of the public through acceptance first of the individual, leading to a breakdown of erroneous conceptions, taboos, and prejudices; through public discussion meetings; through dissemination of educational literature on the homosexual theme.

3. Participation in research projects by duly authorized and responsible psychologists, sociologists, and other such experts directed towards further knowledge of the homosexual.

4. Investigation of the penal code as it pertains to the homosexual, proposal of changes to provide an equitable handling of cases involving this minority group, and promotion of these changes through the due process of law in the state legislatures.[4]

READING 14-D

1968 North American Council of Homophile Organizations

Editor's note: *The North American Council of Homophile Organizations was a nationwide organization pulling together the efforts of local homophile organizations, such as the Daughters of Bilitis and Mattachine, during the 1960s. Its annual Congresses were the first effort to organize a truly national gay movement. In August 1968, seventy-five delegates from forty organizations gathered in Chicago and adopted a "Bill of Rights" representing a national gay agenda. As quoted in the* New York Times *on August 19, 1968, the bill of rights included the following demands:*

•Private sex acts between consenting persons over the age of consent should not be offenses.

• Solicitation for any sexual act shall not be an offense except upon filing of a complaint by the aggrieved party, not a police officer or agent.

• A person's sexual orientation or practice shall not be a factor in the granting of Federal security clearance, visas and citizenship.

• Service in and discharge from the armed services, and eligibility for veterans' benefits, shall be without reference to homosexuality.

• A person's sexual orientation or practice shall not affect his eligibility for employment with Federal, state or local government.

The Times *went on to report that :*

Under "areas for immediate reform," the conference declared that the police should cease entrapment of homosexuals, not notify employers of those arrested for homosexual offenses, keep no files solely to identify homosexuals, and refrain from harassing business establishments catering to homosexuals.[5]

READING 14-E

The 1987 March on Washington for Gay and Lesbian Rights

Editor's note: *The first public protests for gay rights in America were held in 1965, when activist Frank Kameny led picketing outside federal offices in Washington to protest McCarthy-era restrictions on employment of gays.[6] The first large-scale national protest was on October 14, 1979, when gays organized the first March on Washington for Gay Rights. In what would become a regular feature of these marches, the numbers who attended were disputed: the federal Park Police claimed that 75,000 came, while organizers said that over 100,000 marched.[7]*

Outraged by the 1986 Supreme Court Bowers v. Hardwick *decision (see Chapter 15), activists called for a second March on Washington, which was held on October 11, 1987. This march, attended by anywhere from 200,000 (according to the Park Police) to 300,000 (according to organizers), was a much larger affair than the first.[8] In preparation for it, organizers put together a list of demands, which are listed below:*

1. The legal recognition of lesbian and gay relationships.
2. The repeal of all laws that make sodomy between consenting adults a crime.
3. A Presidential order banning anti-gay discrimination by the Federal government.
4. Passage of the Congressional lesbian and gay rights bill.
5. An end to discrimination against people with AIDS or those perceived to have AIDS.
6. A massive increase in funding for AIDS education, research, and patient care. Money for AIDS, not for war.
7. Reproductive freedom: The right to control our bodies, and an end to sexist oppression.
8. An end to racism in this country and apartheid in South Africa.[9]

READING 14-F

Platform of the 1993 March on Washington for Lesbian, Gay, and Bi Equal Rights and Liberation

Editor's note: *Held on April 25, 1993, the 1993 March on Washington for Lesbian, Gay, and Bi Equal Rights and Liberation was, according to some, the largest civil rights demonstration in American history. Estimates of the number who attended vary, from 300,000 by the federal Park Police to 1.1 million by the District of Columbia Police to 2 million according to some organizers.*[10] *Extensive negotiations by representatives from each region of the country resulted in the platform statement, listed below and distributed through the official program given out at the march.*

Action Statement Preamble to the Platform

The Lesbian, Gay, Bisexual and Transgender movement recognizes that our quest for social justice fundamentally links us to the struggles against racism and sexism, class bias, economic injustice and religious intolerance. We must realize if one of us is oppressed we all are oppressed. The diversity of our movement requires and compels us to stand in opposition to all forms of oppression that diminish the quality of life for all people. We will be vigilant in our determination to rid our movement and our society of all forms of oppression and exploitation, so that all of us can develop to our full human potential without regard to race, religion, sexual orientation/identification, identity, gender and gender expression, ability, age or class.

The March Demands

1. We demand passage of a Lesbian, Gay, Bisexual, and Transgender civil rights bill and an end to discrimination by state and federal governments including the military; repeal of all sodomy laws and other laws that criminalize private sexual expression between consenting adults.

2. We demand massive increase in funding for AIDS education, research, and patient care; universal access to health care including alternative therapies; and an end to sexism in medical research and health care.

3. We demand legislation to prevent discrimination against Lesbians, Gays, Bisexuals and Transgendered people in the areas of family diversity, custody, adoption and foster care and that the definition of family includes the full diversity of all family structures.

4. We demand full and equal inclusion of Lesbians, Gays, Bisexuals and Transgendered people in the educational system, and inclusion of Lesbian, Gay, Bisexual and Transgender studies in multicultural curricula.

5. We demand the right to reproductive freedom and choice, to control our own bodies, and an end to sexist discrimination.

6. We demand an end to racial and ethnic discrimination in all forms.

7. We demand an end to discrimination and violent oppression based on actual or perceived sexual orientation/identification, race, religion, identity, sex and gender expression, disability, age, class, AIDS/HIV infection.[11]

QUESTIONS/ACTIVITIES

1. Trace the history of a single demand from one of the early lists. Does it continue to reappear? If not, why not? You may need to do additional research to find out why the item does not repeat, if it does not.

2. Conversely, do new demands appear in later lists not found in earlier ones? Why do these new concerns appear? Additional research may also be needed.

3. How does language evolve? Look for key words that reappear, or words that evolve ("urning" to "homosexual" to "gay," for example). Why do these changes occur?

4. How do tactics change in different eras? Why?

5. What demands on the 1993 list will still be likely to appear if a march is held in 2003? Which ones might disappear? Why?

6. Imagine you are the author of an early list, and you time-travel to find one of the later readings. What would you as the person from the earlier time make of the later demand? Of the language, demands, and tactics employed?

7. Watch videos of the 1987 and 1993 marches to gain a sense of the feeling of the events (see footnotes for availability). Do the documents and the events seem to match in mood? What are the shortcomings of relying on written documents to recapture an event? Try to interview a person who attended one of these marches and ask them to recollect the event. How does his or her memory compare to the video or document?

CHAPTER 15

Bowers v. Hardwick and the "Right to Be Let Alone"

INTRODUCTION

Many Americans feel that what people do in the privacy of their own homes is their business. As the old saying goes, "A man's home is his castle," they argue: he should be free to do as he wishes there, as long as what he is doing hurts no one else. However, there is another train of thought in American history as well. Dating back to colonial times, governments have made laws that restrict what people can do in their homes, particularly with regard to sexual activity. A whole body of laws, called "sodomy laws," were instituted in colonial times, threatening individuals with penalties ranging up to death for engaging in certain sexual activities with other consenting adults. As of this writing in 1993, twenty-three states continue to have such laws, which often apply to both heterosexual and homosexual acts.

In the early 1980s, gay and lesbian activists decided to challenge the constitutionality of these laws in court, arguing that they violated the "right of privacy" to which citizens are entitled. A "test case" was launched, designed to result in a judicial decision declaring that all such state laws violated the "Supreme law of the land" (the federal Constitution). Journalist Randy Shilts describes the incident that triggered the case called *Bowers v. Hardwick*:

> The debate centered on a twenty-nine-year-old bartender named Michael Hardwick, arrested by Atlanta police on the night of August 2, 1982. The police officer had knocked on Hardwick's front door to serve a warrant for public intoxication; a house guest pointed the officer toward Hardwick's bedroom door. The policeman opened the door and saw Hardwick engaged in oral sex with another man. When the policeman said he was serving his warrant, Hardwick explained that he had already cleared the matter with the court and offered to show the officer his receipt. That no longer mattered, the policeman said, because he had found Hardwick engaging in a

violation of the Georgia law that banned oral and anal sex. Hardwick and his companion spent the next twelve hours in jail.[1]

The charges against Hardwick were later dropped by a county prosecutor. Seeing an ideal opportunity to challenge the constitutionality of the law itself, though, the American Civil Liberties Union worked with Hardwick to file a suit against the state. This suit challenged the right of the state to make such a law in the first place. Hardwick won his case at the 11th District Court of Appeals. Georgia attorney general Bowers then appealed to the Supreme Court for a final verdict on whether or not Georgia had the right to make such laws.

The Supreme Court heard the case in 1986. In a 5–4 vote, it upheld the constitutionality of "sodomy laws." As is the custom, one justice (in this case, Justice Byron White) was assigned to write the Court's "decision," explaining the views of the majority. Justices who oppose the decision have the right to write a "dissent" explaining their reasoning, written in this case by Justice Harry Blackmun. In both "opinions" (as they are called), the justices refer to specific Constitutional Amendments as well as the Georgia sodomy law itself. Key laws referred to in the case are listed in Reading 15-A. Justice White's decision is Reading 15-B, with a "concurring" (supporting) decision written by Chief Justice Warren Burger in Reading 15-C. The dissent by Judge Blackmun is Reading 15-D.

READING 15-A

Text of Important Laws Relating to the Case

Below are listed several clauses of the Constitution to which the justices refer in their decision, as well as the sodomy law of the state of Georgia:

First Amendment. Congress shall make no law respecting an establishment of religion, or prohibiting the free exercise thereof; or abridging the freedom of speech, or of the press; or the right of the people peaceably to assemble, and to petition government for a redress of grievances.

Fourth Amendment. The right of the people to be secure in their persons, houses, papers, and effects, against unreasonable searches and seizures, shall not be violated...

Ninth Amendment. The enumeration of certain rights shall not be construed to deny or disparage others retained by the people.

Fourteenth Amendment, Section I ["due process" clause]: All persons born or naturalized in the United States, and subject to the jurisdiction thereof, are citizens of the United States and of the state wherein they reside. No state shall make or enforce any law which shall abridge the privileges or immunities of citizens of the United States, nor shall any state deprive any person of life, liberty, or property without due process of law, nor deny to any person within its jurisdiction equal protection of the laws.

Ga. 16-6-2 [Georgia sodomy law]: "A person commits the offense of sodomy when he performs or submits to any sexual act involving the sex organs of one person and the mouth or anus of another."

READING 15-B

Majority Opinion, by Justice Byron White

In August 1982, respondent Hardwick (hereinafter respondent) was charged with violating the Georgia statute criminalizing sodomy by committing that act with another adult male in the bedroom of respondent 's home. After a preliminary hearing, the District Attorney decided not to present the matter to the grand jury unless further evidence developed [that is, the charges were dropped].

Respondent then brought suit in the Federal District Court, challenging the constitutionality of the statute insofar as it criminalized consensual sodomy. He asserted that he was a practicing homosexual, that the Georgia sodomy statute, as administered by the defendants, placed him in imminent danger of arrest, and that the statue for several reasons violates the Federal Constitution...

...[The Federal District Court] went on to hold that the Georgia statute violated respondent's [Hardwick's] fundamental rights because his homosexual activity is a private and intimate association that is beyond the reach of state regulation by reason of the Ninth Amendment and the Due Process Clause of the Fourteenth Amendment ... We agree with petitioner [the state of Georgia] that the Court of Appeals erred, and hence reverse its judgment.

This case does not require a judgment on whether laws against sodomy between consenting adults in general, or between homosexuals in particular, are wise or desirable. It raises no question about the right or propriety of state legislative decisions to repeal their laws that criminalize homosexual sodomy, or of state-court decisions invalidating those laws on state constitutional grounds. The issue presented is whether the Federal Constitution confers a fundamental right upon homosexuals to engage in sodomy and hence invalidates the laws of the many States that still make such conduct illegal and have done so for a very long time...

We first register our disagreement with the Court of Appeals and with respondent [Hardwick] that the Court's prior cases have construed the Constitution to confer a right of privacy that extends to homosexual sodomy and for all intents and purposes have decided this case ... [W]e think it evident that none of the rights announced in those cases bears any resemblance to the claimed constitutional right of homosexuals to engage in acts of sodomy that is asserted in this case. No connection between family, marriage, or procreation on the one hand and homosexual activity on the other has been demonstrated, either by the Court of Appeals or by respondent [Hardwick]...

Precedent aside, however, respondent [Hardwick] would have us announce, as the Court of Appeals did, a fundamental right to engage in homosexual sodomy. This we are quite unwilling to do. It is true that despite the language of the Due Process Clauses of the Fifth and Fourteenth Amendments, which appears to focus only on the processes by which life, liberty, or property is taken, the cases are legion in which those Clauses have been interpreted to have substantive content ... recognizing rights that have little or no textual support in the constitutional language...

...[However] the Court has sought to identify the nature of the rights qualifying for heightened judicial protection. In *Palko* v. *Connecticut* ... (1937), it was said that this category includes those fundamental liberties that are "implicit in the concept of ordered liberty," such that "neither liberty nor justice would exist if [they] were sacrificed." A different description of fundamental liberties appeared in *Moore* v. *East Cleveland* ... (1977) ..., where they are characterized as those liberties that are "deeply rooted in this Nation's history and tradition."...

It is obvious to us that neither of these formulations would extend a fundamental right to homosexuals to engage in acts of consensual sodomy. Proscriptions against that conduct have ancient roots ... Sodomy was a criminal offense at common law and was forbidden by the laws of the original 13 States when they ratified the Bill of Rights. In 1868, when the Fourteenth Amendment was ratified, all but 5 of the 37 States in the Union had criminal sodomy laws. In fact, until 1961, all 50 States outlawed sodomy, and today, 24 States and the District of Columbia continue to provide criminal penalties for sodomy performed in private and between consenting adults ... Against this background, to claim that a right to engage in such conduct is "deeply rooted in this Nation's history and tradition" or "implicit in the concept of ordered liberty" is, at best, facetious.

Nor are we inclined to take a more expansive view of our authority to discover new fundamental rights imbedded in the Due Process Clause. The Court is most vulnerable and comes nearest to illegitimacy when it deals with judge-made constitutional law having little or no [re]cognizable roots in the language or design of the Constitution ... There should be, therefore, great resistance to expand the substantive reach of those Clauses, particularly if it requires redefining the category of rights deemed to be fundamental. Otherwise, the Judiciary necessarily takes to itself further authority to govern the country without express constitutional authority. The claimed right pressed on us today falls far short of overcoming this resistance.

Respondent [Hardwick], however, asserts that the result should be different where the homosexual conduct occurs in the privacy of the home. He relies on *Stanley* v. *Georgia* ... (1969), where the Court held that the First Amendment prevents conviction for possessing and reading obscene material in the privacy of one's home: "If the First Amendment means anything, it means that a State has no business telling a man, sitting alone in his house, what books he may read or what films he may watch."...

Stanley did protect conduct that would not have been protected outside the home, and it partially prevented the enforcement of state obscenity laws; but the decision was firmly grounded in the First Amendment. The right pressed upon us here has no similar support in the text of the Constitution, and it does not qualify for recognition under the prevailing principles for construing the Fourteenth Amendment. Its limits are also difficult to discern. Plainly enough, otherwise illegal conduct is not always immunized whenever it occurs in the home. Victimless crimes, such as the possession and use of illegal drugs, do not escape the law where they are committed at home. *Stanley* itself recognized that its holding [judgment] offered no protection for the possession in the home of drugs, firearms, or stolen goods ... And if respondent's [Hardwick's] submission is limited to the voluntary sexual conduct between consenting adults, it would be difficult ... to limit the claimed right to homosexual conduct while leaving exposed to prosecution adultery, incest, and other sexual crimes even though they are committed in the home. We are unwilling to start down that road.

Even if the conduct at issue here is not a fundamental right, respondent [Hardwick] asserts that there must be a rational basis for the law and that there is none in this case other than the presumed belief of a majority of the electorate in Georgia that homosexual sodomy is immoral and unacceptable. This is said to be an inadequate rationale to support the law. The law, however, is constantly based on notions of morality, and if all laws representing essentially moral choices are to be invalidated under the Due Process Clause, the courts will be very busy indeed. Even respondent [Hardwick] makes no such claim, but insists that majority sentiments about the morality of homosexuality should be declared inadequate. We do not agree, and are unpersuaded that the sodomy laws of some 25 States should be invalidated on this basis.

Accordingly, the judgment of the Court of Appeals is *Reversed.*

READING 15-C

Concurring Opinion by Chief Justice Warren Burger

I join the Court's opinion, but I write separately to underscore my view that in constitutional terms there is no such thing as a fundamental right to commit homosexual sodomy.

As the Court notes ... the proscriptions against sodomy have very "ancient roots." Decisions of individuals relating to homosexual conduct have been subject to state intervention throughout the history of Western civilization. Condemnation of those practices is firmly rooted in Judaeo-Christian moral and ethical standards. Homosexual sodomy was a capital crime under Roman law ... During the English Reformation when powers of the ecclesiastical courts were transferred to the King's Courts, the first English statute criminalizing sodomy was passed. Blackstone described "the infamous *crime against nature*" as an offense of "deeper malignity" than rape, a heinous act "the very mention of which is a disgrace to human nature," and a "crime not fit to be named."... The common law of England, including its prohibition of sodomy, became the received law of Georgia and the other Colonies. In 1816 the Georgia Legislature passed the statute at issue here, and that statute has been continuously in force in one form or another since that time. To hold that the act of homosexual sodomy is somehow protected as a fundamental right would be to cast aside millennia of moral teaching.

This is essentially not a question of personal "preferences" but rather of the legislative authority of the State. I find nothing in the Constitution depriving a State of the power to enact the statute challenged here.

READING 15-D

Dissent by Justice Harry Blackmun

JUSTICE BLACKMUN, with whom JUSTICE BRENNAN, JUSTICE MARSHALL, and JUSTICE STEVENS join, dissenting.

...[T]his case is about "the most comprehensive of rights and the right most valued by civilized men," namely, "the right to be let alone."

The statute at issue, Ga. Code Ann. § 16-6-2 (1984), denies individuals the right to decide for themselves whether to engage in particular forms of private, consensual sexual activity. The Court concludes that § 16-6-2 is valid essentially because "the laws of ... many States ... still make such conduct illegal and have done so for a very long time."... Like Justice Holmes, I believe that "[i]t is revolting to have no better reason for a rule of law than that it was laid down in the time of Henry IV. It is still more revolting if the grounds upon which it was laid down have vanished long since, and the rule simply persists from blind imitation of the past."... I believe we must analyze respondent Hardwick's claim in the light of the values that underlie the constitutional right to privacy. If that right means anything, it means that, before Georgia can prosecute its citizens for making choices about the most intimate aspects of their lives, it must do more than assert that the choice they have made is an " 'abominable crime not fit to be named among Christians.' "

I

... A fair reading of the statute and of the complaint clearly reveals that the majority has distorted the question [that] this case presents.

First, the Court's almost obsessive focus on homosexual activity is particularly hard to justify in light of the broad language that Georgia has used. Unlike the Court, the Georgia Legislature has not proceeded on the assumption that homosexuals are so different from other citizens that their lives may be controlled in a way that would not be tolerated if it limited the choices of those other citizens ... The sex or status of the persons who engage in the act is irrelevant as a matter of state law. In fact, to the extent that I can discern a legislative purpose for Georgia's 1968 enactment of § 16-6-2, that purpose seems to have been to broaden the coverage of the law to reach heterosexual as well as homosexual activity. I therefore see no basis for the Court's decision ... to defend § 16-6-2 solely on the grounds that it prohibits homosexual activity. Michael Hardwick's standing may rest in significant part on Georgia's apparent willingness to enforce against homosexuals a law it seems not to have any desire to enforce against heterosexuals ... But his claim that § 16-6-2 involves an unconstitutional intrusion into his privacy and his right of intimate association does not depend in any way on his sexual orientation...

II

"Our cases long have recognized that the Constitution embodies a promise that a certain private sphere of individual liberty will be kept largely beyond the reach of government." *Thornburgh* v. *American College of Obstetricians & Gynecologists* ... (1986). In construing the right to privacy, the Court has proceeded along two somewhat distinct, albeit complementary, lines. First, it has recognized a privacy interest with reference to certain *decisions* that are properly for the individual to make ... Second, it has recognized a privacy interest with reference to certain *places* without regard for the particular activities in which the individuals who occupy them are engaged...

A

The Court concludes today that none of our prior cases dealing with various decisions that individuals are entitled to make free of governmental interference "bears any resemblance to the claimed constitutional right of homosexuals to engage in acts of sodomy that is asserted in this case."... [T]he Court's conclusion ... ignores the warning in *Moore* v. *East Cleveland* ... (1977) ... against "clos[ing] our eyes to the basic reasons why certain rights associated with the family have been accorded shelter under the Fourteenth Amendment's Due Process Clause." We protect those rights not because they contribute, in some direct and material way, to the general public welfare, but because they form so central a part of an individual's life. "[T]he concept of privacy embodies the 'moral fact that a person belongs to himself and not others nor to society as a whole.' " *Thornburgh* v. *American College of Obstetricians & Gynecologists* ... (1977). And so we protect the decision whether to marry precisely because marriage "is an association that promotes a way of life, not causes; a harmony in living, not political faiths; a bilateral loyalty, not commercial or social projects." *Griswold* v. *Connecticut* ... We protect the decision whether to have a child because parenthood alters so dramatically an individual's self-definition, not because of demographic considerations or the Bible's command to be fruitful and multiply ... And we protect the family because it contributes so powerfully to the happiness of individuals, not because of a preference for stereotypical households ... The Court recognized in *Roberts* ... that the "ability independently to define one's identity that is central to any concept of liberty" cannot truly be exercised in a vacuum; we all depend on the "emotional enrichment from close ties with others."...

Only the most willful blindness could obscure the fact that sexual intimacy is "a sensitive, key relationship of human existence, central to family life, community welfare, and the development of human personality," *Paris Adult Theater I* v. *Slaton* ... (1973) ... The fact that individuals define themselves in a significant way through their intimate sexual relationships with others suggests, in a Nation as diverse as ours, that there may be many "right" ways of conducting those relationships, and that much of the richness of a relationship will come from the freedom that an individual has to *choose* the form and nature of these intensely personal bonds...

In a variety of circumstances we have recognized that a necessary corollary of giving individuals freedom to choose how to conduct their lives is acceptance of the fact that different individuals will make different choices. For example, in holding that the clearly important state interest in public education should give way to a competing claim by the Amish to the effect that extended formal schooling threatened their way of life, the Court declared: "There can be no assumption that today's majority is 'right' and [that] the Amish and others like them are 'wrong.' A way of life that is odd or even erratic but interferes with no rights or interests of others is not to be condemned because it is different." *Wisconsin* v. *Yoder* ... (1972). The Court claims that its decision today merely refuses to recognize a fundamental right to engage in homosexual sodomy; what the Court really has refused to recognize is the fundamental interest all individuals have in controlling the nature of their intimate associations with others.

B

The behavior for which Hardwick faces prosecution occurred in his own home, a place to which the Fourth Amendment attaches special significance ... [O]ur understanding of the contours of the right to privacy depends on "reference to a 'place,' " *Katz* v. *United States...*, "the essence of a Fourth Amendment violation is 'not the breaking of [a person's] doors, and the rummaging of his drawers,' but rather is 'the invasion of his indefeasible right of personal security, personal liberty, and private property.' " *California* v. *Ciraolo* ... (1986)..., quoting *Boyd.* v. *United States* ... (1886)...

..."The right of the people to be secure in their ... houses," expressly guaranteed by the Fourth Amendment, is perhaps the most "textual" of the various constitutional provisions that inform our understanding of the right to privacy, and thus I cannot agree with the Court's statement that "[t]he right pressed upon us here has no ... support in the text of the Constitution"... Indeed, the right of an individual to conduct intimate relationships in the intimacy of his or her own home seems to me to be the heart of the Constitution's protection of privacy.

III

...It is precisely because the issue raised by this case touches the heart of what makes individuals what they are that we should be especially sensitive to the rights of those whose choices upset the majority.

The assertion that "traditional Judeo-Christian values proscribe" the conduct involved ... cannot provide an adequate justification for

§ 16-6-2. That certain, but by no means all, religious groups condemn the behavior at issue gives the State no license to impose their judgments on the entire citizenry. The legitimacy of secular legislation depends instead on whether the State can advance some justification for its law beyond its conformity to religious doctrine ... Thus, far from buttressing his case, petitioner's [the state of Georgia's] invocation of Leviticus, Romans, St. Thomas Aquinas, and sodomy's heretical status during the Middle Ages undermines his suggestion that § 16-6-2 represents a legitimate use of secular coercive power. A State can no more punish private behavior because of religious intolerance than it can punish such behavior because of racial animus. "The Constitution cannot control prejudices, but neither can it tolerate them." *Palmore* v. *Sidotti* ... (1984). No matter how uncomfortable a certain group may make the majority of this Court, we have held that "[m]ere public intolerance or animosity cannot constitutionally justify the deprivation of a person's physical liberty." *O'Connor v. Donaldson* ... (1975)...

Nor can § 16-6-2 be justified as a "morally neutral" exercise of Georgia's power to "protect the public environment," *Paris Adult Theater I* ... Certainly, some private behavior can affect the fabric of society as a whole. Reasonable people may differ about whether particular sexual acts are moral or immoral, but "we have ample evidence for believing that people will not abandon morality, will think any better of murder, cruelty and dishonesty, merely because some private sexual practice which they abominate is not punished by the law."...

This case involves no real interference with the rights of others, for the mere knowledge that other individuals do not adhere to one's value system cannot be ... an interest that can justify invading the houses, hearts, and minds of citizens who choose to live their lives differently.

IV

...I can only hope that here, too, the Court will soon reconsider its analysis and conclude that depriving individuals of the right to choose for themselves how to conduct their intimate relationships poses a far greater threat to the values most deeply rooted in our Nation's history than tolerance of nonconformity could ever do. Because I think the Court today betrays those values, I dissent.

IMPORTANT TERMS

sodomy laws
right of privacy
constitutionality
test case
"due process" clause

QUESTIONS/ACTIVITIES

1. Look closely at the documents in Reading 15-A. Remember that the Constitution automatically overrules any state law that conflicts with its principles. Does the Georgia law violate a constitutional principle, in your opinion? This is *not* asking whether or not you like the law: the question is, is the law *constitutional?*

2. Look at the specific circumstances concerning Michael Hardwick's arrest. Does this arrest itself seem constitutional, in light of Reading 15-A? Were his rights respected, in your opinion?

3. Justices White and Blackmun present the two very different interpretations of the case. Outline those views by answering the following questions:

- What does each justice say is the central issue in the case?
- Why does he say this is the central issue?
- Why does he rule the way he does, in light of this issue?
- What are the reasons for his ruling in this manner?

4. After answering #3, return to Reading 15-A and render *your* ruling on which justice seems to be closer in his reasoning to the principles set forth in the Constitution. Write a letter to the justice with whom you disagree, explaining why you feel his interpretation is wrong.

5. How does Justice Burger justify his views on sodomy? How does Justice Blackmun answer this argument?

6. Divide the class in two and debate the case. Another way to do this is to have nine students role-play the justices, researching what they can find out about the justice to whom they are assigned and using this knowledge to explain his or her vote.

7. Write letters to the editor detailing your personal reaction to the Court's decision.

8. Draw up lists of activities within the home that you feel the government has no right to intervene in, and activities in which you think it may intervene. Compile lists on the board. Explain your

reasoning and ask others to give feedback. How far should the government be able to go in regulating citizens' private lives? You might also want to research whether or not these activities are legal. Are there any surprises in what you discover?

9. Research earlier Supreme Court decisions that were later viewed negatively. These may include: *Dred Scot v. Sanford; Plessy v. Ferguson; Schenk v. the United States;* and *Korematsu v. the United States*. Do written or oral presentations on the circumstances of a case, the decision of the Court, and why it was later viewed as a mistake. Will *Bowers* one day join this list?

10. Read excerpts of Bob Woodward's *The Brethren* to gain an understanding of the workings of the Supreme Court in this time period, for either extra credit or for class.

CHAPTER 16

"Gays around the Globe": Portraits of Lesbian and Gay Life in Other Nations

INTRODUCTION

While the bulk of this reader has focused on the United States, it is important to remember that gay and lesbian people are found in every nation. The United States is neither the best place to be gay, nor the worst. Take the example of the military: many Western nations have policies far more accepting of gays than America does. Nations like Norway and Denmark have legalized gay marriage, and the European Community officially discourages discrimination on the basis of sexual orientation in its member states.

In many countries, though, gays are invisible or persecuted. States such as Iran still enforce the death penalty for homosexuality, and few nations outside Europe ban anti-gay discrimination. In many nations, there is still a long way to go before a visible, secure gay community emerges.[1]

The readings in this chapter introduce us to the range of experiences gays have in nations around the globe. In Reading 16-A, journalist Neil Miller gives us a portrait of Denmark, the first country to legalize gay marriage and perhaps the most pro-gay state in the world. In Reading 16-B, journalist Lena Sun looks at the conditions for gays in China. In Reading 16-C, the first article is by an Indian studying in America, writing under the pseudonym "Kim," who gives his views on the status of gays in his country. A second article gives the perspective of two Indian lesbians still residing in their homeland. Finally, in Reading 16-D, a Muslim college student of Pakistani descent in speaks of the stresses involved in his "dual identity" as a Muslim and a gay man. These divergent viewpoints give us a sense of how homosexuality is treated in four very different cultures.

READING 16-A

Gay Marriage in Denmark

from *Out in the World: Gay and Lesbian Life from Buenos Aries to Bangkok,* by Neil Miller

The Bryllupsalon, or "wedding chamber," located on the second floor of the heap of turn-of-the-century brick that is Copenhagen's town hall, is a particularly beautiful room — all low vaulted ceilings and graceful Romanesque arches. The walls are covered with murals, primitive in style, that depict various Danish folktales and ballads. The murals depict a world where forests are deep green and skies a deeper blue, where the women are golden-haired and wear long dresses and the men are clad in tunics with swords on their belts. The erotic is suggested only obliquely. In one mural, the groom combs the locks of the bride's hair; in another, a family surrounds a canopied wedding bed; in still another, a young woman is transformed into a bird of fabulous plumage. The decor would be trite — a Scandinavian version of a New Age greeting card — if it didn't have such a mysterious quality, if the colors weren't so vivid, the mood so consistent.

Vibeka Nissen was married in the Bryllupsalon — twice. On the first occasion, twenty years ago, she married a man. The second time, four months before my visit to Copenhagen, she pledged herself to Inge-Lise Paulsen, her partner of seven years.

As of October 1989, Denmark became the first country in the world to give legal recognition to same-sex partnerships. Since then, more than eight hundred lesbian and gay couples have married in Copenhagen's Radhaus and in other town halls throughout the country.

In Copenhagen, where many people don't get married in church these days, civil marriages take place in the Bryllupsalon. On Tuesday and Thursday mornings, heterosexual marriages are scheduled at ten o'clock; gay and lesbian partnerships follow promptly at eleven. Straight and gay couples fill out the same forms. The same phraseology is used when they take their vows; solemn words about the importance of "mutual affection and tolerance" and of "living together in a harmonious way." After the ceremony, the newlyweds and their friends and relatives gather on the outdoor steps that front on the Town Hall Square, amidst confetti and the popping of champagne corks and the clinking of glasses.

In Denmark, the equivalence between heterosexual marriage and same-sex partnership goes beyond the ceremonial. Registered gay and lesbian couples have the same legal rights as married couples with respect to taxes, inheritance, insurance, and pension benefits. They have the same responsibilities, as well — to support the other economically, if need be, for instance. To receive a divorce, homosexual partners have to go through the same process as heterosexual couples do: They must either claim their spouse was unfaithful, in which case a divorce can be obtained immediately, or they must wait six months. (As of January 1, 1991, only seven lesbian and gay couples out of 718 registered at the time had applied for divorce.) Even the bigamy laws apply equally to married heterosexuals and to same-sex partners: Straight or gay, the penalty is three to six years in prison.

In most of the world, all this might sound like the fulfillment of everything for which lesbians and gays have been struggling. But, instead of rejoicing about their recent marriage, Vibeka and Inge-Lise couldn't stop apologizing.

Vibeka blamed their banker. "We have this socialist bank—" Vibeka explained.

"Anarchist bank," interjected Inge-Lise.

"Anarchist bank, okay," continued Vibeka. "Whenever we'd ask anything about our finances, the banker would say, 'It's not possible what you ask. Why don't you two marry?' And we'd just scream, 'We don't like marriage!' "

Inge-Lise elaborated, "It happened several times. He would say, 'It would be much easier if you married.' And then the idea grew. It became something possible to do. I don't know what happened. I still don't know why we did it. In philosophical or political terms, I don't believe marriage is a very good idea."

Inge-Lise and Vibeka had bought an apartment together. That was the problem.

The apartment, which was located in a pleasant suburban neighborhood of red brick houses with peaked roofs, was spacious and airy. There were polished floors, jade and rubber trees, a violin on a stand with sheet music open to "Ragtime Annie," and a FREE TIBET sign on a door. It was tasteful, comfortable — worth marrying for, one might say...

They prided themselves on being flexible and being independent, and now they had bought this apartment together and gotten married.

"You see, if I die," Vibeka explained, "Inge-Lise couldn't stay in this apartment if we weren't married. Because she doesn't own my part. My family would come and take everything, and the law would come here and take everything." Denmark has some of the highest inheritance taxes in the world, as high as eighty percent in cases where you wanted to leave property or money to someone who wasn't a blood relative or legal spouse. Ironically, a law had been passed in 1986 — before same-sex marriage had been approved — that exempted gay and lesbian cohabiting couples from these taxes. But now, with the legalization of partnerships and the equality of straight and gay relationships in the eyes of the law, that special exemption had been abolished. If you didn't register your partnership, your lover risked losing your share of the property. The effect of the new legal situation was to make it almost impossible for gay couples *not* to marry.

Another incentive was the matter of pensions. Vibeka had a private pension from the time when she worked as a government employee; but, as long as she remained unmarried and had living relatives, she wasn't allowed to sign it over to anyone else. Now, with the legalization of gay and lesbian partnerships, Inge-Lise could have the pension should Vibeka die.

"One of the reasons behind my decision to marry is my age," said Vibeka. "I never used to think about saving for my old age. But I am forty-four. Now I can imagine that I can get sick and things like that." The demographics of lesbian and gay partnerships indicated this was a factor for many people. Most of the couples who registered under the new law were in their forties and fifties...

But what Inge-Lise and Vibeka — and many Danish lesbians and gays — most disliked about the new law was that it stated categorically that registered same-sex partners could not adopt children — not even the biological child of the other partner. That was a compromise agreed to by the lesbian and gay organization, LBL, Landsforeningen for Bosser og Lesbiske, to ensure passage of the law. Other concessions included a statement that the law did not authorize church weddings for same-sex partners and that one member of a registered couple had to be a Danish citizen. "It was a typical Danish compromise," said Vibeka disparagingly. "Society says it is okay to be a lesbian but we are too dirty to be around kids. So we're still not okay."...

One of the odd things about same-sex partnerships in Denmark is that, because no other country recognizes such arrangements, once you leave the country you are in effect no longer married. At Easter, shortly after their marriage, Vibeka and Inge-Lise went on a trip to England. As they were walking down a London street holding hands, they began to worry about antigay laws recently enacted by the Tory government. Did these laws apply to public displays of affection? "I said to Inge-Lise, 'They can't arrest us, because we're married,'" recalled Vibeka. "And Inge-Lise answered, 'No, we're not married. We're in England. We're not married.'"

"There are funny problems," said Inge-Lise. "What happens if you move to another country? When they get older, Danish heterosexual couples sometimes move to southern Spain. What happens to gay couples in that case? Suppose you work for Danish Railways? Does your spouse get free tickets? And what happens if the train crosses the border?"

By now, Vibeka and Inge-Lise were warming to their subject. They had to admit how remarkable it was that little Denmark had actually come up with this trailblazing law. At the time the partnership bill was being debated, a Gallup poll showed that sixty-four percent of the Danish public supported it. Increasingly, Inge-Lise noted, lesbians and gays from other countries wanted to come to Denmark to marry. "Gay men from the Soviet Union write to LBL all the time," she said. "They want to use Denmark as a refuge by marrying. They think it is easy. But if you are not a Danish citizen, you have to live with the person you marry for two years. The government actually comes and checks you out. To many people from abroad, that is what Denmark is like — you find someone and you get married and your problems are solved."...

It was easy to lose sight of how much had changed in Denmark. When the LBL was started back in 1948 in the northern city of Alborg, its founder, Axel Axgil, had been practically run out of town. He lost his job and apartment. One afternoon in Copenhagen, I went to visit Axel and his spouse, Eigil Axgil. They had had the honor of being the first couple to be married under the new partnership law.

Axel and Eigil had been a couple for forty-one years. "We've been engaged for forty years and married for one and a half," they joked. They had taken the same surname — a combination of their first names — way back in 1958. The day after they married, on October 1, 1989, a Swiss newspaper printed a picture of them sitting in a carriage in front of Copenhagen Town Hall, giving one another a kiss. In the photo, Axel and Eigil were both wearing suits, with carnations in their buttonholes. The headline said, ROMEO AND JULIO.

They remembered the good times and the bad: the first LBL meeting in Copenhagen in 1948, attended by some two hundred people, after Axel had fled Alborg; how they first met, at a party, two years later; serving time in prison in 1957 in a pornography scandal; the passage of what gays called the "ugly law" in the early 1960s, which banned homosexual prostitution and could land you in jail if you so much as gave another man a cigarette or bus fare home following a sexual encounter. And after all that, many years later, the passage of the antidiscrimination law, the partnership law, their own marriage.

For lesbians and gays, Denmark today was a very different country than it had been in 1948 or 1968 — or even 1988 — and much of that had to do with the efforts of Axel and Eigil. "So many things have happened," they said. "The young people just have no idea."...

By the 1980s, the controversies of the past had been forgotten ... Today, they were heroes, role models for young lesbians and gays. When Axel turned seventy, the LBL held a month-long tribute to him, with lectures, parties, and other events. The organization wanted the Danish government to give the Axgils a medal. Axel and Eigil showed me a letter they received shortly after their wedding, from two gay German medical students. The letter was addressed simply "Axel and Eigil Axgil, Copenhagen, Denmark." Even the post office knew who they were.

Ironically, the partnership law had hurt the Axgils financially. Unlike Inge-Lise and Vibeka, they were actually losing money as a consequence — some twenty thousand kroner (a little more than three thousand dollars) a year. A married couple received less money in government old-age benefits than two single people did. But the Axgils still had savings from the sale of their hotel and could absorb the financial loss. "It's no problem," said Eigil.

The enactment of the law after all those years had been "fantastic, proof that we weren't discriminated against any longer," according to Axel. "Danish society has changed very much. But people worked very hard to make it happen." Yet today they were a little disillusioned with Danish gay politics. The LBL no longer had a vision, they felt. Now that the organization had achieved its goal, it didn't know what to do next. "Nothing much has happened since the passage of the partnership law," Axel said. "We are saying to each other that we should fight for adoption rights — but next year. We should do it now!"

Whatever one thought about lesbian and gay marriage as a thing in itself, it had played a major role in the transformation of Denmark's gay community. Eventually, the inequalities that Danish gays had had to accept to achieve passage of the partnership law would be overturned. As Inge-Lise had put it, "The people who have fought for this, have fought for it not because they necessarily believe in marriage. They believe in equality. Even if they felt marriage was a bad thing, they would fight for it anyway because the others should have this right. That is the main point. The equality point."

The week before, Axel had given a speech about issues facing gays and lesbians to a Copenhagen Rotary Club luncheon. Eigil accompanied him. Rotary Club members, a group of businessmen not exactly known for progressive social views, open each meeting with a song. The week Axel and Eigil were their guests, the members got up and sang a Danish hymn that is traditionally performed at church weddings. Its name was "Det Er Sa Yndigt At Folges Ad": "How Lovely It Is to Be Together." Axel and Eigil stood at the front, facing the audience and glowing. They had triumphed.

READING 16-B

Gays in China

articles from the *Washington Post* (Nov. 4, 1992)

"Gay Millions: China's Silent Minority
Despite Official Denials, Many Lead Secret Lives"
by Lena H. Sun

BEIJING — For years, the tall, good-looking social scientist dated a succession of girlfriends. Each time, he hoped she would be the right woman to help him hide his dark secret. But each time, he found he had no real interest in her.

Then came the Chinese army crackdown in 1989, which changed his outlook forever. As he was fleeing Tiananmen Square that night, he narrowly escaped being shot by Chinese soldiers.

"I thought, 'I could have been killed. Why should I live with this mask? Even if this is not what people like, this is what I am, this is my way of life,'" he recalled with a bitter smile.

The 38-year-old man is a homosexual, a member of a community shunned by most Chinese. In few places in the world does a person with a deviant lifestyle face greater pressure than in China. In a country of communist controls and Confucian morals, homosexuals are considered immoral, abnormal objects of disgust and ridicule.

To keep their secrets, many Chinese homosexuals must lead double lives — marrying and even having children, because to have no heir is, within Chinese culture, a major affront to one's own parents.

They must hide their sexual preference from spouses and families. If found out, they risk their jobs, their housing, their Communist Party membership, and become social pariahs. Shame of discovery has driven some to suicide, others to leave the country. One gay couple from China last month became the first homosexuals to be granted asylum in Australia based on sexual preference.

At the same time, homosexuals in China, one of the world's most repressive countries, have a surprising degree of freedom. Officially, authorities deny that homosexuality exists, which may be why China has no laws or regulations on it.

As a result, most Chinese have virtually no awareness of homosexuals, although at least 2 percent of China's 1.13 billion population — more than 20 million people — are believed to be gay or lesbian. Chinese do not talk about "same-sex love," as homosexuality is called. It is rarely mentioned in the official media.

That general ignorance and the gray area in the law make China "a paradise for gays" in some ways, said one 31-year-old office worker, whose apartment has become a regular gathering place for gays to talk about their troubles.

The lives of homosexuals offer an unusual window into the pressures and values of a society grappling with the social consequences of more than a decade of economic reform and increased contact with the outside world.

Like the rest of the world, China is slowly waking up to its burgeoning AIDS problem. Although infection levels here are statistically low, they are rising fast, forcing officials to give some attention to homosexuality. This summer, for the first time, AIDS prevention workers in Beijing started distributing "safe sex" pamphlets to homosexuals in a downtown park. The city's new AIDS hotline has been flooded with calls from homosexuals.

Even the official media have begun reporting on homosexuals as normal people rather than as psychiatric cases.

Earlier this year, police in a small town in central China's Anhui province finally gave up trying to put a lesbian couple on trial, the Shanghai *Evening News* reported. After transferring the case to Beijing's Ministry of State Security, local officials were told to leave the women alone because there were no laws covering their alleged offenses.

"This society should not overlook such a large portion of the people," said Li Yinghe, a U.S.-trained Beijing University sociologist, who has written a book on the subject with her husband.

Chinese sociologists and homosexuals say the gay community spans all classes and all ages. In general, homosexuals tend to be better educated than the average Chinese, according to a study conducted recently in the city of Nanjing. Homosexuality exists in the countryside, in Buddhist temples and even in the military.

"The military doesn't know how to deal with it," said sociologist Li.

Much more seems to be known about male homosexuals than lesbians, who tend to guard their privacy more closely. Shanghai sexologist Liu Dalin recently finished a major survey of 254 homosexuals in six major cities. He said a researcher had to approach one lesbian — a woman who had married to protect herself from gossip — five times before she was willing to talk to his associates. Liu's survey found that more than 60 percent of the homosexuals had been married.

China has no gay bars or discos, and privacy in most homes is nonexistent. But homosexuals say every Chinese city has certain parks, public toilets and bathhouses where they meet. In some cases, these are also places where they have sex.

In Shanghai, one well-known pickup place is a long, glass-encased newspaper billboard not far from the famous riverfront known as the Bund. One recent night, two men had a rendezvous in a dark alley after completing an elaborate ritual of subtle hand and body signals at the billboard. No words were exchanged. To the causal observer, the scene looked like nothing more than two men, leaning close together, reading a newspaper.

Beijing has several parks where homosexuals meet. One in particular, in downtown Beijing, is known all over China as well as to foreigners as a gathering place. There, young men sit in clusters on the park benches near the men's toilet. Some wear tight jeans and spotless white sneakers. Some wear diamond studs in their ears or gold rings on their fingers. Sometimes there is a hint of eye-liner. One young man had a perm and one lock of hair tinted orange-red, matching his orange jacket and his orange and white polka-dot shirt.

"I just want to find someone who can understand me," said one man, 31, ducking his head shyly. "It is hard to find someone I can talk to about this deepest, darkest secret."

Certainly for China, homosexuality is nothing new.

Chinese literature is full of references to homosexuality dating as far back as the Yellow Emperor, about 46 centuries ago.

One of the most famous stories is about Han Dynasty emperor Ai Di (6 B.C. to 1 A.D.), whose male lover often slept in the imperial bed. Once, when the two were taking a nap, the emperor awoke to find the long sleeve of his gown caught under his sleeping lover. Instead of waking him, the emperor extricated himself by cutting his sleeve from the gown. Since then, the Chinese term for "cut sleeve" has been synonymous with homosexuality. [See Chapter 3]

Much later, during the Ming and Qing dynasties, merchants and aristocrats kept servant boys not only for household duties but to satisfy their sexual desires.

The great classical Chinese novel of the mid-18th century, "The Dream of the Red Chamber," describes homosexual affairs in great detail. Today, a modern novel that glorifies homosexual affairs among Qing dynasty court officials and opera singers is a best-seller in many cities.

Even as late as the 1930s, British novelist Christopher Isherwood described how male customers of Shanghai bathhouses were erotically washed and massaged by young Chinese men.

But under the Communists, the atmosphere became much different. There is no gay-bashing, but there are also no advocacy groups. Basic knowledge is virtually nonexistent.

Police and court officials are clearly aware of homosexual activity in public parks, but often leave them alone unless someone wants to press charges. The crime is almost always "hooliganism," but sentences can be as stiff as seven or eight years in jail.

Many doctors still consider homosexuality a mental illness. Although hospitals no longer use electric shock therapy as a treatment, many still inject homosexuals brought in by police with powerful drugs to induce vomiting in hopes of discouraging erotic thoughts.

Because there is so little information about homosexuality, several men interviewed said they did not realize they were homosexual until they were seduced by others, even though they knew early on they were different.

Shanghai sexologist Liu says Chinese homosexuals tend to be less sexually active than their counterparts in the West. In his survey, only 35 percent of homosexuals said they had sex with their partners.

In Beijing, the man with the tinted hair, 24, a private entrepreneur, said he only had sex three times a month because he is so busy. Like others interviewed, he said he uses condoms, but is afraid of getting AIDS.

By far his biggest fear, however, is being discovered.

"If you are caught, it will be all over," he said. "You can't work, you can't face your parents, the police will tell the neighborhood committee and then the whole neighborhood will know. Then you can't live there anymore."

The pressure becomes particularly intense by the time an individual approaches marriage age — 24 for women and 27 to 28 for men. The social scientist said he was so desperate that he considered marrying a lesbian.

Homosexuals "are forced to get married, have children and live with spouses they don't love," said Wan Yanhai, who runs the AIDS hotline in Beijing.

Marriage brings practical benefits. If an individual does not get married, it is much more difficult to get housing, enter the Communist Party and get promoted.

For some homosexuals, the growing awareness and fear of AIDS is making them more willing to demand better treatment from society.

"I'm not brave enough to tell the government how I think about gays," said a social scientist at Beijing University who is gay. "I do not want to expose myself."

"But the Chinese government cannot ignore the existence of gays. They should be more realistic, give more advice to gay people, encourage them to have safe sex, like in the West," he said. "I'm a human being too."

"One Man's Story: 'What We Just Did, Is This Homosexuality?' " by Lena H. Sun

BEIJING — It was during his second year in college that he had his first sexual encounter with another man. One day during rehearsal, the tenor in his barbershop quartet lunged at him.

"All of a sudden, he hugged me," recalled the man, now 31 and an office worker in a joint venture company. "I was excited, but I was also uncomfortable, and pushed him away."

That classmate became his first lover. Only then did the office worker realize he was a homosexual.

"We were lying on the bed, and I asked him, 'What we just did, is this homosexuality?' And he said, 'What do you ... think you are anyway?' Then I thought, how can I become like this?"

Later, after he read his partner's love letters to another man, he realized he, too, wanted to find such a relationship.

"I burst into tears, I felt so unfulfilled," he said. "This was a kind of self-affirmation. I was so emotional, I jumped into the bathtub and poured a basin of cold water over myself."

Like many other homosexuals here, he never told his parents or siblings about his sexual orientation because of the deep social taboos against homosexuality.

But two years ago, he became seriously involved with another man. Because the office worker was sharing the family's extra apartment with his sister, he was afraid he and his lover would be discovered. One night he told his sister, who became so upset she blurted his secret to their parents immediately.

"It was like a bomb had exploded in my family," he recalled.

For more than a week, his family members railed against homosexuality. His father, a military academy instructor, warned he would turn into a dirty old man who would sodomize young boys. His mother sobbed that it was all her fault for leaving the family for a higher-paying job in the southern city of Shenzhen.

"I knew something was wrong that night when I walked into the house," he recalled. "My mother started hugging me and saying she didn't want money anymore, she only wanted her son back."

Over the next few days, his mother flip-flopped on the issue. One day she would promise wedding rings and a new quilt for her son and his partner. The next day, she would forbid them to have relations and urge him to have a thorough medical checkup in the hospital.

Finally, over a period of months, his parents gave up and agreed not to interfere with the lifestyle of their only son.

He does not plan on getting married, and he wants to become more involved in gay rights. He knows he is lucky to have such support from his family.

"Now I feel more free because my mom and dad accept me," he said. His parents can even joke about it.

"When we changed apartments, my father said, 'We shouldn't put those two refrigerators together — they might become gay.'"

READING 16-C

South Asians Lesbians and Gays

from *A Lotus of Another Color: An Unfolding of the South Asian Gay and Lesbian Experience,* edited by Rakesh Ratti

"They Aren't That Primitive Back Home" by Kim

I would love to get back home to the gay scene in India and get away from the clinical isolation of the U.S. scene. Even gay Indians settled in the U.S. are surprised that there is a massive, vibrant, and exciting gay scene in India, primarily in metropolises like Bombay, Delhi, Madras, Calcutta, and Bangalore. Of course I speak of the scene as it prevailed over a year ago — I have been in the U.S. for over a year and a half now. I have stayed in regular contact with my friends back home, however, and the scene in India seems to have progressed and developed even more.

I had been actively gay in India since 1980, when I first returned home from engineering college. No, I did not turn gay, nor was I coerced into being gay at my hostel. That history runs further into my past, but I shall not delve into that now; that subject deserves an entire book! When I say "gay," I refer to open cruising and attending gay parties. I have had gay experiences and encounters both before and after "coming to terms with my gayness."

India lives up to the theory of 10 percent, underscores it, validates it emphatically, and, I should say, stretches it more than a wee bit. In India there are gays everywhere, just as it is in the U.S. They don't simply shop and commute, they cruise unabashedly in ways that would make an American bathhouse seem demure and conservative ... I could go on and give you a detailed list of where all you could unearth pink triangles on the Indian subcontinent.

To begin with, there are no rules ... At one level, "gays don't exist"; "homosexuality is a social and psychological aberration"; "homosexuality is a Western phenomenon." Indian men are "real men," and the ones who sit on the fence, if they exist, are *hijras* [transvestites or transsexuals]. This is, fortunately and unfortunately, the broad opinion held by the masses and, surprisingly, by many of the intellectuals.

The prevalence of this opinion is unfortunate because enlightenment could bring with it a certain broadening of outlook that would possibly benefit Indian gays. On the other hand, we gays are not bothered too much by the world around us, because straights tend to dismiss our existence or deem us as being inconsequential. Without being militant like American gays, we manage to live a life of unbridled joy and virtual bliss. So what if we don't have gay churches, gay bars, and a score of societies and magazines in India? We don't draw undue attention to ourselves, for with attention come rednecks, homophobia, and everything else that gays do not want in the first place.

Now, now, I can see you falling off your seats, livid. I can hear you saying, "Something needs to be done for our poor brethren out there"; "This is outrageous"; "You mean that gays have no rights and are persecuted." Before we start casting value judgments, picketing, and dragging out all the other cute props of expressing one's political awareness, let's hit the brakes. For once, let's not impose our templates of what a blissful society should be on those halfway around the world. Let us endeavor to become aware of the situation there, try our utmost to comprehend how affairs evolved to their current point, and give consideration to the thought that maybe the gays in India are actually better off than we are!...

In the Indian cities mentioned earlier, and to a certain extent in other cities, towns, and villages, there are not hundreds but thousands of gays. One only needs to do a bit of math to work out that for a country of nearly a billion people a conservative gay estimate of 10 percent would amount to a whopping 100,000,000 people!...

India has no gay movement and perhaps never will. There are no gay magazines; perhaps they don't need them. There are no gay bars *per se;* again, perhaps they are not necessary...

When I was in Bombay, we used to have gay parties each month; often one had a choice of three or four parties on a Saturday. People kept their networks alive this way ... When we felt the need to have a gay bar or two, we converted a few straight bars. We accomplished this by simply spreading the word. Each Saturday, for instance, we would meet after nine at Amigo or Gokul's. Soon the straights would stop visiting these bars. The owners would be only too pleased, for their revenues would actually skyrocket ... In fact, I met my lover, whom I was with for two years, at one such bar I had converted...

There are instances of gay bashing; groups of straights may suddenly appear in public toilets frequented by gays and beat them up. The incidents are few and far between and they tend to make gays cautious, but they never serve to dampen their spirit. Police also engage in such sweeps, but only with the intent of extorting money through intimidation. Hardly anyone gets arrested, though being caught partaking in homosexual activity is illegal...

...[Indian] policymakers are prudes. Kissing is taboo on the Indian screen, and pornography is banned. But that in no way limits the attitudes of the people. Unlike China and the Far East, where people are loathe to show affection in public, Indians are usually rather permissive. Gays are not chastised or socially ostracized. They may not be praised, but neither are they outcast. It is a fact of life that people have grown to live with. However, people (gay and straight) are confused about homosexuality. Ignorance is so prevalent that gay men are often classified as *hijras,* the rationale being that they must want to be women...

I am not trying to imply in this article that any one system is better than any other. I am merely trying to compare and contrast the gay scenes of India and the United States. I am urging you to comprehend the differing scenarios and take each for what it is. There is a world of joy in savoring the cuisine of each country, but try to serve a Big Mac with curry, and you get more than just indigestion.

"Breaking Silence": an interview by Sharmeen Islam

Dupitara Chowdhury and Nandini Datta are two lesbians living and loving together in Bombay. The following interview is excerpted from a longer article published previously.

SHARMEEN: How did you come to know you were gay and to accept yourself?

NANDINI: Looking back at my childhood, I can make connections to my homosexual feelings. I grew up among girls; we used to get physically very close on picnics or day trips, but I didn't know about homosexuality. Not until I went to college and started reading about it. I read and supported progressive discussions of literature about gay rights, but I was scared to probe my personal feelings. However, when I got involved in the left political scene in India, I started developing strong feelings toward a woman "comrade." I was courting my future husband at the time, but the feelings couldn't compare. My comrade and I worked together in the trade union and we spent a lot of time together. We were subjected to a lot of laughs about out constant intimacy. We ourselves cracked jokes!

SHARMEEN: You mean you cracked jokes about being lesbians?

NANDINI: Yes. But we thought it was safe, since [lesbianism] was a "distant, Western phenomenon." Later she married another activist. After her wedding, I was very disheartened. I went off to Sri Lanka and had several unsatisfactory affairs with men. When I came back to India, I knew I had to have a female companion. So, I started to look for a mate who would share my children, my household, and my life with me. And that's how Dupitara came into my life!

DUPITARA: And here I am! My past is very similar as far as close bonds with women are concerned. I come from a conservative Muslim family in the village. The concept of an alternate sexuality or lifestyle is unheard of! I mean, people accept women being with other women — as long as it is not in a sexual context...

All my life I've been close to other women. But, I think it's only lesbians who are free to touch other women freely and in places they would like to touch. Every other woman is scared out of her mind...

I met an Indian lesbian who lives in the States. Then I met another who lives in New Delhi; she gave me a lot of strength. Our feminist friends were very hostile toward Nandini and me. They didn't say much to Nandini, but I was young and vulnerable. They advised me to leave the relationship, to stay away from her. Despite their efforts, we survived and became closer!...

[Now] we are hearing of many lesbians who are not urban, middle class. Recently, two nurses hung themselves because they loved each other and would not be married off. In another village, two women registered their union as a "marriage of friendship," called *Maitrikarar.*

SHARMEEN: Tell me about *Maitrikarar.*

NANDINI: For women, the whole thing started with the two policewomen in Bhopal. It struck the minds of lesbians throughout the country. Two primary school teachers from Gujarat registered their union as *Maitrikarar. Maitrikarar* is an old, heterosexual concept used by businessmen to wed their mistresses in order to give them some commitment.

SHARMEEN: Is sex between people of the same gender punishable by law?

NANDINI: Homosexuality between men is defined in terms of penetration and it is punishable by ten years [incarceration]. But, when they wrote the laws, they didn't even think of homosexuality between women. That's why the police tried and failed to indict the female police officers on a ten-year sentence for being homosexual.

SHARMEEN: It's amazing that lesbianism is not punishable! Moreover, it's okay for two women to marry each other under *Maitrikarar.*

NANDINI: In Bhopal, the homophobic tank commander said that marriage is all about sex and those two women couldn't possibly have a "real" marriage. But the police commissioner said that marriage is a union between two souls — and the soul has no gender! In the midst of this confusion, people of the same gender are fortunately being allowed to celebrate some sort of a union.

However, the system is very conscious of refusing to legalize, institutionalize, and give social acceptance to lesbian and gay people.

DUPITARA: Actually, there is extensive evidence of lesbian sexuality before the British Victorian culture came to India. When I told my aunt of the Bhopal marriage, she shrugged her shoulders and said it's quite normal. Recently, we got to know about a lesbian couple working as prostitutes. When one of them came down with AIDS and died, her lover spent her life savings on her funeral and grave site...

NANDINI: You see, women in India need to be independent, allowed to earn their own livelihood, set up their own households; only then can they explore their sexuality. Otherwise, they never have the strength to come out of the closet. How can they?

SHARMEEN: Is the number of single, young working women increasing at all? If not, what can be done to encourage women to be independent and to come out of the closet?

NANDINI: Only in urban areas are women living independently. A lot of these women have high education and well-paying jobs. They are only a handful. I think if women can develop themselves, if they can take charge of their lives, other things would fall into place.

SHARMEEN: What is the hardest part about being gay at this time in your lives?

DUPITARA: I think the fact that I'm not married. You see, Nandini was married and has two kids. Nobody bothers her about remarriage. But, most people question why a young woman like me is living with another woman with children. And why am I unmarried? I think the hardest part is that I can't tell anyone I'm a lesbian. Everywhere I go, people ask why I am not married, who is my boyfriend. It is humiliating and disempowering. I cannot share any of my happiness or problems with them. It's like I am two different people. Another complication is that I am Muslim. Nobody understands why I am living with a Hindu woman, away from my family.

NANDINI: I feel I'm in a slightly different position than Dupitara. I have come out to people at work. I really don't have many problems being a lesbian here. People are more willing to accept me because

I have been married and have two children. I never give a het [heterosexual] image to my family and friends. They come to my household as it is. In a way, I don't care too much for acceptance. I think a little distance from my family is good. Sometimes, though, I'm scared that when I die, my house, children, and everything will go to my ex-husband.

DUPITARA: I also think I miss having a community. Sometimes, I feel we are not growing because we have nobody except each other in our relationship. No one to go and talk to safely.

NANDINI: The Trikone chapter [in Patna, Bihar] and the lesbian marriage both took place in economically depressed regions of India. I think that, ultimately, the revolution will spread from rural India. I think one day we will be free.

READING 16-D

The Islamic World: "My Own Private Islam"

by "Yusuf al-Hallaj"

"Yusuf al-Hallaj" is a pseudonym, drawn from the name of a Sufi Muslim killed for "apostasy," or betrayal of his fellow Muslims.

As I write this article, the majority of my one billion fellow Muslims are fasting from dawn to dusk in this, the holy month of Ramadan. In the past, I have fasted myself and have felt an extraordinary sense of self-purification as well as a strangely transcendent identification with Muslims all over the world. But as I question certain precepts of orthodox Islam, my commitment to fasting has dwindled. Today, the fourth day of the ninth month of the 1413th year of Islam, I will indulge in three square meals, and I will not feel guilty, for a very simple reason: I am gay, and my religion, or more particularly, my co-religionists, say that I have sinned, and not only will I be punished in the afterlife, but I should be punished in this world too — lashing, imprisonment, or death, depending on the discretion of the state ruler, in accordance with Islamic law. I feel no compulsion to identify, transcendently or otherwise, with my fellow Muslims, my brothers and sisters who would condemn me for loving a man.

Islam's condemnation of homosexuality has not precluded homosexuality in Islamic societies, past or present. Iran in particular has had a long history of male-male sex and love (less is known about lesbianism in Muslim nations). Nineteenth-century Egypt saw European travellers visiting not just to see the Pyramids and the Nile, but to look for pretty Egyptian boys, too. Sufism, a mystical branch of Islam, has a history of tolerance of homosexuality, and in Pakistan there is a province where they say all the men are fags, a stereotype not entirely devoid of factual basis. Needless to say, gays and lesbians "out of the closet" are today unheard of in Muslim countries. In places like these, closets are for clothes, and then some.

To be a Muslim in the U.S., irrespective of sexuality, is to confront a daily assault of ignorance with respect to Islam. In the media, in the classroom, and in people's minds persist some of the most inaccurate and utterly stupid notions of Islam. I often feel like Islam's most ardent defender, a religious vanguard writing to newspapers with tallies of the number of times they have used "Muslim" and "fundamentalist" and "extremist" and "terrorist" interchangeably in a given week; correcting professors on the meaning of the word "jihad"; explaining why *Aladdin* is grossly offensive. I sometimes forget that the majority of the people I am defending would think me an abomination if they knew about my orientation, and would even want me killed. As harsh as the world is to Islam, Muslims are by and large ten times more so toward gays and lesbians. These are my people.

Of course, I am Islam's strongest critic as well, or more precisely, I am among the strongest critics of Muslims, particularly those who start every other sentence with "The Quran says..." or "The Prophet said..." In general, I know better than they what the Quran says, or what the Prophet did; the dissident always knows the history of his or her people better than do others, if only by necessity. And yet, these are dangerous times. Too harsh a criticism of a Muslim is often taken as an attack on Islam, and one need only recall the furor provoked by Salman Rushdie to realize the peril in this.

For most, coming out of the closet is difficult enough without the threat of religiously sanctioned bodily harm. I greet my fellow Muslim with the same hand with which I caress my lover, but they will never know it. Nor will they ever know the joy I feel or the love that I share with my man. For my part, I will never know what it is to be accepted by the only community I have ever really known.

There is a profound cowardice inherent in my closeted way of life, but ultimately I am more comfortable defending Islam than myself. Rushdie is not the only one driven into hiding by Islam.

QUESTIONS/ACTIVITIES

1. Write a one-sentence thesis statement for each nation addressed, summarizing the experience of being gay there based on the evidence you have read.

2. In looking at Reading 16-A, what practical reasons would a gay couple have for getting married? List as many benefits as possible that the Danish couples gained by having this right.

3. Inge-Lise and Vibeka actually express some reservations about marriage, and Axel and Eigil suffered financial losses because of their decision to marry. Why, then, did they support the law? What does Inge-Lise mean when she says, "Even if they felt marriage was a bad thing, they would fight for it anyway, because the others should have this right. That is the main point"? Why is marriage "the main point," to many, for gay liberation?

4. In China, what pressures exist for gay people? List as many examples as you can from the readings, then classify them: are they "heterosexist" or "homophobic" pressures?

5. How do gays in China cope with these pressures? Be specific.

6. Why is there new awareness of gays in China? Cite as many reasons as you can discover in the reading for this growing awareness.

7. In Reading 16-C, Kim writes, "Let us give consideration to the thought that maybe the gays in India are actually better off than we are." What evidence does he present for this point of view? Do you agree with his conclusion?

8. Does the picture of gay life in India presented by Nandini and Dupitara agree with that drawn by Kim? Where are their views the same? Where are they different? Why? What factors might account for their differences?

9. Nandini says, "You see, women in India need to be independent, allowed to earn their own livelihood, set up their own households

... Otherwise, they will never have the strength to come out of the closet." Why does she cite these factors as prerequisites for "gay liberation"? Are there other conditions you see in these readings that are necessary for a "gay community" to emerge?

10. For many gays and lesbians, the stresses of a "dual identity" — which means belonging not only to the gay community but also to another identifiable "minority" — create other issues. Such stress is intensified when that minority is intolerant toward gays. How is this stress shown in Reading 16-D? Why is Yusuf drawn to Islam? Why is he repelled by it? How does he resolve this conflict?

11. Imagine that you are one of the following people: Inge-Lise, Vibeka, Axel, Eigil, the unnamed Chinese man (in the article "What We Just Did, Is This Homosexuality?"), Kim, Nandini, Dupitara, or Yusuf. Role-play a meeting between them in class, where each talks about their nation's attitudes about gays and then discuss their differences together.

12. Interview a recent immigrant from one of the countries discussed in this chapter, asking them about attitudes toward gays in their homeland.

13. Research a country about which you are curious but which is not addressed in this chapter. Resources for information might include: that nation's embassy; the United Nations; Amnesty International; and the International Gay and Lesbian Human Rights Commission, in San Francisco.

CHAPTER 17

Gay and Lesbian Youth: Voices from the Next Generation

INTRODUCTION

Like all movements, the gay and lesbian movement changes when the "torch" is passed from one generation to the next. The generation coming of age in the 1990s, benefiting from the work of those who came before, is one where "coming out" is happening at a younger and younger age. Previous generations had little access to information about gay people; today's gay youth are much more likely to hear news stories, see films, or read books that depict openly gay people and their concerns. In turn, these gay youth have often become activists in their own right, building a series of community-based support groups across the nation, founding in-school groups such as "Gay-Straight Alliances" and Project 10, and supporting political initiatives like the Massachusetts Governor's Commission on Gay and Lesbian Youth, the nation's first statewide body charged with improving the lives of gay youth. For older lesbians and gay men, watching gay and lesbian adolescents speaking out on television and at rallies, fighting for their rights in schools, and going to the prom with same-sex dates reveals a generation gap of truly immense proportions, as such actions were simply inconceivable even a decade ago.

Despite these hopeful signs, however, being a gay or lesbian youth is still hard. What makes gay and lesbian youth different from other traditional "minority" groups (such as Jews, African-Americans, or Latinos) is that they do not grow up with people like themselves. The products of heterosexual families in the vast majority of cases, most lesbian and gay youth come from communities where few lesbian or gay adults are visible, attend schools with no openly gay staff, and belong to friendship groups where "fag" is the favored insult and "that's so gay" is a common put-down. According to Professor James Sears of the University of South Carolina, the average student realizes his or her sexual orientation at age thirteen.[1] For a straight student, many avenues of support — family, friends, school, and community — exist to help with any difficulties that arise. By contrast, gay students rarely feel able to ask their families, friends, schools, or communities to help them out, fearing the possible response they might get. Many of the above-cited efforts to make things better have taken place in urban centers, far from where many youth live, meaning that progress is yet to be felt in the lives of many gay adolescents. Often feeling completely isolated, these gay and lesbian youth still face difficult lives.

Some statistics make a little clearer the difficulties gay youth face:

1. Violence. According to the U.S. Department of Justice, "Homosexuals are probably the most frequent victims" of hate crimes, which are crimes directed against people because they belong to a certain group (racial, ethnic, etc.).[2] Lesbian and gay youth are hardly immune to this society-wide phenomenon: a survey by the National Gay and Lesbian Task Force found that 45 percent of gay men and 25 percent of lesbians reported being harassed or attacked in high school because they were perceived to be lesbian or gay.[3]

2. Verbal Abuse. It comes as no surprise to any teenager that gay and lesbian students are often subjected to verbal abuse. Comments like "fag," "dyke," and "that's so gay" are used so regularly in high schools (often even by teachers) that few even notice such hateful language as being anything out of the ordinary. According to a survey conducted by the Massachusetts Governor's Commission on Gay and Lesbian Youth, 97 percent of students at one suburban high school had heard homophobic language used in school.[4] Another Commission survey found that 43 percent of students said they heard such language "often," 51 percent "sometimes," and only 6 percent said "never."[5] Finally, 53 percent of the students surveyed said they had heard teachers use such language.[6] Few teachers sympathetic to gay youth feel able to intervene to stop such harassment for, as one teacher put it, "Most teachers, gay or straight, are afraid to speak up when they hear homophobic remarks. They're afraid people might say, 'What are you, gay?,' which remains a frightening question in today's climate."[7]

3. Homelessness. Many families react badly when they find out one of their children is lesbian or gay. A University of Minnesota study found that 26 percent of young gay men reported being forced to leave home because of conflict over their being gay.[8]

4. Substance Abuse. Under such stress, many gay and lesbian youth turn to alcohol or other drugs to escape from their problems. The University of Minnesota study found that 58 percent of the young gay men surveyed could be classified as having a substance abuse disorder.[9]

5. High Drop-out Rates. The United States Department of Health and Human Services found that 28 percent of gay youth drop out of high school altogether, usually to escape the harassment, violence, and alienation they face at school.[10]

6. Suicide. Often, young gay men and lesbians feel so hopeless that ending their lives seems like the only solution to their problems. According to the United States Department of Health and Human Services, gay and lesbian youth are two to three times more likely to *attempt* suicide than heterosexual youth (with 500,000 suicide attempts in the United States annually). Up to 30 percent of *successful* teen suicides each year are by lesbian or gay teens (1500 out of a total of 5000 deaths). Using the Department's statistics, this means that a gay or lesbian youth tries to kill him- or herself every thirty-five minutes in the United States, and that a gay or lesbian youth succeeds in killing him- or herself every six hours.[11]

These statistics are frightening and point out how hard it can be to grow up gay in the United States today. However, statistics are a poor substitute for actual stories that show how a real person copes with these stresses. The readings in this chapter are all writings by gay youth. They give readers a feeling for the range of experiences people have — everything from triumphing over oppression to suicide. It is important to remember that, while gay youth do face many problems, the majority of them do survive and overcome the obstacles they face to become healthy adults. The readings below give a "personal" view on the abstract forces we have discussed above.

READING 17-A

Chris Muther

Testimony before the Massachusetts Governor's
Commission on Gay and Lesbian Youth, Nov. 18, 1992

My name in Chris Muther. I'm twenty-three and a reporter in Greenfield, Massachusetts, and I'd like to read a column that I wrote for the paper I work for.

"When my mother told me about a piece of mail that arrived two weeks ago, my heart sank into my stomach. It was the invitation to my five-year high school reunion. It's not that I dread seeing the members of the Athol High School Class of 1987; it's the memory that the reunion brings and a date that I made five years ago for the upcoming August reunion.

"When I think about my years in high school one person who immediately comes to mind is my friend Richard. Richard and I met in junior high and quickly became friends. We had a lot in common. We were both shy, tall for our age, and more interested in being different than trying to be like everybody else, something that anyone who has ever been a teenager knows can be pretty traumatic. This became even more apparent as we entered high school. We were shunned by many of our classmates for being, as many saw us, just plain weird. In a fit of small-town teenage rebellion, Richard and I were out to shock all those around us. At first it was subtle. We liked different kinds of music. We tried to dress like the rock stars we saw on MTV.

"We were also picked on. We were called queer and faggot and a host of other homophobic slurs. We were also used as punching bags by our classmates just for being different, something that sent us into further isolation. Many times we had only each other and our small group of friends to rely upon. Because we thought we had nothing more to lose, we got even weirder by our peers' standards. Richard dyed his light brown hair jet black while I experimented with blue, red, and green. I came to know his family almost as well as my own. I went to the senior prom with his sister and he came on vacation with my family to Maine. Every Christmas I would go to his grandmother's house with the rest of the family to exchange gifts. When we'd go to concerts, our mothers would go out to eat and go shopping while they waited for the concert to get over with.

"Through the church youth group that we were both members of, we went to New York City and Montreal. Although most people outside of his immediate family and our group of friends really didn't know him, Richard was always making people laugh and the two of us were always up to something, usually no good. To the outside world we were shy and withdrawn, but when we were together we were usually getting into trouble.

"Eventually Richard and I made it through Athol High School. At our graduation, we made a date. Since most everyone in our class picked on us for being gay, as a joke we would go as each other's date to the reunion and give our classmates a real shock.

"The longer we were out of high school, the more our reliance on each other decreased. He went to Mount Wachusett Community College in Gardner, and I ended up in Amherst at the University of Massachusetts. I was finally living away from Athol and enjoying life in the U-Mass dormitories. Richard was still living in Athol and struggling with his sexuality.

"Just when it seemed he was beginning to accept himself as a gay man, he hit rock bottom. At the time we were both twenty and Richard would frequently come to U-Mass for concerts and to visit. But when he arrived that night in November 1989 there was something different about him. He wasn't glad or joking to be in Amherst like he usually was when he came to visit me. He was quiet and there was no spark in his eyes. When I asked him what was wrong, he simply shook his head. Eventually, with tears in his eyes, he told me he'd been badly beaten up. When I looked closely, I could see that he'd tried to cover a black eye with makeup. He said as he was leaving the Athol Public Library earlier that week, two people were waiting for him in the backseat of his car. He didn't see them as he got in, ready to make the five-minute drive back to his parents' house. An arm came out of the dark, pulling Richard's neck tightly against his seat. Another arm came out of nowhere and began punching against his ribs. Defenseless and scared, he could do nothing as he was beaten in his own car. When it was over, he was too ashamed to go home because his parents would see his black eye and his bloody nose, so he drove around in pain. He said he had no idea who beat him. The only word his attackers had said was 'faggot.'

"Despite the obstacles, Richard finally did accept himself and told his family he was gay. After three years of college, he figured out what he wanted to do — help other people through social work. He transferred to Fitchburg State College. It seemed like things were looking up for him.

"That's why, when my sister called me three days after Christmas this year, I couldn't believe what she was telling me. She told me Richard had driven his maroon Ford Escort to a deserted Athol street and left the engine running, killing himself. I didn't understand why. There seemed to be no reason for his death and for weeks after I, like much of his family, was inconsolable.

"It has been five months since his death and I just hope that Richard has found a place where he can be himself without being picked on and beaten up. Most of all I hope he's happy. Instead of going to my high school reunion in August, I'll visit my favorite person from the class of 1987. I'll go to the cemetery where Richard is buried and keep our date."

I'd like to read a small update. I wrote that column in May. It's been almost a year since Richard's death and things haven't changed much. It's difficult when I visit with his family. I know Richard's mother doesn't sleep very well anymore. She didn't sleep at all after he first died, staying up all night watching television or cooking and then going to work full-time. She's taking naps now but I doubt she's slept a full night in the past year.

Richard's older sister Karen is also having a difficult time. Shortly after her brother committed suicide, Karen told her parents she's a lesbian, which helped her, but she's still unable to deal with her brother's death. She's told me she suffers from panic attacks and has been attending a support group for families of suicide survivors.

The difficulty I can best tell you about is my own. When the shock first began to wear off last winter that Richard was gone, the pain and depression were almost overwhelming at times. I would come home from work early, get into bed, and cry for hours. I believed the pain would subside in time but it hasn't — if anything, it's gotten worse. There are certain songs and certain bands I can't listen to anymore, and others that open up a floodgate of memories that I don't know how to deal with. Sometimes when I hear a good concert coming to the area or I'm planning a party, I remind myself to invite Richard, then realize that I no longer can.

READING 17-B

Devin Beringer

Testimony before the Massachusetts Governor's Commission on Gay and Lesbian Youth, Nov. 17, 1992

My name is Devin Beringer and I am a seventeen-year-old senior at Concord Academy.

Almost from the beginning, I knew I was somehow different from the other guys. I was always an outcast at school. Books were my best friends. I ostracized myself from the rest of the world because I felt as if I could trust no one, not even my parents. The pressure of feeling so alone manifested itself in fits of manic depression, hysterical outbreaks, and, eventually, suicidal tendencies. I would spend hours sitting on my windowsill, wondering whether jumping would make things better and wishing that someone would help me. All that I needed to be told was that my feelings were normal and I wasn't the only one who had them. Finally, I couldn't stand it anymore. I had to get out. I convinced my parents that I hated school and life at home. A year later they let me go to Eaglebrook, an all-boys boarding school. It turned out later that my parents thought I left because I hated them when in reality I was afraid of them hating me.

At Eaglebrook, homophobia and hazing were rampant. I had to be adamantly heterosexual and had to make dehumanizing comments about girls or else be labeled a faggot. I had to prove my masculinity by hazing the underclassmen. Others found pushing wasn't enough and so turned to whiffle-ball bats. Once someone was rolled down cement steps in a laundry bag for the fun of it. The psychological torture was the worst. Any expression of emotion was taboo, and I would get teased or hazed if I slipped up and let on that I was homesick or felt any other so-called "weak" emotion.

I was constantly denying the feelings I had for other guys. In the process of hiding these feelings, I repressed all emotions. I refused to admit why it was I couldn't help staring at the boy in my geometry class. I was unable to deal with the truth, so I just convinced myself that the attraction was an exception and that he just had a magnetic personality.

Concord Academy changed all this. It was the first place I encountered that was even slightly gay-positive. When I arrived, an openly gay faculty member was assigned to be my advisor. He was the first openly gay person I had ever met. Through him, I learned that being gay is not the horrible and disgusting thing that society makes it out to be but just a normal and natural part of me.

For me, coming out was not the traumatic and terrible experience that it is for many gay and lesbian teens. I lost a couple of friends along the way but there was no real negative response. I have still to come out to my parents, though. We have grown distant in the five years I have been away and we hardly know each other anymore.

Regardless of Concord's positive atmosphere, there is no escaping the internalized homophobia, the self-hatred that comes with the realization that you've just joined what the Justice Department calls "probably the most frequent victims of hate crime in America." This self-hatred is what causes the outrageously high rates of suicide and drug abuse among gay youth. I've spent more than one lonely night sobbing while downing shot after shot, and I've also planned out my suicide more than once. Fortunately, I was not alone. There were gay faculty and students to whom I could go for help. My story is one of success but, for instance, yesterday, as I was writing this speech, a homophobic epithet was scrawled upon my door. We still have a long way to go.

READING 17-C

Stefanie Johnson

Senior Chapel Talk, Choate Rosemary Hall,
Wallingford, Connecticut, May 1992

Imagine that you are looking at the world through the bottom of a glass. The image you get is distorted, twisted, and sometimes frightening, and who you are and your life experiences color the way you see things. I look at my life in this way: each part of me is a tint that is put in front of the glass and shades everything around me.

Imagine now that I am looking and there is a black tint to the glass. This color, this blackness, represents my race and my background. I come from Harlem, New York. I am a first-generation American, my family being from Jamaica and, without any exaggeration, we are poor. We are on welfare. There are eight of us who live in a two-bedroom apartment with three beds to share. I am a part of the America most people don't want to see and never encounter unless it is through the media or while driving through my neighborhood, safely tucked away in their cars. Imagine how baffled I was when I set foot in Wallingford, Connecticut, to attend Choate. Carefully manicured lawns and for the first time in my life I had my own room, my own bed, my own space. Imagine how angry I was last year when a carload of kids drove by and screamed, "Nigger, go back to Africa!" Sometimes, looking at the world through this glass, I lose faith in it and its people. How can some people have so much and others so little? How can some people be so ignorant and malicious?

Can you see through the black-tinted glass I am looking through?

Now imagine there is a pinkish tint to the glass. This pink stands for my sexual identity. I am a lesbian. To break it down even further for you, I love women, I don't hate men, I just love women. But getting to the point where I could say this was not easy. Before I came to terms with my homosexuality I had to get rid of my own internal homophobia and a lifetime of anti-homosexual programming. Growing up I had feelings for other women. I didn't know what they meant, but I knew it was something I was taught was not right, and I hated myself for it. I thought I was the most disgusting thing on the face of the earth, not worthy of being loved or of even existing. This winter I had a long talk with a good friend of mine. With her I started a process of questioning, reflecting, and eventually coming out to myself. And now here I am.

What does all of this mean? Well, four years ago I would never have said any of this. Four years ago I was ashamed of my background and terrified that someone might find out I was from Harlem. Four years ago I couldn't even accept that I was a lesbian. But I have changed and gained strength from the faculty members and friends I have met at Choate, and I feel you can learn something from my experience. Take risks. Be proud of who you are, every part of you. Dare to be different, dare to be who you are. And even though the glass that we all look through may be frightening, tinted, or for some even broken, it doesn't always have to be that way.

READING 17-D

Lee Fearnside

Senior Chapel Talk, Concord Academy,
Concord, Massachusetts, February 1992

One day at the Mountain School, a guy walked up to my friend and asked her, quite innocently, if she was afraid to live in a dorm with a lesbian. One starry night, last semester, I was walking home on my street in Lexington, where I've lived all my life, and some guys in a pickup truck whizzed past me screaming "dyke!" I go to school every day, afraid of violence, feeling that I can't be honest, that I have no right to be proud, that I am a second-class citizen.

One of my friends asked me why I couldn't just "hang out for another year" — why was it such a big deal to come out if I was going to be treated like pond scum? By staying silent, I was confirming the self-hatred and disgust that were consuming me. I was justifying ignorance and fear. I relinquished the power of response, my strength. My closet wasn't a refuge, it was a prison, and it was killing me.

There is one difference that sets sexual minorities apart from other minorities — that is that we can be invisible, and are assumed to be part of the heterosexual majority until we blatantly and publicly declare otherwise. Some of you might think this to be a boon — I can just pretend to be straight and avoid all this discomfort. I tried that for a while, going so far as to use a guy to try to prove to myself that I could be straight if only I tried hard enough. But instead of being accepted into the mainstream, I lost my self-respect.

I felt completely isolated from my friends and family. It appeared that I was the only one who ever had these "queer" feelings. I couldn't come out to anyone, for surely they wouldn't want to be friends with anyone as sick and deranged as I. I, and all of us, are presented with images of gays as degenerate, shameful, and perverted until I accepted them as truth. Not only does society shout at me that I am bad, but an inner voice, internalizing these homophobic stereotypes, whispers it as well. I felt that I could only be a real lesbian if I dressed like a man, shaved my head to the scalp, hated men, and liked whips, chains, and little girls. In other words, do things I despised. I couldn't, and still can't, think of a single positive image of lesbians in our society, so I was forced to rely on negative stereotypes for role models. How could I identify with those images and maintain a shred of self-respect?

This initiated a downward spiral of self-hate and anger motivated by homophobia. I hated myself for being what seemed to be everyone's worst nightmare, a homosexual. I was angry because no matter what I did I couldn't change that. I was angry because I felt I had no right to anger. I created impassable walls, shutting out love as well as hate. I grew increasingly cynical, to try to stave off hurt, and bitter, because I felt no one would try to see the person behind the sexual label, for while straights aren't identified by their sexuality, gay people are. I virtually branded myself with the message "Stay back!" I was an ice queen, a wicked witch of the west, a live bomb, or perhaps a blade forged of overheated steel — a hard blow, and I would shatter. For me, my silence equalled the death of my sanity. I'm not telling you this to make you feel sorry for me, the poor, disillusioned lesbian, or to preach at you, but because I want to give you an idea of what it is to be ostracized from society because I don't conform to its standards of "normal."

And now that I've been out for a few months, have I found the solution to all my problems? Of course not. I have a better grasp of my identity, a sense of self, a pride, and a tiny corner of happiness and relief. Aside from an academic education, this school has taught me a lot. From the acknowledged homophobe to the politically correct, you have increased my bitterness and cynicism by dancing around the issue and ignoring my sexuality because it is an uncomfortable and sensitive issue. It seems I will always have to fight for what should be self-evident truths. Someday, I hope people will accept all of me, not accept me *in spite of* my lesbianism. Someday, I hope I can run across a field of flowers into the arms of my lover like straight couples do in the movies. Someday, I hope everyone will be able to say the words gay, lesbian, and bisexual without cringing. Someday, I hope that I won't just survive, I'll thrive.

READING 17-E

"In My Own Space" by Calvin Glenn

from *Brother to Brother: New Writings by Black Gay Men,* edited by Essex Hemphill

When I arrived on [my small Northeastern college] campus, I was sure I had not done a great job of selecting a college. The college was just as conservative as the school back home. I had looked for a small campus where I hoped to explore my identity without inhibition. The day I graduated from high school, I made a pact with myself to "come out" on campus before returning home for winter break. I had no fears. I had come this far and didn't care what anyone else might think of me. My parents knew I was gay, which I considered to be a plus, but being typical black parents, they first berated me, then alienated me, then sent me to a psychologist to be cured. The local Baptist minister was called in to scare the sickness out of me. (If there had been any sickness there, believe me, he would have scared it out.) My parents have simmered down since then, but I am not sure they accept my sexuality; we simply don't discuss it.

I got off the bus in early September, feeling very good about being at college, away from the stifling silence that engulfed my home. I looked around a bit, and finally mustered the courage to ask someone for directions to my dorm.

"It's straight down the road," a fellow student instructed me. "You'll know it when you get there," he continued. "It's the only building that doesn't look old." I thanked him and proceeded on my way.

When I found the new-looking dorm, I walked in and went up to the second floor to search for room 204. I found it and entered. I was assigned to a triple — three rooms, to be occupied by three very different roommates. One was Jim, a quiet fellow from the Midwest. My other roommate, Sam, was a pseudo-jock from the South. And, of course, there was me. When I moved into my room, I had no idea that Jim and Sam would never become my friends.

A couple of weeks into the school year, I decided that my room was just a little too drab. Everyone else had vivid posters and cutouts from magazines plastered all over their walls. I thought I should do that, too. It took two weeks to complete the job. I started out, innocently enough, with a poster of a lion that I hung directly over my bed (with that image, anyone would think twice about upsetting me). And I progressed from there; being a typical teenager, I put up posters of my favorite rock bands. And, then, it dawned on me; there was something I really wanted but didn't have on my walls: a picture of the perfect man. I looked through my various catalogues and ordered the most innocently seductive poster I could find. When it arrived, I closed the door to my room and tacked up the poster. "There," I said with satisfaction, "now the walls all have a spirit that is purely me."

Later that week, Jim came in to talk with me. "Great posters you've got," he said, walking in. "Kinda perks the place up." We sat on my bed talking about our classes and complaining about our social lives. And then it happened. He turned and spotted the poster on my door. He asked hesitantly, "What — who is that?"

"Some model. It's just a poster. But he is gorgeous." When those words came from my mouth, Jim gasped and jumped up from the bed. I became wide-eyed, and somewhat offended. I asked, "What's wrong?"

The fear in his eyes was apparent. What was he afraid of? I'm sure I hadn't touched him at all since he waltzed in commenting on the new scenery.

"Are you—," he started, then hesitated. He sighed and continued slowly, "Are you gay?"

Equally slowly, I replied, "Yes, I am gay." Jim looked as though his heart had stopped. I had prepared, somewhat, for this confrontation, but I didn't know how to handle his fear. "Calm down," I said, but he just stared at me, his eyes bulging out of his head and his mouth agape. He turned quickly and left. I sat looking at myself in the mirror. What could he have seen to make him so afraid?

It was not long before Sam knocked on my door and entered. I was still sitting on my bed facing the mirror when he walked in.

"Jim told me about the poster you have up on your wall. Where is it?"

"Turn around; it's behind you," I said wearily.

He looked at the picture and gave it a few nervous taps. Pointing at the poster, he said, "You *can't* have this picture up." His plea was in vain. He looked at me with desperate eyes as though I had physically abused him.

"Why can't I have it up?"

Sam paused to search his fears for coherent reasons. "Look, Chris, when people see this up they'll think you're a homosexual."

"But I am gay."

Sam's nose began to twitch. "Why the f*** didn't you tell us?"

"What the f*** does it matter?"

"I can't believe this!" he screamed, putting his hands on his head. "I'm living with a black faggot." He slammed the door behind him as he left. That was the end of our short friendship.

The next day my roommates confronted me. The said they had been conferring and they had come to a conclusion. They put it simply: I had to move out.

"No."

"Come on, Chris," Jim urged. "Wouldn't you be happier in a single?"

"I'm comfortable where I am," I replied.

"But you'd be more comfortable in a single," Sam added.

"You guys are out of your minds. I'm not moving out." I got up and went to my room. "F***ing idiots!" I yelled, as I slammed the door. What the h*** was their problem? I hadn't made any advances at them; I didn't even think either was attractive. I hadn't even had any overnight visitors. "How the h*** am I bothering them?" I asked myself.

I woke up the next morning feeling lousy, and when I left my room I became angry. Someone had written the letters *F* and *G* around the *A* sticker on my door. I had never been so angry. I went back to my room and pulled out a sheet of paper and began to write. But I stopped. "I'm not going to let myself stoop to their level." I crumpled the paper and went on with my life.

There was a small gay and lesbian organization on campus, and I attended the weekly meetings. I told some of the members about the situation with my roommates. They couldn't believe it. Nothing like it had ever happened before. But then, they told me, none of them had ever had the courage to "come out" to their roommates. "Why?" I asked. "Am I the only one who isn't afraid? Am I the only one who is tired of hiding?"

The next week I received a letter from the director of student life. I was told that my roommates had brought complaints against me to her attention. I had to report to her office the next morning for a conference.

The director called us in separately to get an overview of the circumstances. Then we all sat down; Jim and Sam on one side of the room, me on the other, and the director at the head.

"Now what seems to be the problem?"

"Well, a couple of weeks ago we found out that Chris ... he's a homosexual," Jim began.

"He put up this big poster of a guy on his door," Sam added. "Everybody can see it."

"We think he would be more comfortable in a single," Jim concluded.

The director looked at me. "Is this so?"

"Yes, I am gay," I replied, "but I'm comfortable where I am. There's no reason for me to move out."

"But think about us, Chris," said Jim.

"I'm not hurting you." I paused, and then added, "You mean to tell me that I can't put up a poster of a man in my own space?" There was silence. "I don't even bother you. Unlike Sam, I don't even have people staying overnight," I sneered.

Sam yelled, "If the guys finding out I'm living with a fag—"

"That's enough!" the director interrupted. "It seems to me that this is a very simple case. Chris is gay, and according to this school's policies, there is nothing wrong with that. He's done nothing wrong, as opposed to you two. You will both share the expenses to have his door repainted, and you both may possibly appear for disciplinary action if Chris plans to pursue harassment charges. Finally, I cannot, and will not, force Chris to move out of his room."

"But what can we do? He makes us feel uncomfortable."

"Gentlemen, you will have to learn to handle your own insecurities. But, if you feel so uncomfortable, I suggest that *you* move out."

QUESTIONS/ACTIVITIES

1. It may be useful to use Chapter 1 to set the context for these readings. In particular, taking the "Heterosexual Questionnaire" (Reading 1-A) might help as preparation.

2. "Visualize" growing up gay. Close your eyes while your teacher leads you through life in a society where heterosexuals are 10 percent and gays 90 percent. Reverse ordinary experiences of gay youth (not being able to talk to your parents, never seeing people like you on TV, etc.) to become those of heterosexual youth. Be as specific as possible. Write how you feel when you have finished (spend 10–15 minutes on it), and then discuss this with your classmates.

3. Set aside a period for an exercise that explores your and your classmates' experiences of discrimination. Write down any characteristic for which you have suffered discrimination (race, gender, height, intelligence, looks, etc.). List these on the board. Form a group with at least one other person who has shared this experience (if no one has had exactly the same experience, try to choose something closely related). Answer three questions:

- What was bad about this experience?
- What is good about being a member of this group?
- What would you want people who aren't members of this group to know about you?

Have groups report back. Do not question or debate what others present: this is their experience, and others may not devalue it —

only they are the experts on their experience. Keep lists (on the board, on paper) to look for common themes that accompany oppression. What do people who have experienced different forms of oppression have in common?

4. Keep a journal detailing your reactions to each reading.

5. In the Introduction, numerous stresses on gay youth are cited. Using the readings themselves, cite examples of these from the stories, and explain how they affected the authors.

6. Write a letter to the author of the story that most moved you, explaining what you have learned from the story and how it made you feel.

7. Look for things in the stories that "made it better," compiling a list of the actions that could be taken to better the lives of gay youth.

8. Analyze the role of adults and friends in these stories. Did they act appropriately? Find specific examples.

9. Analyze the similarities and differences in the stories. What factors (race, gender, location, etc.) account for the differences?

10. Write a history of when and how you became aware of gay people. Where did your first impressions come from? Where did you get your information? Where does homophobia seem to come from?

11. List on the board all homophobic epithets you have ever heard. Analyze these, placing them in categories. How would such language affect someone's feelings about himself or herself?

12. Using the concept of "unearned privilege" (the privileges we all get because we belong to certain groups but which we did nothing to earn), make lists of heterosexual privileges you see in your school, community, or home. What can heterosexuals do that gays can't? What can they take for granted?

13. Research your school and community for its attitudes on gay youth issues. Share research and compile a report based on findings of the class. Are there needs that could be addressed, or actions that should be taken? Problem-solve! Choose among these and other possible research projects:

- Monitoring language for a week to check it for homophobic epithets

- Investigating curriculum for its representation of gays and for heterosexism (math problems that feature only opposite-sex couples, etc.)
- Investigating policies to see if nondiscrimination clauses exist, etc.
- Researching what resources are in the library
- Monitoring TV and radio for representation of gays and for heterosexism
- Interviewing peers, school, officials, and community leaders for their views on gay youth issues.

14. If possible, interview someone gay about his or her experience of growing up gay. What similarities or differences with the accounts in this chapter arose?

15. Other resources for reading are Bennett Singer's *Growing Up Gay,* Ann Heron's *One Teenager in Ten: Writings by Gay and Lesbian Youth,* Aaron Frick's *Reflections of a Rock Lobster: A Story of Growing Up Gay,* and Paul Monette's *Becoming a Man.* Films include Robert King's *The Disco Years* and *Oranges Are Not the Only Fruit,* based on Jeanette Winterson's autobiographical novel.

APPENDIX

Notes for Teachers

This appendix is designed to raise some issues for teachers to think about in teaching individual chapters. They provide general context, from a teacher's point of view, on classroom issues that might arise. Specific curriculum ideas are found at the end of individual chapters.

PART 1

The readings in this section are the most academic and difficult in the book. Teachers may wish to read them as background material, and present the material themselves if they feel the readings are simply too difficult for their students. The highly academic nature of the readings makes it harder to come up with creative curriculum ideas. The unfamiliarity of the cultures discussed can also make it difficult for students to make connections to their own lives and experiences. For its resources to be used most effectively, this section undoubtedly calls upon the teacher to be most creative in lesson planning.

Chapter 1

These readings may question deeply held beliefs of students. It is important that students work as partners in this exploration, allowing them to join in a process of discovery rather than making them feel they are being harangued. Using their ideas as resources as much as possible will help in this matter. It is important to avoid assuming that the students are all heterosexual: try to be inclusive in language, and avoid allowing discussion to be about "them" ("the gays"), as this will perpetuate isolation and invisibility of gay youth.

Chapter 2

This is perhaps the single most difficult reading in the entire book. Most students will probably find it very difficult to follow. One strategy to make it more accessible might be to distribute vocabulary lists of difficult words to students ahead of time. Teachers may wish to read it for their own knowledge and simply present in class the information it contains, rather than assigning it as a reading. In either case, its content is revolutionary, and it should be introduced to students in some fashion.

Chapter 3

This is a difficult reading of a highly academic nature. Teachers should review it carefully to determine if their classes will find it accessible.

The content of Hinsch's work may be so at odds with some students' conception of how gays were regarded in the past that they may simply refuse to believe it. This may be especially true for those who come from this particular cultural tradition. Teachers should keep students focused on Hinsch's evidence as a way of skirting these reactions.

Chapter 4

Written by a college professor, this reading may be a bit difficult for some students. Two important things need to be kept in mind. First, students must be helped to understand the difference between a person's "sex" (which is a result of biology) and a person's "gender" (which results from society telling one how to behave, based on their sex). There are only two sexes, everyone knows, but students may find it confusing that there are societies with more than two genders. Second, students need to try to understand Indian categories on their own terms, instead of filtering them through the lens of our ideas about gender in twentieth-century America. Otherwise, it will be easy for some to simply say Indians are "weird" and discount the entire lesson.

Chapter 5

This reading is inherently fascinating because of its unusual content. It is also more accessible in style than other readings in this section. It does run the risk of making students think of the people discussed in it as "freaks," however. Teachers must take care to stress the exceptional nature of these individuals. It also blurs lines of gender and sexuality. Teachers must also be careful not to leave students with the impression that all these individuals were necessarily lesbians, or that lesbians all really want to be men.

Chapter 6

These accounts offer an excellent chance to introduce students to the heart of what historians do. Students need to look carefully at the evidence each writer presents and the interpretations offered, and then judge whether a writer's conclusions are justified. The materials introduce students to the difficulties involved in gay history specifically and social history in general, allowing them to grapple with the dilemmas actual historians face in their daily work.

PART 2

The readings in this section are generally much more accessible to students. Drawn from oral histories and less academic sources, they demand less sophisticated reading skills than Part 1's selections do.

Chapter 7

This account touches a key moment in gay history: the beginning of the emergence of gays as a "minority group." The concept of "group consciousness" is important for students to understand and should be emphasized.

Chapter 8

The Holocaust stirs strong emotions, and teaching about it must be done with the utmost care. This excerpt, with its graphic description of conditions in the concentration camps, is obviously highly charged. It is vital to consider the composition of one's class and to be prepared to allot more time for personal reflection and sharing than one might normally set aside. Having taught about the Holocaust to classes that included the children of survivors, I cannot emphasize enough the importance of listening carefully to, and empathizing with, student concerns.

The rationale behind the activities in this unit is that we can best understand the Holocaust if we can put ourselves in the place of the people involved — both victims and perpetrators. This is a risky strategy, one that can evoke strong feelings and possibly offend. Teachers need to judge for themselves the maturity of their students and their ability to deal appropriately with such exercises. These exercises could also easily be turned into questions for students to think about while reading, since these questions ask students to put themselves in the mindset of key characters at different junctures of Heger's narrative.

Chapter 9

This unit presents a unique opportunity to contrast a primary and a secondary source on the same subject. It also is crucial in terms of helping students understand the genesis of the American gay movement, while casting war (an event usually thought of in terms of battles) as a phenomenon that affects society in a much broader way.

Chapter 10

This report is a truly rich resource for examining the paranoia of the McCarthy era as well as the prevailing attitudes toward gays. Its straightforward organization and argumentation should make it easy for most students to follow. It is important, however, to not let its thoroughly discredited "findings" be taken too seriously.

Chapter 11

The straightforward, easy-to-read story line of this selection makes it accessible to many students and engages the imagination. It can be used effectively to help students recapture the feeling of a very different time, and to understand the problems involved in starting a political movement.

Chapter 12

The richness of these stories make them ideal for classroom use. They help students understand the lives of another generation, and bring to light the experiences of lesbians, which have been somewhat neglected in lesbian and gay studies to date. In addition, the diversity found among them should help explode any notions of a uniform "gay experience."

Chapter 13

Duberman's account is a bit long and perhaps should be spread over two days. His frequent use of gay slang may confuse some students: terms such as "queen" (referring to a gay man who frequently adopts the dress and style of the female gender) may need to be defined ahead of time. Because of its pioneering nature as the first comprehensive history of the Stonewall Riots, this account offers the teacher an excellent chance to talk with students about the process of writing history and what problems one can run into when doing so.

PART 3

The readings in this section are the most likely to evoke powerful emotions and feelings, as they deal with still-unresolved issues. Teachers should be prepared to deal with strong reactions. With the exception of Chapter 15, the reading levels are accessible to most students.

Chapter 14

These documents are useful for comparative historiography, helping students gain a sense of the development of a movement over time. They could also be used separately, in conjunction with appropriate chapters in Part Two. One obvious note of caution: be careful to distinguish between the types of documents offered. Organizational mission statements are obviously going to be less pointedly political than march demands will be. Context and intent affect the style and content of each document, and students need to understand this.

Chapter 15

Because these are Supreme Court opinions, they may be difficult for many students to grasp. They have, however, been edited to remove some of the more abstruse sections, and they are accessible to students if used properly. Students should have the readings in front of them, should be led through them with reference to specific excerpts, and should be offered chances to ask questions about confusing segments. The opinions strike at the heart of fundamental questions on the role of the government in citizens' private lives. If employed properly, they can raise vital issues for students to think about.

Chapter 16

These readings only touch on the international gay and lesbian movement. It is important to beware of ethnocentrism in approaching these societies, so that we do not impose our own standards upon them.

Chapter 17

These stories are obviously powerful narratives that offer multiple opportunities for discussion. One caution is necessary: the majority of us have no openly gay students in our classes, and sometimes slip into an assumption that we are talking to an all-heterosexual audience. This can be very damaging to gay youth, for such an assumption perpetuates their invisibility. Try to make it clear, in your language, that this is not a discussion about "them" but about "us." It might be helpful to list a local gay-youth support group or a national hotline number on the board, without too much fanfare, for students who might need to avail themselves of such services. It is also important not to put students on the spot in a way that "who's the queer here?" becomes the focus of attention. This can be done by focusing on the documents so that the discussion does not become personalized. However, it is important not to stifle those students who may find their voice through reading these documents.

NOTES

PART 1

Introduction

1. It is hard to pick up works of gay history without encountering this debate. For those interested in reviewing it, see Martin Duberman, Martha Vicinus, and George Chauncey, Jr., editors, *Hidden from History: Reclaiming the Gay and Lesbian Past* (New York, 1989), pp. 1–64, and Edward Stein, editor, *Forms of Desire: Sexual Orientation and the Social Constructionist Controversy* (New York, 1990), entire.

2. Jonathan Katz, *The Lesbian/Gay Almanac* (New York, 1983), p. 16.

Chapter 1

1. Sources for Reading 1-B are listed as:

References for Left-handedness:

DeKay, James T. *The Left-Handed Book*. New York: M. Evans and Company, Inc., 1966.

DeKay, James T. *The Natural Superiority of the Left-Hander*. New York: M. Evans and Company, 1979.

Fincher, Jack. *Sinister People: The Looking-Glass World of the Left-Hander*. New York: G.P. Putnam's Sons, 1977.

Gould, George M. *Right-Handedness and Left-Handedness*. Philadelphia and London: L.B. Lippincott Company, 1908.

Wagner, Anthony P. *Popular Associations of Right and Left in Romantic Literature: A Dissertation*. Baltimore: J.H. Furst Company, 1912.

Wile, Ira S. *Handedness: Right and Left*. Boston: Lee & Shephard Company, 1934.

References for Gays and Lesbians:

Bullough, Vern. *Homosexuality: A History*. New York: New American Library, 1979.

Haeberle, Erwin. *The Sex Atlas: A New Illustrated Guide*. New York: Continuum Publishing Co., 1982.

Katz, Jonathan. *Gay American History: Lesbians and Gay Men in the U.S.A.* New York: Avon Books, 1976.

Klaich, Dolores. *Woman and Woman: Attitudes Toward Lesbianism.* New York: Simon & Schuster, 1974.

Walker, Mitch. *Men Loving Men: A Gay Sex Guide and Consciousness Book.* San Francisco: Gay Sunshine Press, 1977.

Wallechinsky, David; Wallace, Irving; and Wallace, Amy. *The People's Almanac Presents The Book of Lists.* New York: William Morrow, 1977.

Wittman, Carl. "A Gay Manifesto" in *Out of the Closets: Voices of Gay Liberation,* edited by Karla Jay and Allen Young. New York: Douglas/Links, 1972.

Chapter 2

1. Robert Maynard Hutchins, editor, *Great Books of the Western World,* volume 7 (Chicago, 1952), pp. 157–158.

2. The literature on homosexuality in the ancient world is voluminous. I have chosen John Boswell, *Christianity, Social Tolerance, and Homosexuality* (Chicago, 1980) and Eva Cantarella, *Bisexuality in the Ancient World* (New Haven, 1992) as the two exemplars for the purposes of this introduction. Another essentialist position is found in Kenneth Dover, *Greek Homosexuality* (London, 1978); constructionist interpretations are found in David Greenberg, *The Construction of Homosexuality* (Chicago, 1988) and David Halperin, *One Hundred Years of Homosexuality* (New York, 1990).

3. Cantarella, *Bisexuality in the Ancient World,* p. vii.

4. *Ibid.,* chapter 2, pp. 17–53.

5. *Ibid.,* p. 78.

6. *Ibid.,* p. 78.

7. *Ibid.,* pp. 173–186.

8. Boswell, *Christianity, Social Tolerance, and Homosexuality,* pp. 171–174.

9. *Ibid.,* chapters 7–9, pp. 169–268.

10. *Ibid.,* p. 295.

11. *Ibid.,* p. 295.

12. *Ibid.,* chapter 10, pp. 269–302.

13. Cantarella, *Bisexuality in the Ancient World,* pp. 221–222.

Chapter 3

1. Bret Hinsch, *Passions of the Cut Sleeve* (Berkeley, 1990), p. 2.

2. *Ibid.,* p. 20.

3. *Ibid.,* p. 1.

4. *Ibid.,* p. 19.

5. *Ibid.,* p. 33.

6. *Ibid.,* pp. 173–178.

7. Vivian Ng, "Homosexuality and the State in Late Imperial China" in Duberman, Vicinus, and Chauncey, *Hidden from History,* p. 76.

8. Ng, "Homosexuality and the State in Late Imperial China" in Duberman, Vicinus, and Chauncey, *Hidden from History,* pp. 76–89, explains this transition well.

9. Hinsch, *Passions of the Cut Sleeve,* p. 167.

10. Stuart Timmons, *The Trouble with Harry Hay* (Boston, 1990), pp. 96–97.

Chapter 4

1. Will Roscoe, editor, *Living the Spirit* (New York, 1988), pp. 217–222, provides a complete list. This volume also contains an excellent collection of primary source material on gay American Indians.

2. Jonathan Katz, *Gay American History* (New York, 1976)), p. 285. Katz has compiled an excellent collection of documents concerning gay Native Americans and berdachism, in chapter 4, "Native Americans/Gay Americans," pp. 281–334.

3. *Ibid.*, p. 286.

4. *Ibid.*, p. 287.

5. *Ibid.*, pp. 301–302.

6. Will Roscoe, "The Zuni Man/Woman," *Out/Look,* Summer 1988, p. 57.

7. Katz, *Gay American History,* p. 282.

8. *Ibid.*, p. 289.

9. *Ibid.*, pp. 286–287.

10. *Ibid.*, p. 292.

11. Walter Williams, *The Spirit and the Flesh* (Boston, 1986), p. 2. The excerpt concerning berdaches used here deals exclusively with men. For women who occupied an alternative gender role, see chapter 11, "Amazons of America," pp. 233–251.

Chapter 5

1. John D'Emilio and Estelle Freedman, *Intimate Matters* (New York, 1988), entire, provides a comprehensive history of sexuality to document this.

2. Katz, *The Gay/Lesbian Almanac,* pp. 85–86.

3. Katz, *Gay American History,* has an excellent collection of documents on passing women, pp. 209–280.

Chapter 6

1. Randy Shilts, *Conduct Unbecoming* (New York, 1993), p. 18.

2. Details about Roosevelt's life are taken from Blanche Weisen Cook, *Eleanor Roosevelt: Volume One, 1884–1933* (New York, 1992).

3. Deidre Carmody, "Letters by Eleanor Roosevelt Detail Friendship with Lorena Hickok," *New York Times,* October 21, 1979, p. 22.

4. *Ibid.*

5. *Ibid.*

6. *Ibid.*

7. Kenneth Lynn, "The First Lady's First Friend," *London Times Literary Supplement,* July 11, 1980, p. 787.

8. *Ibid.*

9. Carmody, "Letters by Eleanor Roosevelt Detail Friendship with Lorena Hickok," p. 22.

10. *Ibid.*

11. Lynn, "The First Lady's First Friend," p. 787.

12. *Ibid.*

PART 2

Introduction

1. For those who date this phenomenon earlier, examples include Randolph Trumbach, "The Birth of the Queen: Sodomy and the Emergence of Gender Equality in Modern Culture, 1660–1750," and Arend Hussen, "Sodomy in the Dutch Republic During the Eighteenth Century," in Duberman, Vicinus, and Chauncey, *Hidden from History,* pp. 129–149.

2. Katz, *Gay American History,* p. 52; pp. 39–53, contains numerous documents speaking of the "gay underworld" in the late nineteenth and early twentieth centuries in America.

3. D'Emilio and Freedman, *Intimate Matters,* pp. 202–221, explains the "social control" movements of the nineteenth century and the conditions which produced them.

4. Katz, *The Gay/Lesbian Almanac,* p. 16.

5. Ronald Bayer, *Homosexuality and American Psychiatry* (Princeton, 1987) and Kenneth Lewes, *The Psychoanalytic Theory of Male Homosexuality* (New York, 1988), both analyze the history of psychiatry with regard to homosexuality.

6. Katz, *The Gay/Lesbian Almanac,* p. 144.

7. Katz, *The Gay/Lesbian Almanac,* p. 157.

Chapter 7

1. Details of Ulrichs's early life are found in Hubert Kennedy, *Ulrichs* (Boston, 1988), chapters 1–6 (pp. 13–100).

2. Details of Ulrichs's later life are found in Kennedy, *Ulrichs,* chapters 7–13 (pp. 101–230).

Chapter 8

1. Richard Plant, *The Pink Triangle* (New York, 1986), p. 181.

2. David Feinbech's Introduction to Heinz Heger, *The Men with the Pink Triangle* (Boston, 1980), summarizes the historiography of the gay Holocaust, pp. 1–7.

3. Plant, *The Pink Triangle,* p. 29.

4. *Ibid.,* p. 29.

5. Barry Adam, *The Rise of a Gay and Lesbian Movement* (Boston, 1987), p. 19. Adam's chapter on the German gay rights movement (pp. 17–25) is a good, concise account.

6. *Ibid.,* p. 19.

7. *Ibid.,* p. 23.

8. Plant, *The Pink Triangle,* p. 43.

9. Adam, *The Rise of a Gay and Lesbian Movement,* p. 25.

10. *Ibid.,* p. 50.

11. Plant, *The Pink Triangle,* p. 4.

12. *Ibid.,* p. 51.

13. *Ibid.,* pp. 45–48.

14. *Ibid.,* p. 108.

15. *Ibid.,* p. 113.

16. *Ibid.,* pp. 116–117.

17. Adam, *The Rise of a Gay and Lesbian Movement,* pp. 52–53.

Chapter 9

1. Shilts, *Conduct Unbecoming,* p. 11.

2. Allan Bérubé, *Coming Out under Fire* (New York, 1990), p. 147.

3. *Ibid.,* p. 2. Bérubé's introduction, pp. 1–7, offers a concise summary of the impact of the war on the military, domestic life, and gay people.

4. *Ibid.,* p. 6.

5. *Ibid.,* pp. 146–147.

6. *Ibid.,* chapter 5, "The Fight for Reform," pp. 128–148, explains the change in military policies during World War II.

7. *Ibid.,* p. 147.

Chapter 10

1. John D'Emilio, *Sexual Politics, Sexual Communities* (Chicago, 1983), p. 41.

2. "Perverts Called Government Peril" in *New York Times,* April 19, 1950, p. 25.

3. Katz, *Gay American History,* reproduces these articles and numerous other useful documents relating to this era on pp. 91–105.

4. Nicholas von Hoffman, *Citizen Cohn* (New York, 1988), entire.

5. "Pervert Inquiry Ordered" in *New York Times,* June 15, 1950, p. 1.

6. D'Emilio, *Sexual Politics, Sexual Communities,* p. 44.

7. Bérubé, *Coming Out under Fire,* p. 276.

8. Shilts, *Conduct Unbecoming,* p. 106.

9. Bérubé, *Coming Out under Fire,* p. 269.

10. *Ibid.,* p. 270.

11. *Ibid.,* p. 270.

12. Accounts of Turing's life include Andrew Hodges, *Alan Turing* (New York, 1984).

13. Eric Marcus, *Making History* (New York, 1992), p. 102.

Chapter 11

1. Details about the early period of Hay's life are taken from Timmons, *The Trouble with Harry Hay,* chapters 1–8, pp. 3–171.

2. Details about the later period of Hay's life are taken from Timmons, *The Trouble with Harry Hay,* chapters 9–14, pp. 172–297.

3. D'Emilio, *Sexual Politics, Sexual Communities,* p. 81.

4. *Ibid.,* p. 115.

5. D'Emilio, *Sexual Politics, Sexual Communities,* provides a clear, succinct account of DOB's fifties history on pp. 101–107.

6. *Ibid.,* p. 115.

7. Shilts, *Conduct Unbecoming,* pp. 108–111.

8. D'Emilio, *Sexual Politics, Sexual Communities,* p. 125.

Chapter 13

1. Martin Duberman, *Stonewall* (New York, 1993), pp. ix–xx.

2. Duberman, *Stonewall,* chapter 7, "Post-Stonewall: 1969–70," pp. 213–280, details these events.

Chapter 14

1. Kennedy, *Ulrichs,* pp. 87–89.

2. Certificate no. 8018, State of Illinois, Office of the Secretary of State, Commercial Dept., Springfield, IL, reproduced in Katz, *Gay American History,* p. 387.

3. *One* magazine. Sept. 1962, pp. 5–10, reprinted in Katz, *Gay American History,* p. 389. Pp. 385–397 in Katz, *Gay American History,* provides a comprehensive account of the Society for Human Rights' history.

4. *The Ladder,* October 1956, p. 4. Katz, *Gay American History,* pp. 420–433, presents excellent background on DOB, as does Marcus, *Making History,* pp. 104–126 and D'Emilio, *Sexual Politics, Sexual Communities,* pp. 101–107.

5. "Homosexuals Ask Candidates' Ideas," *New York Times,* Aug. 19, 1968, p. 29.

6. Marcus, *Making History,* pp. 93–103, includes an important interview with Kameny.

7. "Homosexuals Ask Candidates Ideas," *New York Times,* Oct. 15, 1979, p. A-14.

8. "200,000 March in Capital to Seek Gay Rights and Money for AIDS," *New York Times,* Oct. 12, 1987, p. 1.

9. Cited in film *For Love and for Life: The 1987 March on Washington for Lesbian and Gay Rights,* by Joan E. Biren. This film of Biren's excellent slide show is available from Moonforce Media, P.O. Box 2934, Washington, D.C. 20013.

10. Jeffrey Schmalz, "Americans Throng Capital in Appeal for Rights," *New York Times,* April 26, 1993, p. 1. Videos of the 1993 March abound: *Washington '93: Marching for Freedom* from Project 1993, 2020 Pennsylvania Ave. NW, Washington, D.C. 20006, and *Prelude to Victory: The 1993 March on Washington Video,* from Grand Video, 1331 F St. NW, Suite 250, Washington, D.C. 20004, are two of many.

11. Committee for the March on Washington, program guide, "A Simple Matter of Justice," p. 16.

Chapter 15

1. Shilts, *Conduct Unbecoming,* p. 522.

Chapter 16

1. Stephan Likosky, *Coming Out* (New York, 1992), contains an excellent collection of primary source materials on the international gay and lesbian movement, while Adam, *The Rise of a Gay and Lesbian Movement,* provides a good secondary survey, although it only extends until 1986.

Chapter 17

1. James Sears, *Growing Up Gay in the South* (New York, 1991), p. 443.

2. United States Department of Justice, "Response of the Criminal Justice System to Bias Crime" (Washington, 1987).

3. National Gay and Lesbian Task Force, "National Anti-Gay/Lesbian Victimization Report" (Washington, 1984).

4. The Massachusetts Governor's Commission on Gay and Lesbian Youth, "Making Schools Safe for Gay and Lesbian Youth" (Boston, 1993), p. 46.

5. *Ibid.,* p. 52.

6. *Ibid.,* p. 51.

7. *Ibid.*, p. 22.

8. G. Remafedi, "Male Homosexuality," unpublished.

9. *Ibid.*

10. The Massachusetts Governor's Commission on Gay and Lesbian Youth, "Making Schools Safe for Gay and Lesbian Youth," p. 18.

11. United States Department of Health and Human Services, "Report on the Secretary's Task Force on Youth Suicide" (Washington, 1989), pp. 15–24.

BIBLIOGRAPHY

BOOKS

Adam, Barry. *The Rise of a Gay and Lesbian Movement.* Boston: Twayne Publishers, 1987.

Adelman, Marcy, editor. *Long Time Passing: The Lives of Older Lesbians.* Boston: Alyson Publications, 1986.

Bayer, Ronald. *Homosexuality and American Psychiatry: The Politics of Diagnosis.* Princeton: Princeton University Press, 1987.

Bérubé, Allan. *Coming Out under Fire: The History of Gay Men and Women in World War Two.* New York: The Free Press (Macmillan), 1990.

Blumenfeld, Warren, and Raymond, Diane. *Looking at Gay & Lesbian Life.* Boston: Beacon Press, 1988.

Boswell, John. *Christianity, Social Tolerance, and Homosexuality: Gay People in Western Europe from the Beginning of the Christian Era to the Fourteenth Century.* Chicago: University of Chicago Press, 1980.

Branch, Taylor. *Parting the Waters: America in the King Years, 1954–1963.* New York: Simon & Schuster, 1988.

Cantarella, Eva. *Bisexuality in the Ancient World.* New Haven: Yale University Press, 1992.

Cook, Blanche Weisen. *Eleanor Roosevelt: Volume One, 1884–1933.* New York: Viking (Penguin), 1992.

D'Emilio, John. *Sexual Politics, Sexual Communities: The Making of a Homosexual Minority in the United States, 1940–1970.* Chicago: University of Chicago Press, 1983.

———— and Freedman, Estelle. *Intimate Matters: A History of Sexuality in America.* New York: Harper & Row, 1988.

Dover, Kenneth. *Greek Homosexuality.* London: Oxford University Press, 1978.

Duberman, Martin. *About Time: Exploring the Gay Past.* New York: Gay Presses of New York, 1986.

———— *Stonewall.* New York: Dutton, 1993.

———— with Vicinus, Martha, and Chauncey, George, Jr., editors. *Hidden from History: Reclaiming the Gay and Lesbian Past.* New York: New American Library (Penguin), 1989.

Faderman, Lillian. *Surpassing the Love of Men: Romantic Friendship and Love between Women from the Renaissance to the Present.* New York: William Morrow, 1981.

———— *Odd Girls and Twilight Lovers: A History of Lesbian Life in Twentieth-Century America.* New York: Penguin, 1991.

Greenberg, David. *The Construction of Homosexuality.* Chicago: Chicago University Press, 1988.

Halperin, David. *One Hundred Years of Homosexuality and Other Essays on Greek Love.* New York: Routledge, 1990.

Heger, Heinz. *The Men with the Pink Triangle.* Boston: Alyson Publications, 1980.

Hemphill, Essex, editor. *Brother to Brother: New Writings by Black Gay Men.* Boston: Alyson Publications, 1991.

Hinsch, Bret. *Passions of the Cut Sleeve: The Male Homosexual Tradition in China.* Berkeley: University of California Press, 1990.

Hippler, Mike. *Matlovich: The Good Soldier.* Boston: Alyson Publications, 1989.

Hodges, Andrew. *Alan Turing.* New York: Simon & Schuster, 1984.

Holobaugh, Jim (with Hale, Keith). *Torn Allegiances: The Story of a Gay Cadet.* Boston: Alyson Publications, 1992.

Hutchins, Robert Maynard. *Great Books of the Western World,* vol. 7. Chicago: University of Chicago Press, 1952.

Jay, Karla, and Young, Allen. *Out of the Closets: Voice of Gay Liberation.* New York: Douglas, 1972.

Katz, Jonathan Ned, editor. *Gay American History: A Documentary.* New York: Thomas Crowell, 1976.

———— *Gay/Lesbian Almanac: A New Documentary.* New York: Harper & Row, 1983.

Kennedy, Hubert. *Ulrichs: The Life and Works of Karl Heinrich Ulrichs, Pioneer of the Modern Gay Movement.* Boston: Alyson Publications, 1988.

Lewes, Kenneth. *The Psychoanalytic Theory of Male Homosexuality.* New York: Simon and Schuster, 1988.

Likosky, Stephan, editor. *Coming Out: An Anthology of International Gay and Lesbian Writings.* New York: Pantheon Books, 1992.

Marcus, Eric. *Making History: The Struggle for Gay and Lesbian Equal Rights, 1945–1990.* New York: HarperCollins, 1992.

Plant, Richard. *The Pink Triangle: The Nazi War against Homosexuals.* New York: Henry Holt & Company, 1986.

Ratti, Rakesh, editor. *A Lotus of Another Color: An Unfolding of the South Asian Gay and Lesbian Experience.* Boston: Alyson Publications, 1993.

Roscoe, Will, editor. *Living the Spirit: A Gay American Indian Anthology.* New York: St. Martin's Press, 1988.

Sears, James. *Growing Up Gay in the South.* New York: Harrington Park Press, 1991.

Shilts, Randy. *Conduct Unbecoming: Gays & Lesbians in the U.S. Military.* New York: St. Martin's Press, 1993.

———— *And the Band Played On: People, Politics, and the AIDS Epidemic.* New York: St. Martin's Press, 1987.

Steffan, Joseph. *Honor Bound: A Gay American Fights for His Right to Serve His Country.* New York: Random House, 1992.

Stein, Edward, editor. *Forms of Desire: Sexual Orientation and the Social Constructionist Controversy.* New York: Garland, 1990.

Timmons, Stuart. *The Trouble with Harry Hay: Founder of the Modern Gay Movement.* Boston: Alyson Publications, 1990.

von Hoffman, Nicholas. *Citizen Cohn: The Life and Times of Roy Cohn.* New York: Doubleday, 1988.

Williams, Walter L. *The Spirit and the Flesh: Sexual Diversity in American Indian Cultures.* Boston: Beacon Press, 1986.

PERIODICALS, GOVERNMENT DOCUMENTS, ETC.

Carmody, Deirdre. "Letters by Eleanor Roosevelt Detail Friendship with Lorena Hickok." *New York Times,* October 21, 1979, p. 22.

Fosburgh, Lacey. "Thousands of Homosexuals Hold a Protest Rally in Central Park." *New York Times,* June 29, 1970, p. 1.

"Four Policemen Hurt in 'Village' Raid." *New York Times,* June 29, 1969, p. 33.

"The Future of Gay America." *Newsweek,* March 12, 1990, pp. 20–25.

"The 'Gay' People Demand Their Rights," *New York Times,* July 5, 1970, p. E-12.

"Growth of Overt Homosexuality in City Provokes Wide Concern." *New York Times,* December 17, 1963, p. 1, continued on p. 33.

Havemann, Ernest. "Scientists Search for the Answers to a Touchy and Puzzling Question: Why?" *Life,* June 26, 1964, pp. 76–80.

"The Homosexual in America." *Time,* January 21, 1966, pp. 40–41.

"Homosexuals Ask Candidates' Ideas." *New York Times,* August 19, 1968, p. 29.

"Homosexuals in Uniform." *Newsweek,* June 9, 1947, p. 54.

"Homosexuals Stage Protest in Capital." *New York Times,* May 30, 1965, p. 42.

The Ladder, November 1958.

Lynn, Kenneth S. "The First Lady's First Friend." *London Times Literary Supplement,* July 11, 1980, pp. 787–788.

Massachusetts Governor's Commission on Gay and Lesbian Youth. *Making Schools Safe for Gay and Lesbian Youth.* Boston: Author, 1993.

National Gay and Lesbian Task Force, *National Anti-Gay/Lesbian Victimization Report.* New York: Author, 1984.

Nemy, Enid. "The Woman Homosexual: More Assertive, Less Willing to Hide." *New York Times,* November 17, 1969, p. 62.

"Perverts Called Government Peril." *New York Times,* April 19, 1950, p. 25.

"Pervert Inquiry Ordered." *New York Times,* June 15, 1950, p. 1.

"Police Again Rout 'Village' Youths." *New York Times,* June 30, 1969, p. 22.

Remafedi, G. "Male Homosexuality: The Adolescent's Perspective." Unpublished paper, University of Minnesota, Adolescent Health Program, 1985.

Schmalz, Jeffrey . "Americans Throng Capital in Appeal for Rights." *New York Times,* April 26, 1993, p. 1.

Schott, Webster. "Civil Rights and the Homosexual: A 4 Million Minority Asks for Equal Rights." *New York Times,* Sunday, November 12, 1967, pp. 44ff.

"75,000 March in Capital in Drive to Support Homosexual Rights." *New York Times,* October 15, 1979, p. A-14.

Starr, Jack. "The Sad 'Gay' Life." *Look,* January 10, 1967, pp. 30–33.

"200,000 March in Capital to Seek Gay Rights and Money for AIDS." *New York Times,* October 12, 1987, p. 1.

United States Department of Health and Human Services. *Report of the Secretary's Task Force on Youth Suicide.* Washington,DC: GPO, 1989.

United States Department of Justice. *The Response of the Criminal Justice System to Bias Crime: An Exploratory Review.* Washington, DC: GPO, 1987.

Welch, Paul. "The 'Gay' World Takes to the Streets." *Life,* June 26, 1964, pp. 66–75.

"War Role for Homosexuals Sought." *New York Times,* April 17, 1966, p. 12.

ABOUT THE AUTHOR

Cynthia Katz

Kevin Jennings, a high school history teacher, served on the Massachusetts Governor's Commission on Gay and Lesbian Youth and co-founded the Gay and Lesbian School Teachers Network. Now a Klingenstein fellow at Columbia University, he will subsequently return to his home in Cambridge, Massachusetts.

Other books of interest from ALYSON PUBLICATIONS

THE ALYSON ALMANAC, by Alyson Publications, $10.00. *The Alyson Almanac* is the most complete reference book available about the lesbian and gay community — and also the most entertaining. Here are brief biographies of some 300 individuals from throughout history; a report card for every member of Congress; significant dates from our history; addresses and phone numbers for major organizations, bookstores, periodicals, and hotlines; and much more. This new edition has been updated throughout. New sections include a rundown of laws and attitudes in every major country, and a summary of major studies (from the Kinsey reports on) of sexual orientation.

HAPPY ENDINGS ARE ALL ALIKE, by Sandra Scoppettone, $7.00. It was their last summer before college, and Jaret and Peggy were in love. But as Jaret said, "It always seems as if when something great happens, then something lousy happens soon after." Soon her worst fears turned into brute reality.

TRYING HARD TO HEAR YOU, by Sandra Scoppettone, $8.00. Sixteen-year-old Camilla Crawford tells about a crucial summer in which her close-knit summer theater group discovers that two of its members are gay. By the end of summer, she writes, "two of us were going to suffer like we never had before, and none of us would ever be the same again."

GAY MEN AND WOMEN WHO ENRICHED THE WORLD, by Thomas Cowan, $9.00. Growing up gay in a straight culture, writes Thomas Cowan, challenges the individual in special ways. Here are lively accounts of forty personalities who have offered outstanding contributions in fields ranging from mathematics and military strategy to art, philosophy, and economics. Each chapter is amusingly illustrated with a caricature by Michael Willhoite.

BROTHER TO BROTHER, edited by Essex Hemphill, $9.00. Black activist and poet Essex Hemphill has carried on in the footsteps of the late Joseph Beam (editor of *In the Life*) with this new anthology of fiction, essays, and poetry by black gay men. Contributors include Assoto Saint, Craig G. Harris, Melvin Dixon, Marlon Riggs, and many newer writers.

REFLECTIONS OF A ROCK LOBSTER, by Aaron Fricke, $7.00. Guess who's coming to the prom! Aaron Fricke made national news by taking a male date to his high school prom. Yet for the first sixteen years of his life, Fricke had closely guarded the secret of his homosexuality. Here, told with insight and humor, is his story about growing up gay, about realizing that he was different, and about how he ultimately developed a positive gay identity in spite of the prejudice around him.

BETTER ANGEL, by Richard Meeker, $7.00. The touching story of a young man's gay awakening in the years between the World Wars. Kurt Gray is a shy, bookish boy growing up in a small town in Michigan. Even at the age of thirteen he knows that somehow he is different. Gradually he recognizes his desire for a man's companionship and love. As a talented composer, breaking into New York's musical world, he finds the love he's sought.

CHOICES, by Nancy Toder, $9.00. Lesbian love can bring joy and passion; it can also bring conflicts. In this straightforward, sensitive novel, Nancy Toder conveys the fear and confusion of a woman coming to terms with her sexual and emotional attraction to other women.

TORN ALLEGIANCES, by Jim Holobaugh, with Keith Hale, $10.00. Jim Holobaugh was the perfect ROTC cadet — so perfect that ROTC featured the handsome college student in a nationwide ad campaign. But as he gradually came to realize that he was gay, he faced an impossible dilemma: to serve the country he loved, he would have to live a life of deceit. His story dramatizes both the monetary waste, and the moral corruptness, of the military's anti-gay policy.

A LOTUS OF ANOTHER COLOR, edited by Rakesh Ratti, $10.00. For the first time, gay men and lesbians from India, Pakistan, and other South Asian countries recount their stories of coming out. In essays and poetry, they tell of challenging prejudice from both the South Asian and gay cultures, and they express the exhilaration of finally finding a sense of community.

THE PERSISTENT DESIRE, edited by Joan Nestle, $15.00. A generation ago, butch-femme identities were taken for granted in the lesbian community. Today women who think of themselves as butch or femme often face prejudice from both the lesbian community and the straight world. Here, for the first time, dozens of femme and butch lesbians tell their stories of love, survival, and triumph.

COMING OUT RIGHT, by Wes Muchmore and William Hanson, $8.00. Every gay man can recall the first time he stepped into a gay bar. That difficult step often represents the transition from a life of secrecy and isolation into a world of unknowns. The transition will be easier for men who have this recently updated book. Here, many facets of gay life are spelled out for the newcomer, including: coming out at work; gay health and the AIDS crisis; and the unique problems faced by men who are coming out when they're under eighteen or over thirty.

THE COLOR OF TREES, by Canaan Parker, $9.00. Peter, a black scholarship student from Harlem, takes life too seriously at his new, mostly white boarding school. Things change when he meets T.J., a wellborn but hyperactive imp with little use for clothing. Here, in his first novel, Canaan Parker explores the formation of both racial and homosexual identities, and the conflicts created by the narrator's dual allegiance.

LESBIAN QUOTATIONS, by Rosemary E. Silva, $10.00. "Dined with Virginia at Richmond. She is as delicious as ever." —*Vita Sackville-West.* Where are all the quotable lesbians? Author Rosemary Silva has collected the best of lesbian wit and wisdom in one volume. Arranged topically, *Lesbian Quotations* covers subjects ranging from Passion to Pets. A great reference, or just browse through this fascinating compendium for pure entertainment.

THE ADVOCATE ADVISER, by Pat Califia, $9.00. The Miss Manners of gay culture tackles subjects ranging from the ethics of zoophilia to the etiquette of a holy union ceremony. Along the way she covers interracial relationships, in-law problems, and gay parenting. No other gay columnist so successfully combines useful advice, an unorthodox perspective, and a wicked sense of humor.

STEAM, by Jay B. Laws, $10.00. San Francisco was once a city of music and laughter, of parties and bathhouses, when days held promise and nights, romance. But now something sinister haunts the streets and alleyways of San Francisco, something that crept in with the fog to seek a cruel revenge. It feeds on deep desire, and tantalizes with the false and empty promises of a more carefree past. For many, it will all begin with a ticket to an abandoned house of dreams...

BI ANY OTHER NAME, edited by Loraine Hutchins and Lani Kaahumanu, $12.00. Hear the voices of over seventy women and men from all walks of life describe their lives as bisexuals. They tell their stories — personal, political, spiritual, historical — in prose, poetry, art, and essays. These are individuals who have fought prejudice from both the gay and straight communities and who have begun only recently to share their experiences. This groundbreaking anthology is an important step in the process of forming a new bisexual community.

EYES OF DESIRE, edited by Raymond Luczak, $10.00. Coming out is hard enough already. But it becomes a new challenge altogether when one can't take communication itself for granted. Here, for the first time, lesbians and gay men who are deaf tell about their lives: discovering their sexual identities; overcoming barriers to communication in a sound-based world; and, finally, creating a deaf gay and lesbian culture in a world that is too often afraid of differences.

THE GAY BOOK OF LISTS, by Leigh Rutledge, $9.00. Rutledge has compiled a fascinating and informative collection of lists. His subject matter ranges from history (6 gay popes) to politics (9 perfectly disgusting reactions to AIDS) to entertainment (12 examples of gays on network television) to humor (9 Victorian "cures" for masturbation). Learning about gay culture and history has never been so much fun.

LESBIAN LISTS, by Dell Richards, $9.00. Lesbian holy days is just one of the hundreds of lists of clever and enlightening lesbian trivia compiled by columnist Dell Richards. Fun facts like uppity women who were called lesbians (but probably weren't), banned lesbian books, lesbians who've passed as men, herbal aphrodisiacs, black lesbian entertainers, and switch-hitters are sure to amuse and make *Lesbian Lists* a great gift.

BUTCH, by Jay Rayn, $8.00. Michaeline "Mike" Landetti doesn't have a word for what she is, but from the beginning of memory she has played ball with the boys, and fallen in love with the girls. Jay Rayn has written a moving story about growing up butch and learning to make your way in a less-than-accepting world. Originally published by Free Women Press.

LONG TIME PASSING, edited by Marcy Adelman, $8.00. Here, in their own words, women talk about age-related concerns: the fear of losing a lover; the experience of being a lesbian in the 1940s and '50s; the issues of loneliness and community. Most contributors are older lesbians, but several younger voices are represented.

CRUSH, by Jane Futcher, $8.00. It wasn't easy fitting in at an exclusive girls' school like Huntington Hill. But in her senior year, Jinx finally felt as if she belonged. Lexie — beautiful, popular Lexie — wanted her for a friend. Jinx knew she had a big crush on Lexie, and she knew she had to do something to make it go away. But Lexie had other plans. And Lexie always got her way.

THE FIRST GAY POPE, by Lynne Yamaguchi Fletcher, $8.00. Everyone from trivia buffs to news reporters will enjoy this new reference book, which records hundreds of achievements, records, and firsts for the lesbian and gay community. What was the earliest lesbian novel? Where was the first gay civil rights law passed? When was the biggest gay demonstration? For the first time, the answers are all in one entertaining, well-indexed volume.

SUPPORT YOUR LOCAL BOOKSTORE

Most of the books described here are available at your nearest gay or feminist bookstore, and many of them will be available at other bookstores. If you can't get these books locally, order by mail using this form.

Enclosed is $________ for the following books. (Add $1.00 postage if ordering just one book. If you order two or more, we'll pay the postage.)

1.____

2.____

3.____

name:____

address:____

city:______________________________state:________zip:__________

ALYSON PUBLICATIONS

Dept. J-53, 40 Plympton St., Boston, MA 02118

After December 31, 1995, please write for current catalog.